THE
Complications

THE
Complications

ON GOING INSANE IN AMERICA

Emmett Rensin

HarperOne
An Imprint of HarperCollins*Publishers*

THE COMPLICATIONS. Copyright © 2024 by Emmett Rensin. All rights reserved. Printed in the United States of America. No part of this book may be used or reproduced in any manner whatsoever without written permission except in the case of brief quotations embodied in critical articles and reviews. For information, address HarperCollins Publishers, 195 Broadway, New York, NY 10007.

HarperCollins books may be purchased for educational, business, or sales promotional use. For information, please email the Special Markets Department at SPsales@harpercollins.com.

FIRST EDITION

Library of Congress Cataloging-in-Publication Data has been applied for.

ISBN 978-0-06-305722-7

24 25 26 27 28 LBC 5 4 3 2 1

For Jessica

Table of Contents

Part III

Part IV

Foreword

THE EIGHT BALL

On a cold day in the winter of 2020, I received a worried call from J., the then girlfriend now wife, of my longtime friend Emmett Rensin. She asked me if I had heard from Emmett, with whom, she said, she had been enjoying a trip to California until he had simply vanished, taking his car and ignoring calls and texts. I hadn't heard from him, but I offered to call.

Emmett picked up, in a sense. His voice was there but the sense of conviction with which he normally speaks was conspicuously absent, as though he had been mugged of all certainty. He couldn't say exactly where he was or what he was doing. I suggested the word "lost" to describe his situation. He agreed it was fitting but seemed untroubled by its implications. I asked if he had a plan for getting home, but the question failed to register. In building shades of realization I began to understand that this wasn't a quarter-life crisis or a fit of artistic temperament or a burning obligation somewhere far up California's coastline: it was one of those episodes, those periods in my friend's life that he referred to obliquely, with shame and sideways glances, when, by chance, he lost his mind.

I stood by my window above Connecticut Avenue and gazed out into the grey afternoon as though I might find him there, but the man

I knew was in every sense thousands of miles away. When Emmett is well, and he has been, in the years of our friendship, predominantly well, he is witty and winsome, nimble-minded and darkly funny, as fluent in basketball and bullshit as twentieth-century American literature and its inheritors, though he would probably say there's considerable overlap among those categories. I can predict Emmett—somehow both my most incisive and most understanding friend—only so far. This is mainly because he's curious and inventive and only partially because he's prone to losing his mind, which is more common than you might think, in any case.

In fact, every friendship carries a risk of one or both partners going insane; the brief recollection above, which Emmett recounts in this book's chapter "Ordinary Time," only represents my first encounter with the author's symptoms. There is an eerie quality to having a conversation with the version of a friend's self that is available when all higher cognition is fractured by transmissions raining down from every frequency, but the sense of sudden and catastrophic neurological luck I found entirely familiar: I myself am epileptic, something Emmett and I had discussed the first time we met in a diner in Washington, DC, circa 2015. In another era, I had observed, we may have found ourselves housed in a similar institution for the unfit—or canonized as martyrs, he countered, typically clever. That we found ourselves in DC instead was a stroke of good fortune, by a narrow margin.

Indeed the historical conflation of mental illness and epilepsy makes Emmett's happenstance selection of Dostoevsky's *The Idiot* as a balm for troubled thoughts in the middle of the psychotic episode in "Ordinary Time" especially apt: In the passage Emmett happened to read, the epileptic Myshkin describes the wasted days of a man who briefly aspired to greatness in the aftermath of a mock execution, but then fell back into old, dissolute habits despite his brush with fate. By the novel's end, Myshkin's purity of heart, met with the sins of the world, has driven him mad.

Emmett does not believe that madness is indicative of any particular purity of heart, clarity of purpose, or special artistic capacity.

He would dispute that there is continuity, for instance, between his receptiveness to the odd and misleading thoughts that occasionally strike him as true and his superior negative capability, the quality that makes an artist's imagination especially vast and fertile. That, I suspect he would say, is runaway romanticism. Mental illness is not the obverse of genius or a harbinger of unique insight; neither is epilepsy, the once-sacred sickness, now consigned to an ordinary malady: they're both a turn of bad luck, getting caught behind the eight ball.

But all an epileptic need fear is death or injury—relatively dignified fates compared with the vicissitudes of madness. An entire *life* behind the eight ball is a life spent in perpetual doubt of one's perceptions, with a black veil dropped over half the past and all of the future. Contemporary writing on mental illness has incorporated a great deal of therapeutic thought in its approach to the subject, which has translated into an (often explicit) agenda of destigmatization framing the genre. For that reason, madness and blame are often treated as radically distinct, even mutually exclusive subjects; Emmett can't countenance the false estrangement. Guilt, accountability, and repentance are themes he returns to again and again, even as he visits (perhaps too pessimistically) the organic limits of his own judgment and restraint. He is the protagonist, and the villain, of his own story.

Emmett's guilt is expansive. In life you can see it in the slump of his shoulders, the rings around his eyes, the way he drops down while seated to rest his elbows on his knees and hang his head. In his writing, it manifests in his choice of subject matter. Where modern poets of madness, like Sylvia Plath and Anne Sexton, found the fullest expression of their own experiences with mental illness in the illumination of guilt in the (typically sane and typically inhumane) people around them, Emmett seems to most assuredly articulate the private moral experience of going insane when he is reflecting on—appropriating, almost, as though to relieve—the guilt of other people like him. Emmett is acutely sensitive to the fact that his own wrongs, such as they are, could've been—may still someday be—orders of magnitude worse, and he considers the fates of those who have committed heinous crimes in the midst of madness with startling integrity. Here, life behind the eight ball yields a strange gift of perception: Anyone else would view the same people as either pitiful or reprobate; Emmett only finds them familiar, and fully human. They are enlivened by agency in his tellings, awakened from true crime stock figures and other sanitized shades of themselves.

Herein lies an example of one of Emmett's most enthralling traits as a writer and most inviting traits as a friend: His appetite for ambiguity. In her 1971 the *New York Review* essay "On Sylvia Plath," Elizabeth Hardwick noted the poet's preeminence among a class of authors possessed with a "greed for particulars," which expresses itself in the detailed precision of her work. Hardwick viewed Plath and her mid-century contemporaries through the prism of sex, but Plath, Sexton, and even Virginia Woolf, to fetch another of Hardwick's prized writers, were all also compatriots of Emmett's in madness. Through the lens of mental illness, insistence on hard, concretizing detail arrives almost as a reaction *against* the author's condition, as though by documenting reality in spectacular clarity they might hang on to it, and attest their claim to it, even during episodic excommunication from the truth. What is unique about Emmett is how thoroughly he resists that journalistic temptation to offer mainly observations of indisputable and mundane character. Instead he meditates on good and evil, guilt and innocence, the human capacity for failure measured against the teasing flashes of earthly brilliance that suggest we could be more than what we are: dark grey areas of moral life, in other words, that would test the boundaries of anyone's reality.

Still, Emmett's is not a confessional book. He isn't looking for absolution, but rather trying to understand something about himself and a sizable portion of the world's population; untangling his and their place in the great matrix of moral meaning is only a stage of that journey. It is also something unique within his genre, this treatment of mental illness that is equipped with all the accoutrements of contemporary writing on madness—the language and logic of psychotherapy, the bodily mortification of psychiatric medication and treatment, the historical awareness of psychology and its suspect past—yet unwilling to rely on any given one as its moral index. Instead, Emmett makes his broader moral frame—the one in which he is ruthlessly self-critical—the thing to which he adheres despite his condition, whatever chasms open up in his reality, whatever roads he finds himself several hundred miles along and lost upon. Even in madness, he never outruns his own exacting judgment.

Only when it comes to others does his careful accounting of right and wrong soften into something much more generous, forgiving. In his correspondence with a killer, Emmett is suspicious of no one's motives except his own; in his reflections on the man's life and death, he extends shades of mercy seldom set aside for himself. I must confess to you that the experience of reading Emmett is not unlike the experience of conversing with him as a friend, in this key respect: One never derives the sense that they are being judged, only that they are witnessing someone with profoundly sound judgment sorting through the mess of the world, its strange rifts and entanglements and dalliances with nonexistence. He would of course deny that this skill of his was cultivated through the crucible of his condition, but I myself am not so sure. Luck can only explain so much.

Elizabeth Bruenig, October 2022

Part I

The Weather

Charles Thomas was lucky because when police officers found him in an alley beside the street on the South Side of Chicago where he had spent the evening smashing glass doors and windshields with an iron tent spike, they only shot him once. Charles was still manic when they arrived. He ran at the cops, spike still in hand. One of them shouted, *Don't come at me!* but Charles came at him, so the cop put a bullet in his arm.

Charles Thomas was lucky because his mother knew right away what was wrong. The family had a history of manic depression. *To me, it was obvious he was having some sort of psychiatric episode,* she told the *Chicago Sun-Times.* Charles Thomas was lucky that, until that April, he had been a student in good standing at the University of Chicago, and he was lucky that this had brought attention, editorials, letters, and rallies to his cause. He was lucky that his family had money to hire lawyers, and that the lawyers could secure his bail. Charles Thomas was lucky that the bullet only broke one bone, and that although it remained lodged inside him, it didn't lead to further complications.

The next year, while awaiting trial for the aggravated assault of a police officer, Charles violated the terms of his release and fled across state lines. He was lucky that when the cops found him nearly two weeks later, naked in an Indiana cornfield and holding only a brown blanket that he dropped as he tried to run, they only tased him this time.

The mistake that you make when you imagine going crazy is that you imagine the unexpected appearance of bad weather. You imagine a rumble, the smell of iron in the air, a sudden drop in temperature and then a gale force wind blowing down. You imagine thunder and lightning, a hurricane crashing to life; chaos and panic—*Oh my God, I'm going crazy!* Maybe you believe the common myth that the marker of insanity is failing to realize that you're insane, but still, you imagine that just before you are swallowed by the flood, you'll have a moment of terrifying clarity: something is very wrong.

A few weeks before he lost his mind, Charles Thomas told a friend that he'd been feeling anxious. When I went finally and definitively crazy, I was in Chicago too. For months beforehand, I'd told friends what a pain it was to have all of these panic attacks all of a sudden. I was feeling anxious all the time.

The reason that the insane largely do not know that they are crazy is not because there are no signs. It is because very few people have ever thought, *Oh, I'm experiencing the prodromal symptoms of a psychotic disorder.* They think, *I've been feeling weird lately, and I don't know why* instead. Their friends and families do not think, *Oh, she's developing a clinically significant pattern of affective dysregulation.* They think, *She's becoming a little toxic, huh?* Madness isn't like the weather. It doesn't bear down from the front.

Madness is a cat burglar; it lets itself in quietly through the back while you're asleep and closes the door in silence. It disturbs only little things for a while. It moves a glass, misplaces a book, unsettles dust on a counter that you know you haven't touched in years. It moves slowly. It moves out of sight, like a ghost. It takes you over, room by room, until it is in everything, until it is wrapped around the backside of your skull and you can't tell it from how things always were before. You're different, but what it feels like is, *The world is different now.* If you fail to see that you are going crazy, it's because the illness has become your eyes. You don't see it; you see through it. That's what it's like.

Two years after he was shot, Charles Thomas developed COVID-19 symptoms while being held in Cook County Jail. It took several newspaper stories and three separate hearings to find a judge who was willing to fit him with a monitoring device and let him go on bond. He was lucky. Many of his fellow prisoners, sane and insane, and almost all without the money and lawyers and public attention Charles had, got sick in lock-up, too. They weren't so lucky. Almost all of them would remain behind bars and some would die there.

I've been luckier than Charles. I've been beat up but never shot. Arrests have always ended with me in the hospital or in my home. When I was losing my mind at the University of Chicago, seven years before Charles did, I only broke the glass in my own apartment. When I stole a friend's credit card (I don't know why) and used it precisely one time one week later for a seven dollar parking fee (I don't know why), nothing came of it at all. When I broke into the apartment below mine—sure that I lived there and unwilling to leave—the man who woke up to find me standing over his bed just screamed until I ran away. When I stripped completely naked and threw things at the walls and yelled and threatened suicide and cried one night until my girlfriend called the cops, they didn't come until the morning. I was in bed. I talked to an officer from under the sheets in my underwear, sitting up with my back against the wall. Nobody booked me. Nobody tased me. I didn't get sick in jail.

When I was nineteen years old, God commanded me to drive my car into a freeway median and die. But my car bounced off the concrete barrier and went careening back into another car. It was winter. I told the police that my brakes had failed on the icy off-ramp and they believed me. Bad weather, good luck.

Clarity, if it comes, doesn't often come until too late. Until you wake up into yourself one night in April, running down an alley with a tent spike; until you wake up into yourself one night in May, trying to remove your lymph node with a butter knife, like I did. Until you wake up half-awake in a hospital somewhere, committed against your will.

At least Charles and I woke up. In many cases, there's only a long life, a ghost lurking permanently below the threshold of visibility, below the level where anybody says, *Call a doctor.* You're never quite certain why you can't keep a job. You're never quite certain why you can't keep friends, why your family can't stand you, why you do the things you do. You're just slow. You're just weird, just aloof, just sad, just an asshole. Nothing ever seems to work out. There is no sudden, thunderous storm. You never think to seek shelter. No reason to speak to a professional.

Here is when it's like the weather: When you are not the madman but the madman's friend. When the lunatic is your charge, your child, your parent, your employee, your student, your wife. There are long calms and good days. There are light rains and hard storms. Some winters are mild; others are bitter and hard and cold. Experts can provide a forecast, and after a while, you develop an intuition in your bones; there is no way to say for certain when the sky will suddenly open up and soak you. When you imagine going crazy, do not imagine yourself caught in bad weather. You are the bad weather, the rain and the wind and all.

Sometimes the weather is a catastrophe: floods and hurricanes, earthquakes and fires, screaming and crying, property destruction, assaults and suicide attempts, patients gone missing in the night, lost and preyed upon and confused. Sometimes the weather is temperate. Days and weeks and months go by when you would never know, when "eccentric" or even "quiet" might be the strongest word you'd say. Everything is only a little bit harder. Only a little bit harder to predict, like: What will they do today? Will they get out of bed? Will they be okay? Will they ever go to sleep? Can I bring them to this party? Will they embarrass me? It's hard to tell if they're joking right now. Is this a bit, or are they starting to lose it again? They didn't shower today or yesterday or the day before that, either. (Or did they? They say they can't remember if they have.) They won't talk or won't stop talking. Sometimes the weather is even mild. But if you've seen one storm, you're always worried. You look at them. They look at you, too closely. Or they seem to be looking at nothing at all, all day. You over-notice warning signs, then over-correct and fail to spot them. You wonder if this is a little bit like what the schizophrenic feels like, trying to separate out signal from noise.

What I am trying to tell you is that we are talking here about ordinary people in possession of all the ordinary problems, plus one extraordinary one. We are talking here about what you would expect might happen if some hundredth of the population, already varied and limited, variously flawed, woke up one day and found that they were coming apart at the seams. What would happen if they became frightened by sudden, new impulses, and more frightened by their sudden inability to control them. What would happen if they realized that their memories had gone shaky, that something had gone slow inside their brain, that people around them didn't act the same, didn't look the same, might be imposters, that they were suddenly sad or paranoid, angry or confused.

It's like a mudslide that moves down the hill slowly, Charles Thomas's father told a newspaper. *It just doesn't ever pick up steam. It just keeps rolling and rolling.* He was talking about his son's legal process, in particular, but he may as well have been talking about his son's life in general, or a million other lives, or mine.

I was born in California at the end of the twentieth century, in a valley, which, because of the persistent smog, could not be identified from within for lack of a visible hill ring. My parents were forty when I was born. I was born in January. I am an only child. All of these are correlated with an increased likelihood of madness, although I do not know if any of them contributed to my case at all. I was born firmly into the middle class, in a family trending upward. I suppose that with different luck, I would have been a doctor or a lawyer.

I began to have problems when I was thirteen or fourteen years old. I was temperamental and withdrawn and had difficulty keeping friends. Other parents were often wary of me, even then. I was talented at school, but received only middling grades, particularly as time went on. I was institutionalized for the first time when I was seventeen. Like Charles Thomas, I got out of California and went to Chicago, but every year everything became more difficult for me and far more difficult for everyone around me. Although I did not make it one term before my dormitory head referred me for mandatory counseling, I did somehow graduate on time.

By twenty-one, I began suffering complex delusions. When I was twenty-three, I heard consistent voices for the first time, although these voices have very rarely gone as far as issuing commands. At twenty-four, I had what a clinician would call a full, prolonged psychotic episode. I was diagnosed with bipolar disorder type one with psychotic features. Later, this diagnosis would be modified to schizoaffective disorder of the bipolar type. The point is that I have a problem, and that I am a problem, and that this problem is not just mine but the problem and bad luck of some small percentage of every person who has ever lived.

I was lucky, because twenty-four is not an awful time to catch and treat a defective mind. The longer it goes on, the worse it gets. I am lucky because I can afford medication and I believe, as only about half of serious patients do, that it is important for me to take it. I am lucky that I respond to medication. Some patients don't. I am lucky that, even when delusional, and even when I am hearing the sounds leak out of other people's heads, I do not frequently become disturbed or obsessed with these facts, and that this luck accounts a great deal for my classification as a "high-functioning" patient. But I am also glad that I did not become a lawyer. I have limited cognitive resources. I can go from smart to very stupid, very fast. Ask anybody who has ever fired me.

I am luckier than Charles. Charles is luckier than Tyree Davis, another man found by police on the South Side of Chicago. He was tased and shot and killed all at once. Tyree is luckier than someone else, I'm sure. Most people like me will not be caught in time. Many, if caught, will not buy or take or submit to any kind of treatment. Many, like Charles Thomas, will receive treatment for the first time in a prison cell. Forty percent of the seriously insane—themselves some 2 or 3 percent of Americans in general—do not receive any treatment at all. Many do not know they are crazy—not because this is a feature of their illness, but because nobody has ever looked carefully enough to tell them. The difference between them and me is the weather. The difference is luck.

I am told that the climate is changing. We are always talking about *mental illness* these days. Out of the vaunted bad old days of shame and silence, we've emerged like a manic patient caught in pressured speech: we cannot, cannot, cannot shut up about the sensitive, struggling insane. I am told that this is encouraging. People are willing to *open up* and *talk to someone*, they are *willing to seek help*, and the world is ready to *help* them. The shelves are filled with this talking, with inward-looking memoirs and sympathetic profiles, long-reported dispatches, smug correctives, gawking and well-rehearsed *concern*. I walk onto a subway platform and see Olympic swimmer Michael Phelps, demanding that I go get therapy. I open a newspaper and read Selena Gomez finally *telling the world* about her bipolar diagnosis. Diagnoses are at an all-time high. There's never been so much frank confession to a medicated life, particularly among the professional class. I am told that all of this is part of an important fight against stigma. We're very *open* now.

The talk is, for the most part, very bad. Even psychiatry itself is in the state that general medicine was under the reign of the four humors. Causes and courses remain obscure. The likelihood of successful treatments, or even the mechanisms by which known treatment functions, remain obscure. Many diagnoses are like declaring a patient to have "coughing." We have distinguished between transient coughing and chronic coughing, between a light cough and a dangerous one, even between a cough that seems to come from the environment and a cough that seems to come from a defect in the lungs, but all of these are listed in the *Diagnostic and Statistical Manual of Bad Breathing* as variants of coughing. In an effort to reduce stigma, it is now called "Pulmonary Difficulty Disorder." We have invented several variants of cough syrup. We are not certain why it works.

It is even worse outside the clinic. The talkers are talking about a topic that they do not understand and do not want to understand, lest it interfere with the indignant clarity of their talking. They do not know, for the most part, even the ill-defined clinical distinctions between the various forms of insanity they would like to stop us feeling embarrassed by. They do not know the state of public and private amenities for the insane, although they tend to know that they are not ideal. They do not talk much about what ought to be done instead.

The talkers cannot decide if they are talking about a social problem or a moral one. They cannot decide if they are talking about a medical problem or a personal one. They cannot decide if they are talking about a matter of poverty and criminal justice or recognition and access and *respect*, or both—or even what's the difference, if there is one. They do not know if Charles Thomas deserves mercy or a long, slow stay in prison. *You can't criminalize mental health, only actions*, says a commenter on a story about his case. *So I'm glad he's safe. Now he can stand trial*. The talkers do not even know if these are actually the same sentiment in the end.

They don't even know if they want to cure us. They are worried, in a very modern way, if it might bother us to hear that we have a problem to be cured. They do not know if they are talking about a problem related, inexorably, to broader problems of housing and medicine and work and justice, or if this is largely the narrow trouble of too many people using the wrong words. Does the manic-depressive find a job when he is understood to be a person struggling with bipolar disorder? The talkers are very concerned about *stigma*, by which they largely mean the ways that less-respectable lunatics embarrass them by association. But I do not suffer mainly from stigma. I suffer from blunted affect and pressured speech, delusions of reference and violent moods and diminishing cognitive function. I am not mainly invested in being Accepted as Valid, but in staying well enough to stay free and employed so that I can afford thousands of dollars of medication so that I can stay employed and free. So much of the talk has nothing to do with this at all.

It is tempting to turn insanity into another category of marginalized difference. It's an easy contemporary reflex to say, yes, here is a new species of identity to be recognized and protected and milked for New Voices. But madness is nothing like that at all. The problem is not just an uncomprehending world. The mudslide sweeps the hillside bare behind it. One day you are completing your bachelor's thesis at a prestigious university; the next day you are feeling anxious. Now you're smashing the glass doors of your apartment building; now you're smashing cars. Soon you're shot; soon you're fleeing; soon you're sick in jail. Eventually, you're just a cripple, trying to outrun the mud. You were born into a mean world, a world that *marginalizes* you, but in a world of perfect kindness, you'd be sick just the same. One autumn, when I lived in the Midwest, I spent a night in a hospital where the nurses there were very sweet and sensitive and good. They brought me blankets and water and food. They checked in on me more than they had to, and every time I heard their footsteps coming toward the door, I thought, *This time they're coming with the knife to kill me.* I closed my eyes and waited. I was absolutely sure.

There have always been madmen, and we have always been a problem. We have a problem, but we are a problem, too. We are a problem for ourselves and for our friends and for our families; we are a problem for any society. What do you do, precisely, with a group bound in most cases to consume more than they produce? A group who requires more care than they can give? Who tests more patience than any of the patients themselves are liable to have? We are a medical problem and a social problem and a personal problem, a problem of health-care policy and criminal justice and housing and labor, like a series of bizarre thought experiments, designed to test the boundaries of our moral reasoning, brought to life. No society has ever known what to do with us. I don't want to be hated or locked away, of course. I don't want to die. But I have been a hard problem, for myself and other people, too. Sometimes it turns out okay. Three years after he was shot, prosecutors in Cook County, Illinois, dropped the charges against Charles Thomas after he completed a diversion program for first-time criminal offenders. Like I said, he's lucky.

I began writing this book in a cold, white room in eastern Iowa, next to a window overlooking a grey street. Down the grey street is a grey park; past the park is the redbrick wall of the nearest mental hospital. I didn't mean to move so close. It's a small town. I've since moved.

I've been largely stable for the better part of seven years. I am past thirty now; I only need the hospital every eighteen months or so. Some psychotic disorders become milder with age. Others are deteriorating, progressive conditions. Outcomes are difficult to predict. I don't know if I'm lucky or not. Maybe I will be gone someday, made stupid, entirely replaced by the ghost. For now, the medication is working. I am capable of appearing sane most days. Perhaps I will need more medication as I get older. Perhaps I won't need it at all. Perhaps medication will stop working, no matter what I take.

Not long ago, I sat in the middle of packed pews for the midnight vigil before Easter, watching the baptisms of the newly converted, when I heard clapping at irregular intervals coming from somewhere in the church, clapping like a signal, not applause. While the congregation turned their heads—they turned their heads, they'd heard it, too— I smelled a bitter odor in the air, like nerve gas not like incense. I cupped my nose inside my collar and believed that all of us were slurping death, and I believed it for two hours while we celebrated the Stations of the Cross. It smelled like dying, but no one died. I didn't choke. We went forth when the mass was ended. It was just a little slip. I was fine.

We do not know, really, what causes some of us to go crazy. We do not know who will recover and who won't. We do not know what should be done with us. I do not know what will happen to me. But I know that I am lucid enough to write to you right now. I am safe in this cold room, where I can try to tell you what I can about this strange, bad luck while the weather holds calm for a while.

The Year of the Four Emperors

The historian Livy looks backward from the reign of Augustus, turns, and predicts the future: Rome has grown since its humble beginnings, now it is overwhelmed by its own greatness. Fifty years after Livy's death, the Emperor Nero was condemned by the Senate and fled to the countryside in disguise. Unable to bring himself to commit suicide, he ordered his secretary to kill him. *Qualis artifex pereo*—what an artist dies in me! He was the last of the Julio-Claudian line, the last heir of Claudius and Octavius and Julius Caesar. Within a year of Nero's death, four different men would usurp the Imperial title. Each deposed the man before him; each, in turn, swore to cure the chaos brought on by the last. But Rome would never go another generation without a civil war. History calls 69 AD the Year of the Four Emperors. Their names were Galba, Otho, Vitellius, and Vespasian.

When I was seventeen years old, I had four therapists in a single year. I had begun acting out and acting strangely. I was clearly in some sort of trouble, but it was not clear what the trouble was quite yet. My parents had grown more and more concerned. Each clinician promised to help me, to discover what the last had failed to see; each of them said that they could teach me to *feel less overwhelmed*, to *build healthy coping mechanisms*, *adjust to adulthood*, and *better manage my emotions*. Perhaps that would be enough to set me back on a normal course. And if there was more trouble than that, they'd find and treat that, too, they said. I'll call them Galba, Otho, Vitellius, and Vespasian. All four of them failed, and for many years, I resented them their failure. But Livy also wrote that for all we cannot endure our own vices, we likewise cannot endure their remedies. That's closer to the mark.

Galba (reigned January 2007–April 2007)

Galba wonders if I like punk rock (emphasis on "punk") because her son likes punk rock (emphasis on "rock") and maybe I do, too. This is not a helpful question.

She asks other questions, too. How are things at home? Do you like your mom? Your dad? How's school? These would be helpful questions if they were ever followed up on, even pressed if I resisted. But I don't give detailed answers and Galba never presses. I am willing to say more. I'm willing to tell Galba anything. I know something is wrong, but I still believe that it might turn out not to be a very big deal. I just need to be asked. I might struggle articulating what I'm feeling, but I will try if I am asked. But I'm not asked and I'm very shy.

Galba has me bring in albums that I like. We listen to them together. She doesn't like them. She doesn't say that out loud. She asks me how often I feel "down." She asks me, *One to ten, how blue do you feel today?* I tell her that I don't feel blue at the moment. She doesn't follow up.

Galba tells me that it can be difficult to *grow out of childhood*, that it's totally normal, that indeed she has many younger clients who find they suddenly *have a lot of feelings*. We talk for an entire hour about how I never want to wear a jacket. I always say that I'm not cold. This concerns my mother. I own many jackets, but I don't wear them when it's cold out. It was my mother's idea that I go to Galba. She says she has found it helpful to talk to somebody and maybe I'd like to talk to somebody, too. I say yes, but the first time I go to Galba's office, it is cold outside and I refuse a jacket. I have seemed upset lately.

Galba knows, because my parents have told her, that I am not only feeling a little blue. The trouble is my *adjustment difficulties*. Difficulties like: in a just world, I would be failing out of high school. I have been pulled out of C-block English class and threatened with suspension more often than I have attended C-block English class. My old ability to simply memorize academic material on first read—an ability that launched me, during my first two years of high school, into honors courses that I am barely faking my way through by the eleventh grade—has been deteriorating rapidly. Difficulties like: for all the fights I have been starting or provoking, I haven't won a single one.

For several months, I have been coming home from school at four o'clock and passing out on the aging sofa in my parents' living room until I get up and go to bed at ten o'clock. Sometimes I can be roused for dinner, briefly. By March, temperatures in the Valley are running an average of eighty-five degrees, and my face is sticky and stuck to the cracking brown leather of the couch. I will not get out of bed most mornings unless somebody comes in and pleads with me. Or I am already up because I have not been to bed at all. I have been lying to my parents a lot and stealing from my friends. I have been shouting at my friends and calling them in the middle of the night, furious or desperate or demanding. I do not believe my friends are really my friends and I sometimes want to prove this by hurting them. I have a sudden, growing inability to maintain a sense of what I am meant to be doing day to day.

Do I like punk rock? No, not really. I like the Bee Gees, but not the disco stuff. Does Galba like the Bee Gees? She likes the disco stuff, or she used to back in the day. It occurs to me even then that Galba has a strikingly teenaged faith in the correspondence between the bands you like and the state of your soul.

I like Galba. Her office is too dark—there is only one lamp—but the thick green chair where I sit feels good. I am afraid. I do tell her that. I feel afraid when there is nothing to be afraid of, which is almost all the time. The rest of the time I am angry. I think something is the matter with me, but I don't know what. I don't tell her that. I cannot wake up sometimes, and sometimes when I am awake, I feel as if I am sleeping. I feel like I am trying to hold a very small sphere between two fat fingers and something about the way the little orb fits and presses against my hand makes me want to spasm and scream and puke. I have a dream where I am holding the little orb inside of a very long closet. I wake up as I begin throwing up. Galba tells me that teenagers feel afraid sometimes. It's a scary time of life.

I have a profound faith in the healing powers of these conversations. *It's only a scary time*. Okay. *It'll be better soon*. Great. Galba offers that while she's *not going to pretend to understand me*, she'll nonetheless *listen no matter what*. Many adults have made this offer and each of them appears to believe that they are the first one to do so. I like Galba. I want to tell her everything, but I do not even have the words to describe what I am feeling. I don't have any sense of what is relevant or whether any of it would amount to anything at all. Still, I would like her to ask more pressing questions. She does not. She says she'll *listen no matter what*, but I am seventeen years old and she is a professional and she will not tell me what, beyond bad albums, she would like to be *listening* to me say. I keep waiting for her to ask.

During one appointment after two straight nights without sleep, I begin to get caught up on the word *apostle*. The second syllable is caught in my mouth. *Ostle. Stl. Stllll. Sss-tl*. The way the *s* becomes the *t* becomes the *l*; like that. It sticks in a good way. It feels good. I curve my tongue back over itself and hold it with the backside of my top-front teeth and push the s-t-l out that way. I only do this three or four times; it isn't so bizarre. But Galba asks if I feel all right. I say, I just like how the word sounds. She asks what I mean. This is the first follow-up question she has ever asked with any interest. I say I like the consonants at the end. She asks if I get stuck on words like that a lot.

I think it is something in her voice or something in her face or something about the air settling in the dark office that tells me that there are words you cannot take back in a clinician's office, that there is a line where you are no longer speaking only about difficulty adjusting to imminent adult life, and I am suddenly aware that this question is the first step toward that line. Or, I am not *aware*. I feel short of breath. I am afraid and this fear is an instinct saying: *shut up*.

I doubt Galba had anything so significant in mind. If I picked up on anything, it was something in myself, not her. How could this possibly matter? But from then on, I wouldn't have told Galba anything, even if she had asked.

I said, *No, I'm sorry. I'm taking a creative writing class.* (I wasn't.) *I'm just thinking about a story.*

Okay, said Galba. *Just checking.*

I told my mother that therapy was not for me and somehow I stopped seeing Galba. I like to imagine that I was allowed to abandon her on a whim, like piano lessons. But I think that I refused to go. I may have cried or yelled or made threats or run away for a few nights (I did that from time to time). I don't remember. I refused to explain why I did not want to go back, and I made it so unpleasant for my parents that it was easier for them to just give up and let me stop. I never saw Galba again.

Otho (reigned June 2007–July 2007)

I only saw Otho three times, but I remember his face very clearly. He had a memorable face. He had the sort of face about which you might say, *He has a horseface.*

Otho doesn't have an office. He works out of his home in the northern San Fernando Valley, in a bungalow set back from the sidewalk by a large dirt plot. He sees clients in his living room, which is decorated in seventies sitcom plush. Thick carpets and painted walls; mustard yellow, lime green, mud brown. He dresses like his decorations: pumpkin-orange dress shirt and thick corduroy slacks. I remember him blending into his chair like a stick bug: horseface emerging from shag home set.

I'm here because I have been getting worse. I stormed out whenever my parents wanted to talk. Lately, I'd been storming out a lot: out of class, out of practice, out of clubs, out of my parents' house. Once, I left for several days to go to San Diego to attend an internet security convention, despite knowing nothing at all about computers. I spent the three nights getting high with a man who would later go to federal prison and then accept a ride back to Los Angeles with a man from Detroit who would not tell me his real name. I have fucked up the spring semester badly and now I have to go to summer school.

I have been using a lot of very cheap cocaine and sometimes cheaper heroin. My parents have never explicitly acknowledged this, but I suspect it was not as secret as I believed. I am afraid of drugs, but they confirm and amplify certain already-present baseline feelings, so I keep taking them. Every time I do, I am nervous; I half-believe I won't each time. But even when I am not on them, I am all nervous energy, all yes and no but no why before acting. I am all impulse. Or I am scarcely awake or capable of action at all. Over the previous weeks, my impulses and actions have begun alienating me from my old circle of high school friends and from the older friends I've replaced them with. I am rarely speaking to my parents, and when I do, it almost always turns to screaming or threats of running away or crying or violence. I am only in Otho's office because coming here is a condition of retaining my right to go out or drive or do anything at all, and if I am not free to go out, then it will be too difficult to run away from home, which I plan to do as soon as possible.

The first session in Otho's mustard living room is with my father, who carries on a conversation between himself and his tendency to second-guess whatever he's just said. *I think I was like this at his age, although . . . He's always done well in school, but . . . I'm just out of ideas, except . . .* Like that. Otho asks me if there is anything I'm concerned about or if there's anything I would like to say to my father. I say no. We sit there for a minute in silence, so I say no again. Otho then asks if everything is all right with me, and I tell him I'm fine.

I don't remember much else of what my father said. I was very tired. He was scared.

In Otho's office, I believed that if I refused to engage with this exercise, but did so while being *fine*—which I understood to mean sitting in a chair for an hour without evident difficulty—then Otho and my father would see that I was *fine* and stop being afraid. I did not believe there was anything to be afraid about. Since leaving Galba, I had come to believe that nothing was wrong, or at least that if I did not answer any questions, nobody could prove that something was wrong, and everyone would be forced to stop asking.

I spent most of my time in the weeks between the end of the spring semester and the beginning of summer school trying to wake up. The walls in my bedroom creaked wrong. They're fake. I could smell sea air or bus exhaust when I closed my eyes. I was on a beach somewhere. I was imagining all of this. There was an immense curve on the highway over the ocean; go there. Steal every scrap of cash you can find before you go. I spent time sitting at my desk in a black and steel chair, pressing the tops of my hands into the cold undersides of the arm rests. Everyone I knew was talking about me behind my back. I wasn't paranoid; it was true. I had been needy and insulting, calling them and hectoring them and bothering them and then disappearing for a while before coming back, asking if they wanted to *hang out.* By now, this was the only personality that a significant number of my friends had ever known.

Like Galba, Otho said during our first session that he would *always listen,* that he would *try to understand* and *help* with *the problems I'd been having.* During our second session, just me and him, he asked me what kind of music I liked.

Do ya like the Beatles? He had a horse voice, too.

Sure.

Who's your favorite Beatle?

I don't know. Who's yours?

Paul.

Okay.

You like John?

No.

George?

No.

Ringo?

No.

Then who?

Pete Best.

Fuck you.

He didn't say fuck you, but he squinted like he was thinking it. Or he didn't say any of that at all. I remember this conversation as clearly as I remember Otho's horseface, but I also know that I heard this dialogue later, somewhere else, possibly in Chicago, after I had become much sicker than I'd been with Otho. I don't know where it came from, precisely, although I have checked, and it does not appear to come from anything under copyright. The memory has come detached from its origin and has settled into my memory of Otho. I can hear him saying his lines. I don't know what to make of that, but it's funny. It's here for you to laugh.

Otho did ask about the kinds of music I liked. He did ask if I liked the Beatles, but in reality, I didn't say anything back at all. He asked if I was feeling anxious. I didn't say anything for forty minutes straight. I am certain that this is what really happened, but the memory feels no more real to me than the memory about Pete Best. It's only that other people remember this version, too. I didn't say anything for the whole hour. Otho let me go. I got into my car and took my car home and walked back outside on foot. I walked several hours down Ventura Boulevard, across the Valley, and I didn't go home for six weeks.

I stay with three or four different friends in rotating shifts. When one of them goes to a group outing, I tag along, invited or not. I demand attention but do not make much sense. I accompany a group of people I vaguely know to a faraway beach several times in one month by borrowing a car and offering to drive the hour there and back. I show up to drive without asking if anybody wanted me to drive them. Nobody is ever pleased to see me. I call a woman who I have not seen in months from the side of a bridge and tell her that I am going to jump and it's her fault, then I hang up the phone and don't accept incoming calls for several hours. Most days are agitated emptiness.

Most days, I go to the same diner three times, four hours apart, and order a vanilla milkshake. If I can convince someone to join me, I spend the evenings loitering in a public park nearby. One afternoon, I agree to see Otho and drive to his house in the Valley. He says, *Do you want to talk about what's going on?* We sit in silence for thirty minutes straight, then: *Your parents are worried about you.* I say nothing. We sit in silence for thirty minutes more.

I sleep on couches. I pay back my hosts by ransacking their houses for cash. I keep attending summer school (*If I am still going to summer school, the situation is not out of control,* I think). I stay awake all night. On a field trip to a museum of ancient Greek and Roman art, I go through the Corinthian columns at the edges of a reproduced agora and decide that I am having a heart attack. I go to the bathroom to recover. I think, *God is trying to kill me.* And then I think, *All puns are intended by God,* and that this is an urgent and related thought. The middle knuckle on my right hand is very swollen. Several weeks earlier, I had punched my best friend in the face because he would not stop demanding to know a secret I was keeping (I don't remember what the secret was), and when I hit him, his tooth split in half and the bottom part split my knuckle. I never saw a doctor. The swelling went down eventually but the knuckle set wrong. It is still uneven.

Sometime in the middle of the summer, I go home. It is a spontaneous decision. I am vaguely aware that my coming home is inevitable, but I do not know why I choose the day I do to accede to this reality. I have not yet run out of couches or money. I believe, coming through the front door that evening, that everyone will just act as if nothing strange has happened. I am still in summer school. I haven't missed a day. Perhaps all of this, while unpleasant, is not a terribly big deal. Perhaps merely refusing to acknowledge what had happened, by treating any effort to discuss it with contempt, I can force my family to accept that nothing significant has gone on. Even if they do not accept it really, I think that my refusal might serve as a blunt emotional instrument. They might agree to go along with my silence because it would be too exhausting, after all the worry, to fight back.

We have dinner. We do not discuss where I have been or what will happen next. I ask about using the car. My mother mentions that the car needed a new hose of some kind; it might not be available for a while. I think, *Okay, good, this is working.* I go to sleep in my own bed. I sleep one night in my old bedroom. At five in the morning, I am woken up by two large men I'd never seen before. The men tell me that I am going with them. We are going to the airport.

On the way out, one asks me when my eighteenth birthday will be. I tell him it's in January, in six months. He says that I'll probably be back in time.

I don't believe I saw my parents that morning. Or they were right outside my bedroom doorway, watching. Or they were in the kitchen, or they were at the front door for a quick goodbye while the men took me out to the driveway. My father, or maybe not my father. My mother, with my father hiding in his office. It's very early and it's hard to tell what's going on.

Vitellius (reigned July 2007–October 2007)

They call him the Bagel Man because he brings bagels, all kinds. He brings regular bagels and blueberry bagels and onion and cinnamon and chive. You can have as many bagels as you like if you cooperate. If your diet has consisted primarily of rehydrated beans and yellow rice for several weeks now, then you'll take a lot of bagels, thank you. You'll eat a whole sleeve of four or six or eight. You'll eat too many and get sick. When the Bagel Man comes, you'll spend all day in a truck eating bagels and submitting to a battery of psychiatric tests.

The Bagel Man is not Vitellius. The Bagel Man is a psychologist for the wilderness inpatient program I've been sent to in a mountain range in Georgia. If you are a patient at this program, then sometime during your third or fourth week of involuntary commitment, the Bagel Man will arrive in his big truck, and you'll sit with him inside of it and eat bagels while he administers as many psychological exams as he is able in a day.

By the time the Bagel Man comes for me, I have already made three escape attempts. One lasted only five minutes—I ran and a counselor grabbed me. The second involved begging and crying, refusing to take shelter under our group tarp despite a heavy thunderstorm, and saying *Just give me a phone call just give me a phone call* over and over. The third time I manage to slip off early in the morning (they do not expect you to make a run for it before you've been given your shoes back for the day), and I make it some six hours by wading through creeks and staying off the roads. In a small gully with a river, I find an old man and his wife fishing and convince them to give me a water bottle and two cigarettes. I shit under a tree and do not bury it, which is what we are ordinarily obliged to do. Near twilight, I risked going up to a dirt road in search of directions out of the forest, but within a few minutes, a program van somehow finds me. I go limp and refuse to walk and two counselors drag me into the back.

After this attempt, I begin to accept what everyone accepts about these programs after a while: you are no longer in a position to re-fuse. Nobody will concede that you have come here by mistake. I spent the next two weeks on run watch, denied my own tarp and sleeping bag, forced to spend nights swaddled up between two counselors so I couldn't run away.

The program is in Georgia because Georgia is one of the few states that allows parents to sign over temporary custody like this. I was meant to arrive the same afternoon the two men took me, but the flight from LAX to Atlanta was delayed and didn't arrive until evening. From the airport, two new men drove me several hours north to a small town, then handed me off to be processed in an office next door to a salvage yard. Processing involves turning over all my clothes and possessions (I've brought two books I'm not allowed to keep), receiving new clothes and possessions (camping supplies), and packing them in an enormous backpack. A middle-aged nurse, still at work far later than she'd expected to stay that day, drew blood for a drug test and administered an anal cavity search. After I left the processing office, I didn't go inside again for months. The program is entirely outdoors.

My group consists of me and eleven other male patients. We are accompanied at all times by three counselors who rotate in and out every Tuesday when we stop at a proper campsite to resupply. The rest of the week, we hike and cook and participate in group therapy. We carry around some several hundred pounds of equipment, both our own and our communal possessions: cooking supplies, shared food, a large group tarp, and stakes. We move between hillsides and thick woods and underbrush; for the most part, we do not sleep in properly cleared areas. Our equipment does not include flashlights, real tents, electronics of any kind, or any gas or lighters. We have wooden spoons we've made ourselves. We have bows and string and flat stones we've found to drill embers to make fire. If we cannot get a fire going, we rehydrate our beans with cold water. We have paper and one pen per person. We have exercise books, mainly copied from self-help texts or AA pamphlets. We are always together.

Any group that requires its members to tolerate one another's presence at all moments of the day, and that furthermore expects them to provide constant therapeutic reinforcement to one another, must induce shared trust. This is sometimes accomplished with the kinds of trust exercises you might encounter at summer camp or on a corporate retreat. At other times, it is accomplished by way of a self-enforcing disciplinary regime in which patients are conscripted to police themselves.

If he won't hike, we all stand here, no matter how late it gets, until he starts going again. Is that frustrating? Have you communicated how he's letting you down? Stuff like that. But the trick is mainly rigid communication structures. All conversations take place within staff earshot. Certain kinds of conversations—those that valorize past poor behavior or speculate about what we may be doing next—are forbidden. (We are forbidden "future knowledge" in general). We make structured statements: *I feel x because I believe y; when p did q I felt r.* The program is very bullish on the notion that emotional states are a consequence of belief structures, something they have cribbed without context from cognitive-behavioral therapy. There is less guidance on whether we ought to adjust our responses, or our underlying beliefs, or both, or neither, or how such adjustments might be made.

Communal humiliation breeds kinship, too. One group meeting is dedicated to reading my "letter of accountability." Everybody has one. You are given a letter written by your parents. You have not read it before, but you will read it aloud now: a liturgy of disappointments and misbehavior, concern, well-wishes. At the behest of the program, it includes accounts of particular incidents and particular wrongs. It comes down to: *You've hurt us.* It comes down to the fact that you are no longer sitting with somebody willing to *listen* until they sort out whether something has gone wrong. Something has gone wrong already. Now it is your turn to *listen.*

I do not remember anything from the contents of my letter, except a line in which my father reminds me that the night I came home, I demanded, as a condition, that he order a particular kind of takeout meal. This is a small, petty thing, but both then and now it makes me feel as if I have shown you the worst part of myself. I remember crying, my cheeks turning red, both humiliation and shame (and knowing that these are different things), but I was not asked to identify the beliefs that motivated these bad feelings.

It is difficult to remain aloof after this experience. You are part of the group now. Later, you will compose and read a reply to your parents, subject to critique by the other patients. *I feel like you're evading; I wonder if you're not rationalizing here.* All of the critiques include this sort of neutered, clinical language, which is also prominently featured in our therapy and the workbooks we've been given. It is unclear, during these sessions, if your peers are actually concerned with the honesty of your reply, or if they are like any student who has memorized a few key phrases they can offer whenever they are called on to earn their participation grade. You can't talk outside of counselor earshot, so you can't ask. You learn that it is important to show the staff that you've grown since you've arrived, and that you can help the others grow by teaching them what the program has already taught you. *I think you're explaining excuses instead of accepting responsibility.* That was my go-to line.

I come to like my group. How could I not? There is no one else. I come to like Jackson, a wiry barista so obviously bullshitting his way through the program that it is a wonder he is allowed to leave at all. I come to like Rich, who is proportioned like a high school football player too skinny to go pro, and who is somehow capable of simultaneously demonstrating *excellent peer leadership* and always being very slightly in trouble with the staff. When he finds out one morning that he is leaving, he pulls me aside and helps me cheat on a required skill test by giving me a piece of rope he's weaved from bark, capable of holding a fifty-pound sack for at least thirty minutes. *Just tell them you made it*, he says, then promises to call a friend of mine when he gets home. I come to like Doug, whose cognitive limitations prevent him from even faking a cooperative attitude. Weeks into his stay, he will still stop in the middle of hikes and sit down and weep and refuse to go on until he is sent home. I come to like "Cool Mike," who is thirteen years old. His parents had him committed for excessive pot smoking.

During daylight hours, patients are always in sight of at least one staff member. One leads the hike. One brings up the rear. They form a triangle at camp; each one has at least sixty degrees of vision. We are allowed privacy only when we shit or shower (fill a sack with river water, strip, pour over yourself, repeat), but only if we are not on suicide or run watch. There is a catch. When out of sight, we must shout our first name every three to five seconds, loudly enough to be heard at camp. This is precisely as ridiculous as you imagine. Or it is for a while. The extraordinary becomes ordinary far faster than the merely unusual. Shouting your own name, particularly with your pants down, quickly becomes unremarkable. I do not remember much of the therapeutic content of my time in this program. I do not remember the faces of any but three or four staffers, or what we did most days. But I remember this habituation and the extent to which compliance transforms into reflex. I realize that this is the point.

By the time the Bagel Man comes for me, I understand that there was no set stay in the wilderness. You could be gone for three months or for six. You could go home after, or you could continue to a "therapeutic boarding school." I begin to understand that there are two kinds of therapy: the kind for when you have a problem, and the kind for when you are the problem, and that this is the latter kind. I am scared. I think, after a while, that the point is not to get well but to get out. I think, after a while, that perhaps these are one in the same. I will get out and this will prove that I have gotten well.

After a while, I become secretly enamored with the aggression and discipline of this program. Galba and Otho did not force me to get well. But here, nobody will sit back and wait for me to tell them I feel badly. They already know I feel badly, and they will find out the reason why. They will not let me quit or sit silent through appointments. They will compel me to collaborate in my own cure.

The Bagel Man administered, among other tests, the Minnesota Multiphasic Personality Inventory, the Beck Depression Inventory, the Teenage Sentence Completion Test, a Rorschach test, and the Millon Adolescent Clinical Inventory. *Have you ever hallucinated?* No. *How do you feel?* Okay. *Have you ever felt anxious or depressed?* Sure.

When I sit with the Bagel Man, I do not disclose everything, but I disclose more than I ever have before. I do well. I talk with him about myself and about the program; I demonstrate maturity and acceptance. I talk about my relationships with staff and with the other patients candidly; I even offer my own insight into their cases, couched in program language. I talk about my parents and my friends at home. I concede the reality of my situation: something must be wrong if your situation is involuntary commitment in the Georgia wilderness. The Bagel Man and I build a rapport. I walk the line between appropriate insight and not seeming too troubled or crazy. I eat a great number of bagels.

Many years later, I obtained a copy of the report the Bagel Man produced from our day together. It reads, in part:

"Emmett demonstrates an impairment of his ability to perceive events, often forming mistaken impressions of people and what their actions signify . . . [He has] issues with impulsivity . . . poor motivation for therapy and less willingness to explore feelings . . . is defensive . . . fatigued . . . wound up . . . unable to self-focus . . . " and prone to "denial and intellectualization as major defenses" due to "a fear that he may become overwhelmed."

"Emmett describes [his anxiety] as dread, and it appears to be overwhelming for him." The Bagel Man reported that I suffer from "intrusive ideational concerns" and that I "give responses indicative of someone who is experiencing depression" with some "fleeting suicidal ideation."

"An apparent inability to comprehend societal norms," was noted, attributed to "a general feeling of estrangement from his parents and peers . . . He expresses a defensive rejection of the desire to form close ties with others, whom he regards generally as untrustworthy, cynically motivated, or conspiratorial." I have "significant substance abuse issues."

"Emmett is locked in circular arguments and logic, which keep him from being able to work through his emotional difficulties. He had difficulties staying on topic as he wanted to engage in philosophical debates of mental illness . . . His inaccurate perceptions of people and events are likely to lead him to erroneous conclusions and ill-advised actions, and faulty judgment is likely to undermine the adequacy of his adjustment. This is a significant adaptive liability that appears to constitute a chronic and pervasive source of difficulty in his life." This is how the Bagel Man concludes. But he does allow, in his final summary, that I am "a pleasant-looking boy of smaller than average stature." At least there's that.

Vitellius, meanwhile, comes once a week. He is the group therapist who sees us individually every Tuesday evening or Wednesday morning. He reads our mail. He sends for us unless he does not (and he tells you why he hasn't). He gives us any mail we may have gotten from our family or program-approved friends, unless he doesn't and never says. He brings his dog to work and has the friendly affect of a man overestimating his own charm.

Vitellius says I like abstraction too much. He says I need to learn to see the situation around me as it really is. I need to stop evading, he says, and I know that he is right about this. It is possible that he will ask me the questions Galba couldn't, and it is possible that I will answer them. I don't know what I'll do. The second or third time we speak, he says he is putting together a mix CD with one song from each member of the group and he will let us listen to it once next week on a stereo system that he'll bring. He asks who I like. I say, *The Mamas & the Papas*, but he doesn't believe me because I'm lying.

Vitellius is the most skilled therapist I see during the Year of the Four Emperors. He listens well but is clear about what he would like to listen to. He persuades me to accept that I am in trouble. Something has gone wrong. I don't have the words for it yet but in the quiet and routine of the wilderness, the first springs of legitimate insight set in: Something is happening inside of my brain and I cannot pretend that this is simply what it feels like to *adjust to adulthood*. This is not just a benign lump. This is not a normal cold. This will not go away if I ignore it.

Vitellius is capable, programmatic, and deliberate. He is the first to suggest to me that while he is not entirely certain what's wrong, it's not likely to be something that will just fade with time. I will need to begin developing the ability to live a managed life, to adapt to a permanently different reality.

Because there is no risk that I simply won't come back the following week, Vitellius moves slowly. Over the weeks, he tailors his treatment plan to the needs of his patients. He lets me indulge in "abstraction" for a while, then cuts me shorter and shorter each session, requiring me to refocus on myself. His questions become challenges in small, nearly imperceptible degrees: *What happened?* Then, *Why do you think he did that?* Then, *Why do you think you responded that way?* Then, *Why did you spend that way?* Then, *Do you really think that's why he did that?* Then, *Do you think this was an appropriate response, given how much you were assuming about his motives?* Like that. He's empathetic. He has a talent for pushing clients without undermining the sense that we are *on the same team here.* Mainly, his regimen involves learning cognitive-behavioral coping mechanisms, locating the emotional bases of my reactions to events, honing my capacity to consider my initial interpretation of events, and having me jerk him off from time to time on the implicit understanding that I will get out earlier if I do.

There are no mirrors in the wilderness. For months I don't see my own reflection. I catch a distortion of my face in dark, rippling water, or in the steel of the hubcap of the Bagel Man's truck, blasted out by the refracting sun. The glare blinds me when I try to meet my own eyes.

I know my body is changing. My hair is growing longer. I lose weight from hiking then gain it back from exercise. My legs get thick. For all the bags of river water I poured over my own head, my skin gets cracked and caked with dirt. When I put my palm to my face, I feel a beard growing in, although a beard will not grow in on my cheeks yet. I take stock in the manner of the blind: fingertips to jawline to cheekbones to neck. I forget that this is a strange thing. The faculty for tracking incremental differences becomes dedicated to leaves, to rocks, to sky, to the footfalls of other people. By six weeks in, I am waking up long before we are required to. I like the cold air in the forest. I like half-light. My brain feels clean and clear and calm for the first time in the whole year.

I have spoken to many people who attended this program and programs like it in the decade and a half since I have left. You wonder, while you are there, who in the group has *bought in* and who is just cooperating as a means of hiding in plain sight. What you discover, after a while, is that there is very little difference between these two states. Many of the people I've spoken to cannot say which they were doing. I'm not sure what I did. The program is aware of this ambivalence. They know that if you want to believe in God, you start by kneeling.

Rich leaves and Jackson leaves and Cool Mike leaves; eventually, the group I entered has been replaced by a different group of similarly lunatic teenagers with drug problems. One is a former Neo-Nazi. Another is a Jew who came by court order after laying out his own grandmother when she wouldn't let him leave the house. I remember them because both were named Andrew and both were good cooks. By the time they arrive, I have been granted some privileges as a result of completing a number of skill exercises, like *insightful journaling* and the bark-woven rope. I have a very small flashlight and a walking stick inherited from another patient. I am told that I am demonstrating excellent *peer leadership*.

One morning, after an average period of time, I am told that my parents have arrived. I'm leaving. I did not get out early. This stays with me.

My parents drive me out onto the highway, and I am amazed that the drivers trust that the lines on the road are real. I go back to my ordinary high school, although I've missed my senior class picture and had to be photoshopped in. For months, when I sing in the shower, I say my own name every three to five seconds without hearing it at all.

Vespasian (reigned November 2007–September 2008)

I liked Vespasian. I liked him because he was like Galba; he didn't insist that I do therapy. *How are you this week?* Just fine. *How's school?* Okay.

Like that. I felt comfortable with him. He looked like a therapist should look, by which I mean he looked like someone cast to play a therapist in an HBO drama, by which I mean, he looked like Gabriel Byrne, who played a therapist in an HBO drama. I didn't like that I had to see Vespasian, but if I had to see a therapist, I did not mind seeing this one. He's easy. Like Galba, he rarely followed up, and I no longer wished that someone would.

I was required to see Vespasian twice a week until my eighteenth birthday, then once a week until I left Los Angeles for good. I took a drug test every two weeks. Those were the conditions of my return from the wilderness.

This was possible, in part, because I was feeling better. I really did feel fine for most of that year, or at least, I felt better than I had before. I was able to behave as if I was feeling better than I was before the woods. My grades improved slightly. I believed, sincerely, that the trouble had just gone away. A temporary recession of symptoms is not uncommon in psychiatric patients, particularly early on. The crash from an acute episode produces a period of relative tranquility. Many patients are found to be particularly calm in the days and weeks following a suicide attempt or particularly violent episode; the excess psychic energy was released and the disease satiated for a while.

I had a tranquil year. Even my parents behaved as if everything was back to normal. Only occasionally did they betray—in small flashes, unexpected phone calls, indirect but urgent questioning—that they were still afraid this peace would not last. I drifted into an interest in the arts and discovered that "artistic" teenagers, particularly when they are men with messy hair, are afforded a great deal more charity when it comes to eccentric or even troubling activity. I learned to speak less, and less explicitly.

Vespasian never seemed suspicious about my always being *just fine*. I barely recall the contents of any of our conversations at all. He never pressed important questions, and in exchange, I never gave him any cause to think that he should be asking. I saw Vespasian for a year and never once did he ask, if I seemed so stable, how I'd gone through so many professionals, how I'd been sent to the wilderness, how the Bagel Man had written the report he'd written, a report which Vespasian had read years and years before I ever read it. When I turned eighteen, we switched to only once a week. After I left town, I never saw him again.

Omnes Annos Post Hoc (2008–Present)

In the second century AD, the Roman physician Aretaeus of Cappadocia wrote of patients in Greece who oscillated between an *unreasonable torpor* and *excellent spirits* who spoke *untaught astronomy, spontaneous philosophy, and poetry truly from the muses. They sometimes go openly to the market, crowned as if victors in some contest of skill,* he wrote. *At other times they rend their clothes and kill their keepers and lay violent hands upon themselves. Wherefore they are affected with madness in various shapes,* reported Aretaeus, *some run along unrestrainedly and, not knowing how, return again to the same place.*

Every patient learns evasion tactics. Therapy teaches you, after a while, how to avoid therapy. The Year of the Four Emperors taught me how to hide; each emperor instructed me in a more sophisticated way to be left alone. With Galba, I had not meant to conceal myself; I was just unwilling to come out if no one asked me. With Otho, I had learned refusal, which is a blunt and ineffective way to hide. With Vitellius, I learned that it is best to avoid clinical attention by appearing to embrace it. You cooperate to avoid alerting the clinician to the fact that they ought to treat you as a hostile witness to your own wellbeing. By the time of Vespasian, I had gone somewhere beneath the floorboard of myself, and nobody could have pried me out without great effort.

Was this their fault or mine? Psychiatric patients are famously uncooperative. We are famously inclined to deny our need for help and to evade help when it is forced on us. We are not like the patient who wanders nervously into a hospital with a painful, tightening chest, eager to be examined and saved. Surely, each of my four emperors knew this. Surely, they could have anticipated my resistance. I was seventeen years old.

It was seven years from the Year of the Four Emperors to the day that a psychiatrist in Chicago first diagnosed and medicated me. Those seven years constitute, and will, I hope, continue to constitute, the worst years of my life. They might never have occurred at all. I have hurt myself and other people. Perhaps that pain could have been avoided. I have lost cognitive function. Perhaps I could have kept it. I have learned tricks and points of emphasis and conversational performance routines to conceal this fact, but my memory is shaky and my reasoning, particularly under pressure, has degraded. Perhaps I could have been a more pleasant friend.

Each of my emperors had promised to help and none of them did. I do not know if saying that I did not want their help, that I avoided their help and resented their help and resisted their help as best I could, is the same as saying that I made it impossible for them to help me. I was a collaborator in each coup and the failure of each regime, but surely I was not a novel case. I still don't understand what happened. I never went another year without a crisis. I have seen nearly two dozen therapists in my life. I fired one between writing this essay and getting it back in proofs. I'll find another soon enough.

During my last year in Iowa, I spent a year under the care of a doctor who specializes in mood disorders. By then I was a straightforward case: nearly thirty, diagnosed and medicated, good insight. This new doctor's job was just to monitor me week by week for warning signs, and to alert my psychiatrist if she felt a medication change was in order. I told her about my year of the four emperors. The therapist told me that she had previously focused on youth treatment with an emphasis on early detection. Had I been a teenager in her care, she said, I would have been referred to a psychiatrist for a small dose of antipsychotics, and that this may have prevented me from ever getting sick at all. *I have patients*, she said, *who we catch so early that they never have a real psychotic break. They're ill; you can see the early symptoms. The neurological disease is there, but we keep the kindling down so the fire never comes.* I wish she hadn't told me that, and I told her so.

We talked about it for a few more minutes, but then the therapist redirected me back to more practical matters. She wanted me to get eyeglasses. I had been hallucinating recently. I knew these sounds— which sounded, more or less, like the din of background chatter in a restaurant run through a ham radio, and which seemed to emanate from other people's heads—were hallucinations. They were simple to ignore. But my therapist wanted to get them under control while they remained simple. This would likely involve a medication adjustment, but glasses, she said, were essential, too. *It's sensory kindling,* she said. *We want as little of that as possible.* I said, *Okay, I will,* and left, and then put off getting the glasses for six weeks. The demand felt intrusive. I resented it. I am still sometimes only pretending to cooperate.

I bought the glasses eventually. Then a few days later, I called the Bagel Man. It was easy to find his phone number online; he'd transitioned to private practice in a different state. In the conclusion of the report, he'd diagnosed me with a depressive disorder, an anxiety disorder *not otherwise specified*, paranoid tendencies, and oppositional defiant disorder. I wanted to ask him, *Motherfucker, can you add?*

When I reached him, I told him that he'd assessed me in the wilderness a decade earlier. I read back his diagnoses.

And now you've been diagnosed bipolar or something? he asked.

Yes.

Yeah, that happens, he said.

Then, after a pause, he said, *You have to understand that it usually doesn't. You don't want to tag somebody who is just having a hard time in adolescence with a lifelong mental illness.*

Okay, I thought. Then, after a pause, I said, *But this happens enough that you guessed without me saying.*

I told him that it took another seven years before I was diagnosed, and that I wished I'd been put on medication earlier. He told me seven or eight years after initial onset is about average, and by the way, not even inevitable. *Really*, he said, *the problem with teenage boys is that no matter what's wrong with them, the symptom is that they're sullen and pissed off all of the time.*

Okay.

I asked the Bagel Man what the point had been of institutionalizing me for months if it couldn't help me. What was the point if, ultimately, they were reticent to really "label" me in a way that might have been helpful? What was the point?

He explained that a diagnosis and medication aren't the only way people can be helped. They're meant to learn skills that—

Okay.

You wanted it to help you? A lot of younger patients—

Okay.

It's just that the program works best if—

Okay.

In any case, he said, *I'm sorry. You seem okay.*

Yes, I said. *Okay. Thank you. Yes. Okay.* And then I hung up.

Marlon

On a Friday night when I was seventeen years old, I checked in for the first time at the Hotel Alexandria. The Alexandria is an old hotel. It opened in 1906, when downtown Los Angeles was still the center of the city. D.W. Griffith checked in for the first time in 1910. Charlie Chaplin got married there. Several presidents have been guests over the years. But when I went, I wasn't checking in to a hotel room. In 1976, following decades of decline, the building was converted into a Single Room Occupancy (SRO) apartment building for long-term, low-income residents. *Due to its proximity to Skid Row, the building became notorious for drug crime and its generally dangerous character,* a tourist website warned.

The lobby had been plundered, exposed wire hung from a bare ceiling above chipped and missing floors tiles. I had to give my ID to a security guard in the lobby, who had to sign me in before I was allowed to enter the elevator. The guard was not a sign of exclusivity. He existed, mainly, to defend the residents from one another. I had come to visit my friend Marlon, who had just moved in.

Eleven years later, a final visit, when I was twenty-eight years old: Downtown had gentrified again. The Alexandria was restored. The ceiling was in one piece. The security guard was gone. There was a bar in the lobby and a club on the second floor. A famous chef ran a restaurant inside. Marlon didn't live there anymore. But B., another friend of mine and Marlon's, suggested that we check out all the changes. A bouncer outside the new bar asked us for our IDs. B. was already drunk. *Okay, okay, I mean—sure*, he said. *But you know our friend died in this building.*

Okay, said the bouncer. *IDs, please.*

•••

I do not believe, as many do, that tragedy is necessarily significant, even if it occurs when we are young. I do not believe that events we remember as significant are necessarily the most consequential, even when they require mourning. In *Mourning and Melancholia*, Freud writes that when we have first lost an object of love, we turn away from any activity not connected with it. The memory and its attendant grief are all that are left of what we've lost, and so to cease grieving feels like a betrayal. Freud goes on to say that mourning is the process of divesting the dead of their importance. We mourn until we are able to surrender our grief and return to ordinary life. The alternative is melancholia; unable to displace love onto another object, the melancholic fixates until they have identified their lost love entirely within their own ego. The process of divestment, if it occurs at all, becomes an act of self-destruction. The result is sometimes suicide. But I do not believe, as Freud did, that these are the only two possibilities, or even that these are the most common scenarios.

There are also mourners who are not melancholic, those who have, in some sense, "moved on," but who have not truly divested themselves of their grief. The world goes on, but the mourner cannot bear the possibility that the world has not been ruined by the loss. They believe that the ongoing world has not only lost some essential part of its quality but some degree of its *reality* as well. For these mourners, the moment of loss becomes an inflection point. The state of things in that moment—the state of politics, currents of culture, the ambitions of the mourner, the condition of hotels—becomes the authentic version of those things. The loss becomes the central ordering principle by which the mourner interprets all subsequent events. Any changes belong to a grey after-time, tracked only by how far they have drifted from the old and real world. Even Freud, in his later years, conceded the possibility that there was no real dichotomy; that all mourners were melancholic, and no loss leaves the ego entirely unchanged.

A significant tragedy does not reveal the secrets of a life so readily as its victims are liable to believe. Causation is not tidy, nor would it be so sentimental if it were. But the tragedies that we assign significance, the events we misuse as the interpretive instruments of our lives, the particulars of our foolishness and self-deception—these, I believe, can be revealing.

• • •

During my last year in Los Angeles, I attached myself to a group of old friends who did not particularly like me. They didn't know me. They all lived in the San Fernando Valley like I did, but they went to different schools. They were slightly older and had known one another since childhood. They played music together, snuck out together, tried drugs together—and although I was taking drug tests and trying to behave myself, I imagined that these were the sorts of people who would find my institutionalization in the wilderness to be a marker of credibility rather than a warning.

I became their friend by insistence. I turned up. I tagged along. They may have been open to liking me. Maybe some of them did like me. But they learned quickly that I was annoying. I texted and called too much. I rarely had anything to do; I was just seeing what they were up to. I turned up uninvited because I believed that this would lead to being texted and called and invited on purpose. Mainly, it led to a begrudging acceptance of the fact that I was around. But I suspected that even that tolerance was a tenuous and fragile thing, liable to be revoked at any time. I wanted very badly to belong to these people, and so I feared that I did not, at all times.

It was through these new friends that I met Marlon. I had known them for a few months and was driving several of them around near Venice Beach when they instructed me to pull over on the curbside of a residential neighborhood. We were picking somebody up. One of them placed a call, and a few minutes later, a man in a green wig and cheap half-finished zombie makeup came sprinting up, phone in hand. He got inside. Nobody explained to me what he was doing there. I'd gathered that he lived in the Valley, too. He was taller than any of us, but he volunteered to sit in the middle seat. He was very thin.

By the end of the afternoon, I knew the following things about Marlon: He was slightly older, but still in high school. He had a flask with what he said was liquor, but he wouldn't share. He liked movies, which I still believe is a very cool thing to like. He was too insistent when he talked. He got too close to people's faces. He bulged his eyes and jutted his head forward when other people were talking until he got an opportunity to open his mouth; his eyes bugged and darted, as if he were very pleased with himself for keeping one step ahead of a jump. When he got into my car, he began talking to one of our mutual friends about a camera he'd secured. He was terribly excited. He was terribly excited about everything. When he talked, he got ahead of himself, and much of the time, he sounded as if he were just making sounds to buy time until he remembered the sounds he meant to say. He talked so much that it relieved me of my need to talk, but when I did talk, he talked through it. Tight small nods, mainly with his chin. *Yeah, I mean, yeah, yeah, yeah, man, right, I know.*

The year before he began to die, C. S. Lewis wrote that friendship is the least natural species of affection. It *is born at the moment when one man says to another "What? You too? I thought no one but myself."* It is the least biological, the least organic, the least instinctive, gregarious, or necessary kind of love.

...

I had a car and Marlon didn't. He still lived in the Valley then, with his mother and his stepfather and two much younger half sisters—all of whom he seemed routinely motivated to escape, so I would drive once or twice a week the fifteen miles to his neighborhood and pick him up. Once together, we would begin to figure out if anybody wanted to see us. They rarely did, or they did less frequently than we hoped.

We spent a lot of time driving around Los Angeles, waiting to be texted back. This could go on for hours. During these rides, Marlon would tell me exciting facts about himself. He had an incessant need to self-mythologize; he was what Janet Malcolm called the rare self-fabulizing subject. Many of these stories were about ordinary teenage bullshit: women, drugs, encounters with celebrities. But during one car ride, he told me that his father was a Zapatista. He told me this casually, and apropos of nothing. It came between, *Do you want me to call him?* and *Let's just head that way and see if he texts back.*

Most of Marlon's stories were untrue, but they weren't precisely lies. When he told me about his father, I thought it was a kind of juvenile fantasy, like a little girl in a children's book, imagining her real parents are a king and queen. Of course, his father was not a Zapatista. But a decade later, his mother told me that his father was *a kind of Peruvian Scarface.* This was both too close and too far from what he'd told me.

As it happened, nobody wanted to see us that day. Texts came back later, *missed* and *ah, I wish I'd seen this earlier!* I was used to this treatment from our friends; when Marlon wasn't around, I tried to be more strategic about pressing their tolerance for my company. But Marlon had always known these kids. He'd grown up with them. When he began to alienate them, in many of the same ways that I would one day alienate them, too, it must have come as a kind of slow shock: a familiar presence slowly withdrawn until one day he noticed it was missing. He hadn't noticed yet. He was almost always enthusiastic. Even when he was frustrated or annoyed, he was angry with a kind of childish, hopeful energy.

Without anything else to do, we drove up to Mulholland Drive and parked to smoke cigarettes and *figure out our next move* (pray somebody would text us back). I think it was then, inspired by the Zapatista story, that I told Marlon I had a congenital heart condition, inherited via two recessive genes from each parent, and that this condition was liable to kill me before the age of thirty-five. This was the first time I'd told anyone, though I don't know when I'd begun to believe it. I was sure that I had been told by my parents. It had something to do with dentistry. It was a given fact of my life. I know that I believed it for years, and after a while, it was something I told nearly everybody I knew, often casually and apropos of nothing.

Marlon still had hair then, messy blond curls, and he was not yet used to how tall he'd become. When he rolled the window back up after throwing a cigarette out the side, some of his hair got caught between the glass and the door. He didn't roll the window back down, but instead whipped his head sideways, freeing himself but leaving a wad of hair behind. He shifted his chin back and forth quickly under a stationary face. He said, *Ow. Shit*. Several beats too late. Then he laughed for a long time.

...

In its juvenile form, friendship is not a partnership for living in the world, but a means of escaping it. Juvenile friends construct a fantasy, apart from the pressures and obligations of ordinary social life and bound by the importance and indispensability of the friends. With children, this may be a literal fantasy—a shared knowledge of special status or secret rituals, plagiarized, much of the time, from TV, film, or literature—but it may also be, as it often is with adults, a mere suspension of expectation. The juvenile friendship is self-contained. It is a separate world, operating by its own laws and logic. That separate world is precious precisely because it stands apart from or against the real one. Juvenile friends are bonded by defiance—us against the world! Or by desperation: the rest of the world will not have us. We are friends no matter what, perhaps because we are unwilling or unable to win the friendship of other people.

Marlon either dropped out of high school or he was kicked out. I do not know which. He either left his parents' house or he was kicked out. I do not know which. I remember Marlon as a friend and this period before the Alexandria as the most intense phase of our friendship. Why can't I remember how anything of significance happened in his life? I know that sometime after I returned from the wilderness, he rented a room in the Hotel Alexandria, and B. and I went to visit him for the first time shortly after. After the decaying lobby and the menacing hallway, I didn't know what to expect, but I think I imagined something very near the truth. The apartment had one room. The room was very small and almost entirely black. He had a hotplate, a mini-fridge, and an exposed radiator; a twin bed, a small desk, and a table with two stools. He had a bookshelf. There was very little space left. The bathroom was parallel to the entrance, and the two doors next to one another took up nearly the entire wall.

I don't know why he chose that place. The Alexandria was close to a café owned by a friend's mother and Marlon had a job there, but the job came after the move. Maybe it was only because the Alexandria was cheap and felt dangerous and urgent to a teenager. I don't know. I know that when I went up to the fifth floor for the first time to visit, I thought that it all seemed very adult, very free, very cool, very hidden from the brightness and heat and flatness of the Valley and the suggestion, whenever I was stuck there, that I was quickly wearing out my welcome.

Marlon worked during the day. He had fun at the café, he said. He liked his life downtown. *I'm just finally doing real shit*, he told me when I asked him how it was going. *I don't go back to the fucking Valley at night and get tucked in by my parents*, he said. He had begun talking with a hard affect he hadn't had before and did not actually possess now. On the windowsill over the radiator, there was a large bottle of medicine, which Marlon told me was lithium. I still don't know if that was true. The bottle was always full.

One night, we went with B. to buy three very large meatballs and cooked them on Marlon's hotplate. We ate them with spaghetti sauce. Within an hour, B. had thrown up the sauce on his sweater in one tremendous red burst, then moaned from the bathroom that that was his punishment for attending college. Then he passed out. Marlon suggested that if he woke up and didn't remember where the stain came from, he should tell him it was blood. Then Marlon passed out. I didn't pass out. I sat in the middle of the room and threw up in thirty-minute intervals, a few degrees farther to the right each time, until it formed a perfect circle around the stool I perched on.

When I said we cooked the meatballs on the hotplate, I meant we heated them up on the hotplate. They had never been cooked. They were not pre-cooked. I am telling you this because this is the memory where I loved Marlon the most. I don't know why. Maybe because we were very stupid.

• • •

A moment I misunderstood for a long time as an inflection point: A few weeks later, I was back at the Alexandria. But when I arrived, Marlon didn't answer my call. He didn't answer the security guard's call to ask if he's expecting me. He didn't answer when the guard relented and let me up and I knocked on his door for a few minutes straight.

I was thinking of calling somebody else, when Marlon wandered up the hallway in a dress shirt torn off at the left sleeve. *Fuck, sorry, I lost track of time.* He told me he was hanging out with a neighbor down the hall. She's cute, he says, and she works at a bar on Seventh Street. She likes movies, and he thinks she may like him, too.

Marlon built himself a computer. I convinced him, one day, to let me install a medieval war simulator that wouldn't run on my old laptop. I played as the King of France. The Pope ordered me to participate in a crusade. Marlon got impatient and paced behind my chair and shook his head and yelled at me to go rogue and fuck the Pope. He meant kill the Pope. But you cannot fuck or kill the Pope in this game.

• • •

After a while, the apartment in the Alexandria smelled like mucus most of the time. I don't know why. All the black made it get too hot. Marlon circled around the apartment picking objects up at random and flicking a finger against their sides before putting them back down. There was an election coming up, and B. and I were talking about it, but Marlon confessed that he didn't plan to vote. *I don't think I know enough to do that*, he said, and that was the last thing he said for a while. When he spoke again, twenty minutes later, he cut someone off in the middle of a sentence to say, *It's too hot at night.* Then, *Some guys from Skid Row have been hanging around the apartment at night*, he thought they might be looking for him. Then, he found a Chinese liquor store he thought would sell him a gun.

Marlon wanted to buy heroin, but his heroin dealer was not answering the phone. I called around and found the number of a friend of a friend who was said to be holding, and when I called him, he told us to meet him at an address on Sunset Boulevard, which turned out to be a motel overlooking a dirty part of the freeway.

I believe the dealer's name was John. His room was on the second-floor balcony, overlooking the parking lot. B. came along with Marlon and me, even though he didn't take hard drugs. When John answered the door, he said, *I think the cops are watching me. You've got to come in for a while, so it's like we're just friends hanging out.* I don't believe the cops were watching him. In the room, he had several syringes on a small table, a crack pipe in a bedside table drawer, a mountain of empty plastic vials and empty Styrofoam takeout boxes, and around the corner toward the small bathroom at the far end of the suite, a hundred-year-old bolt action rifle, complete with bayonet. B. saw it first. He said, *Hey man, cool antique.* And John said, *Don't touch that shit. It's loaded.*

John's plan, as he explained to us between explanations for his red eyes (he hadn't slept in a while), why he actually needed to call somebody else who could hook us up (business is booming!), and why we all needed to sit down (too many people, like, moving around, like, made him nervous), was that in the event the police showed up, he'd defend himself with the rifle.

Before we could do anything, John needed to clean up (empty plastic vials in the Styrofoam boxes, boxes in plastic bags, bags in the trash bin), text another dealer (to actually secure the drugs he allegedly had to sell us), and tend to the rifle, which he brought out and propped against the foot of the bed where I was sitting—angled toward my head—and unloaded bullet by bullet.

Marlon did most of the talking—the *yeah man, uh-huh, yeah man, yeah mans* between John's scattershot self-narration—one got the impression that John hadn't had an opportunity to express himself to a captive audience in a while—but the two never got very near one another. Marlon would not sit down or sit still. John kept telling Marlon to sit down and sit still. But Marlon kept circling the room talking, while John circled the room cleaning, always on opposite sides, like two repulsing magnetic fields in oblong orbits, hissing and chatting and together constituting one endless stream of interstitial sounds, punctuated occasionally by words.

But it was Marlon who got John to focus. And Marlon who got John to get in touch with who he needed to get in touch with, who got him to send a message, and get one back, and then find an address, and then tell us what it was, and then convince John to give up cleaning and put on a shirt and come to the door and get in the car (my car) so that we could go. We drove downtown, to a street where I had never been before, and it was Marlon who went with John into a decaying apartment building near Skid Row, while B. and I sat in the car in the dark for a long time.

I am telling you this because Marlon can come off as a fuckup in recounting, and I want you to see him do something, even this, as an expert, to see him as someone capable of rising to an occasion.

• • •

One evening during that year, Marlon called me and asked me to get him from a diner near his parents' house in the Valley. He had visited them for dinner, but it hadn't gone well. His cheeks and eyes were both red. I was with a girl we knew, and we took him inside the diner to eat, but he got drunk on the two or three beers they sold him or maybe he was drunk already, and then he spent too long in the bathroom. Afterward, in the parking lot, he took out a switchblade he bought for "protection" and pantomimed jutting it into our throats.

Weeks later, in the Alexandria, I asked about that girl from the building that he liked. *She wasn't really cool, anyway,* he said. *She was kind of fake. She was just whatever, you know, like, you know.*

I didn't know. Maybe she came by. Mucus smell, throw-up stains, big ominous full bottle of pills on the window. Black walls, small room. Maybe he waved the knife around.

I think that Marlon knew, even then, that his life had begun to slide from the controlled, half-affected chaos that appeals to teenagers, into the real, aimless chaos that would leave him behind as his teenaged friends moved on. And I knew, even then, that my life had begun to slide from the troubled but resolvable, toward a future in which something—although I did not yet know what—was coming to permanently strain my ability to live up to ordinary social expectations. I already knew how I got on people's nerves. Marlon sensed that he had begun to get on those nerves, too. So we always texted each other back and ran to meet one another. For a while, the move to the Alexandria had halted Marlon's social decline. For a few months, there was nearly always someone visiting him on the weekends, often several of us at a time. For a little while, he wasn't the last one called. He was the one with his own apartment, in downtown Los Angeles; he was the proprietor of a separate world. I worried, for a while, that Marlon would be the one who would move on from me.

The trouble with juvenile friendship is that it's always uneasy and always defined by the tension between the self-sufficiency of a separate world, proudly insisted upon, and the threat that either party could betray it at any time, and will, so soon as they find purchase in the real, larger fabric of society. Which is to say: somebody will inevitably betray it, and somebody will inevitably feel betrayed.

But after a while, our friends in the Valley didn't want to go to Marlon's apartment so often. They hesitated when somebody suggested a trip downtown. Even when they went, they didn't want to stay. *I can't be there for too long*, one told me on the car ride down. It was claustrophobic, depressing, Marlon was a mess. *I just feel like I'm fucking trapped*, he said. *So don't drink too much because I can't sleep there, and you need to drive me back.* And I said, *Yeah, same. I mean, yeah, I don't want to hang out for too long, either.*

Still, I'm certain Marlon talked shit about me when I wasn't around. I'm certain there are people who will read this and say, You weren't even that close. He didn't even really like you.

•••

A year after Marlon moved into the Alexandria, most of our friends left for college. I was leaving, too, although my school started later than most. Still, I only saw Marlon once or twice that year; I always believed somebody who I actually wanted to see might turn up unexpectedly, although nobody did. I was afraid to leave home, of course, but I also thought that it might make my life in California into somebody else's problem. Marlon got a new job, something to do with checking subtitles. Another friend moved downtown to a building nearby, so he wasn't so frequently alone. He told me he began seeing his parents more often.

One morning, shortly after I left town, Marlon passed out while getting ready for work and fell back-first onto his radiator. He wasn't wearing a shirt. A few minutes later, he woke up, realized the time, scrambled to get dressed, and rushed to the office. He felt strange. An hour or two later, his back began to hurt worse than anything he had ever felt before. All of a sudden, he was screaming. Marlon's boss pulled up his shirt and looked at his back. It was all red and split and stinking skin. The radiator burned halfway through his back. He had been in shock.

His mother had him transferred from one hospital to another with a better burn unit. The latter hospital was not in network. The debt collectors called him for the rest of his life. Later, I'd see the aftermath of this in his apartment: little charred globules of flesh fused onto the iron where he'd fallen. He couldn't get them off. Too hard. Too hot.

• • •

The National Alliance on Mental Illness advises that if you are crazy and looking for love it is important to be honest, open, and understanding with a potential partner, although a few items farther down on the website, they say that you need only disclose your condition if you feel "comfortable" doing so; otherwise, it is okay to stay lying, closed, and confused. The same goes for friends. All advice for the mad goes like this: you should *be honest* and disclose *when they ask you*, but somehow, at the same time, only when you're *comfortable*, when you *feel okay*, and *only when you are ready*. The presumption, always, is that the problem for the patient is that they may not always feel comfortable with their friends, or able to hold up a friendship. Meanwhile, the potential friend is presumed to struggle with their ability to be *understanding*, and the risk that they might bring undue *stigma* to the patient. There is only ever a glancing acknowledgment, if there is any acknowledgment at all, of the possibility that the patient may not just be a pitiable friend, but a poor one; that they might be exhausting or alienating or frightening and that their primary social impediment is not being misunderstood or stigmatized, but being seen for what they are. There is no advice, anywhere that I can find, on how two patients may best approach a friendship with one another.

I have known other crazy people, but I have been close to very few. The ones I have been close with have not become close as a consequence of some shared psychiatric identity or experience, a topic which is rarely discussed at all. Sane friends are always more likely to want to talk about these sorts of things. I don't want many close friends like me, for the same reason I have never understood the assumption—made by a startling number of friends over the years—that I might want to *work with* people like me, or *give back* in some way. I am already exhausted. I do not want to be exhausted further by people like me.

When Marlon and I were friends, I did not know what was wrong with me, and most of what would go wrong had not happened yet. I didn't know what was wrong with him, and to the extent that he said, or suggested, or let on, I don't know how much I believed him or how much I believe him now. Would it have mattered if we had both known? Would we have treated one another differently? Would we have been friends at all? Our friendship was made for the most part out of a shared sense that we bothered most people in our lives, and that at the very least, we were not likely to refuse each other. But we couldn't acknowledge that out loud. We didn't have the language. But even if we had, I don't believe that either one of us was much inclined to say what we both knew to be true.

The year after I left Los Angeles, I read *The Heart Is a Lonely Hunter* for the first time. I reread it every year or two. I've been working on a joke about Marlon and me: *In the town there were two mutes, and they never, ever, ever stopped talking.* It isn't quite there yet.

• • •

I spent a term in college and then went back to Los Angeles for Christmas. That winter, for the first time I could remember in a long time, there were at least a dozen people crammed into the tiny room in the Alexandria. Marlon's back was still not entirely healed, and he was high, but he was in good spirits. All the stools were taken, four or five people sat on the bed, a few sat on the windowsill, the rest on the floor. We played music, poorly. Most of us would only be in town briefly.

Most of us stayed very late. But the toilet was broken; Marlon didn't remember since when. The place still smelled like mucus and spoiled meat and dust. After the music died down and the room was just murmuring and talking, Marlon began pinging between little circles and corners and seating areas, stepping over people as he went, halfway cleaning and halfway scouring for something to do. I think he was very drunk. He lashed out at a friend for touching something (A book? His computer? A coaster?) and threatened to hit him, although he insisted he'd been joking. He calmed down but spent a long time sitting in the open window looking out. Marlon's guests began leaving. He begged one of the women to stay but she didn't. B. and I were among the last to go, and by then, he was more *yeah, yeah, so, yeah, so* than sentences.

I took the elevator down with B. He turned to me and said, *He's got, like, two years max, right?* I said: *Don't say that.*

Two weeks later, I went to a New Year's party in the Valley. Marlon was meant to come, but several people confessed to ignoring his messages asking for a ride. Nobody wanted to drive downtown on New Year's.

The next morning, I woke up on the couch of an old friend. Around 11:00 a.m., we went out barefoot in our underwear and shirts to the storm drain on the side farthest from his father's window to smoke. *What happened to Marlon last night?* he asked. I told him that I didn't think he could get a ride. He probably wound up doing something with his downtown friends. *I told him I'd text him today to hang out,* my friend said. But we decided not to call him. We were hungover and didn't want to drive all the way downtown. We didn't want to deal with two headaches at once.

Sometime between December 31 and January 2, Marlon lost consciousness in his apartment. On January 3, his stepfather paid him a surprise visit. Or his stepfather was concerned because he couldn't reach him. Or they were meant to see each other that day. I don't know; Marlon never told me. Marlon did not answer his phone. Marlon did not answer the knock on his door. His stepfather convinced the on-duty security guard to let him in to the room where he found Marlon's body. Based on the amount of heroin in his system, it is unclear if it was an accident.

By then, I had flown back to Chicago. I took a cab from the airport to my dormitory on the South Side. I was saying hello to my roommate when I got a text from a friend on whose couch Marlon liked to crash when he was out too late in the Valley. It said, *Marlon is dead*, and I thought it was a joke, like, *He's passed out here again. What a mess. What a creep*. But it wasn't.

. . .

I've written about Marlon many times. He's fit any number of contrivances: essays about Los Angeles, decay, loss, fear. I don't look down on contrivance. Contrasts, forced parallels, juxtapositions brought about by careful placement, making the reader go cross-eyed with the unfolding of apparently contradictory ideas in tandem: all of this is what a good deal of writing amounts to. Whether it is good writing or bad writing isn't even a matter of concealment, but of skill. Anybody who is simply unloading their impressions verbatim on a page is making you read their diary. Anybody who is contriving alongside the insistence that they are doing *no such thing* believes, perhaps correctly, that their reader is very stupid. But now I am thinking about Marlon again and about the ways I've used him, in his life and after, and I've come upon the possibility of a more troubling and elemental contrivance: Were we even really friends?

We spent a lot of time together. I knew him. Was this enough? We saw each other because we bothered people in similar ways. We intensely disliked loneliness, even if being around people made us feel bad, too. Even early on, mutual friends talked about Marlon when he wasn't there with some combination of concern, exasperation, and displeasure. He was *interesting* but also tiresome; like something sour best taken in small and well-portioned doses. But these people talked the same way about me when I wasn't there, and I suspect I knew that then.

If Marlon and I were friends, we were friends because the irony of a paranoid personality type is that it provokes whispers about you when you're not around. The most trustworthy friends you can find are the people who are also the victims of these whispers. But then, I don't even remember why he moved into the Alexandria in the first place. I don't remember almost anything about him that didn't have to do with me.

Maybe I was just distracted. I didn't sleep. I took risks. I saw everyone—my therapist, my parents, my other friends—conspiring against me. I made breaks in the middle of the night from one place to another, began entertaining fantasies that all of this was moving to-ward a special purpose just for me—but Marlon was like that, too. Did that make me like him? His dysfunction was so much clearer, so much better corroborated by external signs—the dropout; the small, terrible apartment; the bad luck; the bad jobs—that I could tell myself that I was fine. We spent so much time in his apartment and in my car and in parks and in traffic; I did not, as the cliché goes, feel *judged* by him, and I do not think that he felt judged by me. But I always sat there hoping someone else would call, somebody who *would* judge me and who *had* judged me, and had then, in their judgment, found me worth calling up. I am sure that Marlon had that same hope, too.

I did like him. But I didn't like him for the drugs or the apartment or the dysfunction or the juvenile friendship. I liked him because if you spend enough time with somebody, you will either like them or hate them—and I liked him. I liked him because he had relentless energy and because unlike many allegedly smart people I've known, he was actually curious about the subjects he couldn't already talk about. I liked him because we spent a lot of time together and we had fun, but those memories aren't here because they aren't essential to this contrivance: the story of two sick young men, one of whom dies in a flophouse built into the hollowed-out chest of an old hotel.

I think that Marlon died without accepting that he was going crazy, that if he'd lived longer, it would have gotten worse. He may not have known for certain that anything was wrong at all. Marlon was the first insane man I knew, a man who seemed nothing like an affectation would, who was not eccentric or charming or some wild-eyed malcontent, but a difficulty. And I believed that if insanity was what Marlon looked like, then I must be fine. I was fine. I was fine.

· · ·

A month after I left, I went back to Los Angeles for a memorial service. They held it in a bar, several blocks from the Alexandria, but most of the guests were minors. They wouldn't serve us anything but water. Marlon's mother and stepfather had filled the room with photos and film clips, assembled a playlist of Marlon's favorite songs. But he had not liked any of the songs since he was sixteen years old. There were no photos from the last three years of his life. It was a memorial to a memory that terminates around Marlon's fifteenth birthday; one that only fits if you imagine he died high and alone in a small black box of a room still mainly digging The Strokes and that one early aughts Violent Femmes song. Oftentimes, the mourner who believes the world becomes less real without their lost love is in fact robbing that love of their reality.

Some 90 percent of suicides are believed to result from significant psychiatric dysfunction. For serious disorders, the suicide rate is believed to be between 5 and 15 percent. Substance abuse is the most common compounding factor. What I mean is there are many Marlons. One died in the Hotel Alexandria over a decade ago. One is dying right now. But don't worry. Once they're dead, they'll be remembered fondly. Some of them will fantasize about this fact while they're alive. They will know that once they're gone, the lying and contrivance can begin in earnest.

Every book published about crazy people lately tells the story of Malcoum Tate, a man murdered by his own family when he would not take his medication, when he kept threatening his baby niece's life. They drove him around until he had to piss, then they shot him on the side of the road. It's a sad story, but if Malcoum Tate had lived, he'd just be another pain in the ass, wearing out the patience of his friends and family; another frightening lunatic tolerated from a distance. That would be the story we would tell, if there was anybody interested in the telling.

The further we have gotten from Marlon's funeral, the more the camp and artifice of his memorial has become what remains of his memory. I am sure his other friends have their own memories of him. I am sure they've built their own inflection points, built their own mythology about their *friend who died.* That he and I were both crazy, and I did not know it about myself yet, and he did not believe it about himself, if he knew it at all—this is just an arbitrary way of pairing us. It's a contrivance. I know that now.

After the service, I went back to Chicago and spent the next five years becoming Marlon. I became the difficult one, the insistent one, the erratic one, the one who stayed too late, who flipped out, who yelled, who stole and talked shit and was very afraid of what was plainly true: my friends were my friends, but I was not as close to them as they were to each other because they didn't like me very much. I became the one who crashed on the couch without permission, the one who let his own apartment go to waste. I became the one who called someone forty times until they left a meeting and demanded to know, *What is it?* And I didn't even know so I yelled for a while about nothing and then drove around the city trying to remember for nearly two entire days. I became the one waving the knife around. Except I never bought a knife. I bought what I let people believe was a real gun. What I mean is that when I went to Chicago and became Marlon, I did not, in virtue of my memories, realize what I had become. I did not learn anything at all.

I had better friends than Marlon. Even then. B., who has been haunting this story, was a better friend. He still is. When we met, we had a juvenile friendship, too—two against the world, last invited to the party, pretending not to care—but time had made our friendship a mature thing. I think an adult friend is not somebody who helps you build a barrier against the world, but who acts as your ambassador to it. Who serves as an intermediary, a translator, an apologist, and you act as an ambassador for them? You don't fight the world. You encounter it together. Marlon never apologized for me. I was never brave enough to apologize for him. We had a juvenile friendship and then he died.

• • •

Eight years later, during the same trip home that B. and I took back to the Alexandria, I went to see Marlon's mother for the first time since the funeral. I visited her at her house in the Valley. I stood with her in the kitchen while a dozen of her teenage daughter's friends played on a trampoline outside, celebrating their eighth-grade graduation. We talked for a little while about what we'd been up to. She made salad and poured wine. Outside, on the trampoline, the teenage girls screamed when their playlist switched over to The Strokes. By then, Marlon's stepfather was long gone. Her boyfriend came home and turned on the TV. We watched LeBron James struggle in the finals for a while. The whole house was airy, lots of space between furniture, lots of windows, lots of light. It was easy to breathe in there.

We ate on the front porch and then went back to the kitchen. We talked about Marlon, about his biological father, about our mutual friends. The sun went down. *Marlon loved you*, she said. I don't remember what I said. She said, *You had a lot in common.*

I don't think she meant it that way, but it's true, because I also used. And I also knew, from very young, that something was going very wrong. I knew, like Marlon did, that people were bored and annoyed and terrified of me behind my back, and that much of this was my doing, but that it's very hard to see that from the inside. I too got paranoid. I too saw conspiracy in neighbors and women and old friends; I too acted up and made it worse and spent time in hospitals. I too ignored bills and lost jobs and left lithium untaken for a long time and the only difference is that I didn't die. *So sometimes I believe I stole your dead son's life.* I believed it while I stood there in the kitchen. I still believe it now. Because that's my inflection point, that's my fantasy, my contrivance, my mourning, my point of deviation from what would have been reality: I think I was the lucky one, the stable one, the one whose problems were mild by comparison. And I would have stayed that way but then Marlon died, and I stole his life and lived a really shitty one for the both of us.

Break

All break stories begin with cracks. Lori Schiller was seventeen, she tells us in *The Quiet Room*, when everything *seemed much nicer than it was before*. Colors deepened. Love felt possible. She felt attractive and happy and strong. At summer camp, she could not stop talking and trying to make friends; she kept stopping, mid-activity, to appreciate the sudden, vivid beauty of her surroundings. But over the weeks, her mood darkened. She began to wonder if she was ugly. Maybe she was hideous, unlikeable, unlovable. Maybe she was *fat and disgusting, an object not of romance but of ridicule*, she writes. That same summer, disembodied voices would tell Schiller that she was going to die. She began jumping on a trampoline all night to shut them up. Four years later, after graduating from Rutgers and moving to New York, a suicide attempt put her in the hospital, where she was diagnosed with schizophrenia.

I remember very well the day it happened, recounts "Renee" in *Autobiography of a Schizophrenic Girl*. *We were staying in the country and I had gone for a walk alone as I did now and then. Suddenly, as I was passing the school, I heard a singing lesson. I stopped to listen, and at that instant a strange feeling came over me, a feeling hard to analyze but akin to something I was to know too well later—a disturbing sense of unreality. The* feeling persisted on and off for years. On some days, her whole school-yard felt *limitless, unreal, mechanical, and without meaning;* rooms transformed into *nothing but teeth under a remorseless light.* Friends looked wrong, like strangers or even wild beasts. Years later, while in a sanitarium for TB patients, she began to receive commands from the cold autumn wind.

On occasion, writes Kay Redfield Jamison in *An Unquiet Mind,* her regular periods of total despair *would be made even worse by terrible agitation. My mind would race from subject to subject, but instead of being filled with the exuberant and cosmic thoughts that had been associated with earlier periods of rapid thinking, it would be frenched in awful sounds and images of decay and dying: dead bodies on the beach, charred remains of animals, toe-tagged corpses in morgues. During these agitated periods, I became exceedingly restless, angry, and irritable, and the only way I could dilute the agitation was to run along the beach or pace back and forth across my room like a polar bear at the zoo. I had no idea what was going on, and I felt totally unable to ask anyone for help.*

Elyn Saks writes, in *The Center Cannot Hold, It felt like my mind was falling apart: there was no center to take things in, put them together, and make them make sense.* Her first episode occurred when she was sixteen, but she did not *officially* break down until she was a Marshall Scholar. It was not until Yale Law School that she *ended up forcibly restrained, and forced to take anti-psychotic medication.*

People ask, How did you get here? writes Susanna Kaysen of the mad-house in *Girl, Interrupted. What they really want to know is if they are likely to end up in there as well. I can't answer the real question. All I can tell them is, It's easy.*

It is difficult to know which events and dreams and memories occurring prior to the onset of insanity are significant precursors, and which are only noise. We do know that madness comes on slowly. Most patients pass years between the first cracks and the full break. On their own, many of the cracks would not register as markers of a coming illness at all, and in most cases, they do not indicate anything at all. Manic-depressives and schizophrenics often report years of feeling cloudy, of difficulty concentrating, of slipping grades or job performance, of difficulty speaking clearly and diminished spatial reasoning. A failing sense of smell is common, too. Cracks can include mild depression, anxiety, anger issues, agitation, irritation, sleep abnormalities, hypochondria, suspiciousness, grandiosity, recklessness, hyper-sexuality, compulsive gambling, stealing, lying, spending, drug abuse, waning empathy, repetitive behavior, the flattening of emotions or social withdrawal or inappropriate laughter or crying, a deterioration in personal hygiene—for years, it can be difficult to distinguish an incipient lunatic from a slob or an asshole. The prodromal period is filled with strange feelings, but so is ordinary life.

It is natural to look back and wonder. It is easy to see a line, running through every odd dream and strange mood and disagreeable act, from the earliest memories to the eventual unmistakable emergence of illness. It is easy to believe that this line tracks a story. This kind of reconstruction—the fitting of a sensible mold over a life's worth of events—is the work of both the memoirist and the mental patient. But in both cases, the process is inevitably as much invention as memory.

Renee, in *Autobiography of a Schizophrenic Girl*, reports a recurring childhood dream in which she finds herself inside of an immense, illuminated barn. In the middle of the barn is a needle—*fine, pointed, hard, glittering in the light*—which fills her with excruciating fear. Suddenly, the barn begins to fill up with hay. She can't see the needle anymore, but suddenly it emits a powerful current, electrifying the hay and pushing Renee into a frenzied terror. She wakes up screaming.

Was this dream an early symptom of her schizophrenia? Or was it only a nightmare? All children have strange dreams. It is only after an illness is undeniable, is identified and diagnosed and accepted, that one begins to pour over history, searching for signs.

Crack: I was a very nervous, naked eight-year-old, drawing stars in the fog of my shower door. In crooked rows, I drew every kind of star I knew at the time, which was three kinds total. Five-sided and six-sided and the kind that's a cross with an X across it (eight-sided), like an asterisk or a clock. The only rule I had was that each kind of star had to appear in equal numbers on the shower door. Otherwise, the earth would come up through the pipes and swallow me. Ants would swallow me. The water bursting from the showerhead would be replaced by ants, crashing down onto the tile floor and spreading up the walls in a thick coat. The ants would cover my body. I imagined this vividly. They wouldn't eat me. They'd just keep moving. Up my legs, around my torso, around my throat. Eventually I would need to breathe, and the ants would get sucked in with the air. Ants swishing under my tongue and ants ricocheting against the roof of my mouth and ants cascading down my windpipe. Squiggling frantic sludge, crawling across the insides of my lungs. If I didn't draw the stars, then ants would fill up all the empty space inside of me. I imagined gagging. Ants vomited up colliding with ants being swallowed, crossing paths in the back of my throat. I don't remember when I stopped believing this would happen, or when I stopped drawing stars.

Crack: Between the ages of nine and thirteen, I rarely spoke. Once, after I was compelled to say a few sentences in response to a direct question, a teacher told me that it was the most he had heard me say in years. When I did start speaking, I spoke too much. I began having terrible fights with my parents, worse than the fights I remember hearing about from my peers. Around this same time, I became intensely focused on warm car windows and cold chair arms; I'd press my flat palm against either one whenever I could.

Crack: My grades slipped every year I was in high school. I quit every activity that I could get away with quitting and spent most of my time driving around. Los Angeles felt impossibly large and very small at once, particularly at night. I had the feeling, for years, that everything was terribly urgent, that something significant would happen if I only made the right call, appeared at the right house, knew the right person. I know I started several fights. Maybe I was just an asshole. Recently, I found a message I got back then from another teenager I knew. He wanted to know how I had any friends at all when I *dress unfashionably, have poor hygiene, and ramble on about things that are boring to 99.9%*

of all people. People talk about this, too! he wrote. *Every word I get is . . .* "Oh, I hate that Emmett kid . . . he smells bad . . . he doesn't change his clothes, he's filthy . . . he's a dumbass and hides behind esoteric factoids to mask his stupidity." But the letter writer may have just been an asshole, too.

Crack: A few months after Marlon died, during the end of my first year of college in Chicago, I began to believe that my thoughts did not come from inside of my head. Or, I began to feel, in a scarcely articulated way, that my brain had turned to candle wax or soft clay. I didn't feel dull or stupid, although it was difficult to hold consistent thoughts. It was only that invisible fingers kept pressing on the inside of my skull, softening edges while sharpening others, leaving little bits of oil and the vague charge of static-electric contact on the outside. I felt this way for the first time on a spring afternoon, while walking underneath a gate at the north end of the main quad, en route to my dormitory from a sociology seminar. I felt my brain move inside my skull and felt a soft, static buzz at its outer edges, and thought, *If only it grows a little up and to the right, I can catch what was eluding me in the reading.* But, entering university and believing that one's mind is *expanding* is common enough as a metaphor. I do not remember how seriously I took this feeling. It may only have been a metaphor to me then, perhaps a metaphor I took literally as a kind of joke with myself, only to forget, all of these years later, that I was self-conscious of the gag. I did not spend all my time studying, at any rate. I became very attached to friends and girlfriends. I believed that if I called the same number one hundred times, it meant the call was one hundred times more significant than if I just called once. But then, teenagers often call too much, are too clingy, too invested in the romance of their own connections with other people.

Crack: I liked stealing. I stole quite a lot. I never stole anything too valuable. I stole small change on counters. I stole half-empty bottles of booze and didn't drink them. I stole a razor blade in a friend's bathroom and used it to shave while I was over there but I didn't lock the bathroom door, so I got caught. The world is filled with thieves, but I cannot tell you why I stole, only that years later, when I achieved a therapeutic blood level of lithium for the first time, it never occurred to me to steal again.

Crack: There was a term during my final year in university when I rarely left my apartment. I didn't attend class for weeks. I arranged passing grades where I could. It was a private college; they'll wave you through. Trash piled up in the bedroom and the kitchen and the living room. My roommate began living with his girlfriend. Trash turned into mold turned into stink turned into me abandoning my lease by New Year's. Before I left, I took to ordering the same pizza every day at 4:00 a.m. The delivery man was usually the same: a Russian man in his thirties or forties. He asked, as often as not, if I had any gum he could chew so his girlfriend wouldn't smell the cigarettes he'd been smoking all night on his breath. I never had gum. He usually followed up by asking for a cigarette.

Crack: Sometimes I told people that I wasn't a real person. That I was a widely held intrasubjective hallucination. But this was taken to be a joke. I said it jokingly.

Crack: For a period during my third year at university, I believed that I was seeing a ghost: at parties, in my home, on the street. She had entirely white lips. I am still not certain if I was confused about a real person or if I was only making someone up. Most people began to strike me as mechanical, or empty, or fake. There was something wrong with their faces. There was something wrong with rooms, too. They felt flimsy and false, especially if I stayed in them for too long. This was not a consciously articulated fact. It was only a condition of the world. I once looked into the eyes of an underclassman and told him I could read his mind because he wasn't a real person with a thought-protecting skull. I believed it. Then I insulted him so badly and at such length that he believed it, too.

Crack: The fall that I was twenty, I moved to England for a term abroad: the only study abroad option that did not require me to learn a language or otherwise prove myself competent or responsible prior to approval. While I was there, I wore the same pair of pants every day.

I took them off to sleep, but I never washed them once. One morning, after the snow had started icing the sidewalks to the tube station, I began repeating, over and over, some rhyme about what might happen if I removed my magic pants. I don't remember how the rhyme went, but I remember the idea: the pants absorbed every bit of bile and dirt and pestilence floating in the English air. They were training my body to fight infection off by exposing me only to small doses. Without them I would get too sick, too fast. The pants were old black jeans. Nobody noticed, or at least nobody said anything. When I went home to California, I took them off, wrapped them in a plastic bag, and threw them in a dumpster in Los Angeles.

Crack: The causes of severe psychiatric dysfunction are not thoroughly understood, but it is widely believed that genes are not enough. Some additional event typically precipitates the full break. Trauma, substance abuse, and brain injury are common suspects. When I was twenty-one, during my final year in college, a minor infection on my neck led to a seizure. I was on the north side of Chicago with a friend, who texted another friend of mine at the university, who picked me up eighteen hours later from a hospital. A patch of my hair was missing. I had meningoencephalitis, an infection of the spine and brain, which had caused cerebral swelling and thus the seizure. My prospects were good. This was ordinarily a disease of the very young or very old or terribly immunocompromised, and while the doctors were not sure how I'd gotten it or what damage the swelling and seizure might have done to me, they believed several weeks of intravenous medicine would heal me. I had to quit smoking and quit drinking and start exercising. I did, and after several weeks in constant fear that my brain would swell into my skull, I recovered. I have been telling people about this bout with encephalitis for years.

While writing this essay, I gathered all the medical records I could. I requested records from both the hospital where I was treated after my seizure, and from the hospital where I received weekly treatment for encephalitis. I wanted to check the dates and see if there was some connection between my illness then and my illness now. Did my symptoms become worse shortly after? But the hospitals had no records. I had never been admitted for a seizure, or encephalitis, for any malady of the body. The friend who I was with when it happened, who'd texted my other friend to pick me up from the hospital, and who I had not seen since that night, told me that I left her apartment in a hurry. I kept saying, *I'm having a seizure, I'm having a seizure*, she said. She was sorry she never called, but to be honest all these years later, she said, I was starting to get on her nerves.

When you come to accept that you're insane, you do not receive a document, clarifying what the delusions are in your alleged memories. It is obvious enough, once in the thrall of antipsychotic medication, that you are not actually an alien. But some delusions are attended by so many real verifiers—so many friends who knew I was sick, who drove me from the hospital, who helped me avoid drinking until the infection cleared up—that the core delusion takes on the real bounded architecture of a memory. The missing patch of hair was real. But I don't know how that happened.

I wonder how much of what I still believe I've actually invented. I wonder if there is anything I believe that I've invented but which a perfect record of my life would reveal to be true. I wonder about many small things, small memories, small and ambient facts. In Iowa, I told my psychiatrist about the encephalitis discovery. He asked me if it was unsettling to find out that I never really had it. Of course not, I said. It's not as if having had a brain disease is central to my self-conception.

Crack: After college, I stayed in Chicago. I moved in with two friends on the north side of the city. I had not made any plans to work, but an older woman I knew took pity on me and arranged a six-month gig working at a small publisher, just out of town. The publisher operated out of a suburban home and specialized in subcontracted standardized test design. I hid in the bathroom quite a lot. I left work for lunch and did not come back. I rarely spoke, and I believed, quite firmly, that a fat man whose desk gave him a view of my own was engaged in a prolonged campaign to spy on me and undermine my work. There was another new employee. It was likely only one of us would be brought on long-term. The fat man favored her. Eventually, she won. She was offered a promotion and a raise. When my initial term expired, I was not even given a meeting about the possibility of staying on.

I didn't hold another full-time job of any kind for years. Mostly, I did low-rent theater for free. I took occasional freelance writing gigs and failed to turn most of them in. I felt, more and more, as if it was impossible to hold more than one thought in my head at any given time. If I needed to connect two, I would take firm hold of the first and then reach for the second. With the second in hand, I would lose hold of the first, turn around, be unable to find it, find it, but have lost the second one again.

I would learn later that while the active symptoms of psychosis can be controlled with medication, the condition remains degenerative. It is difficult to stop the loss of cognitive function, particularly spatial and verbal reasoning. I knew, two years after college, that I was becoming stupid. Years later, a series of MRIs conducted as part of a university research study would confirm these moderate brain abnormalities, but at the time, I only knew that when I reached for long-familiar mental resources, I found that they were limited, obscured, or missing. I became very good at picking the situations in which I might expose the state of my intelligence. I became very good at a kind of ostentatious verbal smartness—the telltale digressiveness of a breaking brain can be misinterpreted for a kind of eccentric intelligence—which is to say, I became that much more annoying, that much more tedious to be around.

I remained largely out of work. I drained my savings and bothered my parents for money. I volunteered with an after-school program in collaboration between a theater company and Chicago Public Schools, but after a few weeks, I quit turning up, and a few weeks after that, I stopped responding to messages entirely. I wrote several bad articles. I wrote several bad plays. I believed I was being held up by some mental block not of my own making. I kept trying to find somewhere to sit and write where the signals couldn't interrupt my thoughts, but I never found it.

One night, while at a small get-together with a girlfriend who lived with no internet on the far north side of Chicago, I became convinced that the man whose house we were visiting was not real and that the music he was playing constituted a form of brain-scrambling mind control. I got up and left without saying anything. The relationship did not survive another month. I still worried that I needed to be near other brains. I took the same two-mile walk nearly every day.

One night I took dozens of sleeping pills that I'd purchased from a friend. I didn't want to die, but taking them felt mandatory, like an involuntary mechanical assembly process. I did not die. I became very ill and threw up for hours and passed out. I stayed in bed for days. There was not a moment, like there is in the movies, when I clutched my head and asked myself, *Am I losing my mind?* But there was a fear, always, very near but out of sight, like something waiting to attack. A fear that *something* was wrong, although I could not say for sure. A fear that if something was wrong, that I might have to find out what it was.

Crack: I became interested in the Prophet Elijah. His feast day was my half birthday. He never learned mercy. He was too vengeful even for God. I thought that perhaps he was wandering the world until he learns to be forgiving. I thought maybe that was me, too. I thought: maybe I'm not really hearing other minds, but those prophetic whispers that whisper in a prophet's ear. I thought that perhaps all prophets were made up of other minds.

I asked them how they dared so roundly to assert that God spoke to them, William Blake asked Isaiah and Ezekiel in *The Marriage of Heaven and Hell.* Isaiah replied, *I saw no God, nor heard any, in a finite organical perception; but my senses discover'd the infinite in every thing, and as I was then persuaded, and remained confirm'd; that the voice of honest indignation is the voice of God.*

But I didn't have anything to prophesize. I didn't have anything righteous or indignant to say or do at all.

I began to worry that the Holy Ghost lived inside my body. He was so passive-aggressive, and there were so many tedious, small habits I had to keep or He would abandon me to poison and car crashes and sudden cardiac arrest. I worried about it all the time—but putting it that way misses the essence of a widening crack. No matter what I believed, it never seemed like a sudden new emergency to confront. These were just the given conditions of my life. Like my age or what city I lived in or my plans for the year: barely worth articulating, just facts to build a work schedule and a social life and the appearance of ordinary behavior around.

I do not know which of these events are relevant. I do not know if any of them are relevant. Even in reviewing nearly seven years and telling you about only what seem to be the most obvious signs leaves a lot that I believe may just be noise. It is possible to be in the prodromal period of a psychotic disorder and have a bad personality at the same time. I had other friends, made other friends, dated other people; I was annoying and angry and smelled bad, but I do not think that in the absence of the early stages of a mental collapse, I would have spent this period in the early stages of becoming a very industrious saint.

Most days I wasn't even acting out. I did not feel crazy. I hung out. I went to class. I had a drink with friends. I felt something tight under my skin, something obscure and difficult to articulate but terribly urgent. Perhaps many people feel this way in early life. I suspect many people feel this way. I don't know. I don't have an "ordinary" period of adolescence to compare to my own. Does this line track a story? The neurologists tell us that even a sane man's memory is counterfeit. Plumbing those counterfeits for a through-line is just lying. Every person who has written about themselves with the slightest bit of self-awareness knows this. The presence of madness only makes this plain fact plainer.

Here is what it felt like on most days during those years: Imagine yourself in a room full of strangers at a party. Nobody is paying attention to you at all, but you are suddenly very aware of your hands. You are suddenly very aware of how you're standing. You are suddenly very aware of how you're holding your drink, where you're looking, how you are not in any of the small circles talking. Imagine the small and ultimately unimportant nervousness such situations bring on. It is a little bit like that.

Or imagine the moments when you remember that you will die. That fear that comes in every once in a while, that pits out the stomach and leaks just a little adrenaline into your blood. Imagine that you can't push the fear out of your mind. Imagine that you are sitting in that perilous apprehension forever. Imagine that the universe has begun to feel malicious and particular, imagine it feels more like that every day. Sink into that feeling and stay there for a year, or two, or three. Try to act natural in the meantime. If someone asks if something's wrong, say, *No, I'm fine, sorry, I'm tired, no, my face is just that way, I'm fine.* Then when you walk home, pick up every cigarette butt on the sidewalk while God tells you you've got filthy hands.

Crack: I had just turned twenty-four and was sitting on my bed in my apartment in Chicago, running my fingers over my neck when I found a mass under the skin behind my jawbone. I thought, *Oh, right. This is how it happens. You find the tumor first by accident.*

I pinched the skin and put my fingers on either side of the lump. It was very small, like the smallest thing you'd still call a pebble instead of sand. Semi-circular on one side, flat on the other, like a little model of a little dome. It felt granular, or rough. If I turned my head far to the opposite side, my throat-muscle pushed the lump hard against the surface. It rolled a little under my touch.

I sat on my bed for a long time, trying to un-find it.

As far back as September, I'd started getting light-headed nearly every day. I'd fainted a few times. My heart rate would spike arbitrarily; sometimes I had trouble breathing. When I drove, my whole left side tensed up, which felt like what I think those public health commercials are describing when they say that tingling and pain on your left side is a sign of an impending heart attack. Then I lost twenty pounds in three months for no reason.

I began to notice myself going blank in the middle of conversations.

I was suddenly unable to concentrate or listen or speak at all. I would walk away from conversations and walk around for a while, trying to get my diaphragm to unclench. I had trouble falling asleep, trouble waking up, trouble remembering what I was meant to be doing. I missed several deadlines. Several friends stopped speaking to me for what felt like no reason at all; I remember feeling very wounded. I got an email from a friend at the theater where I worked asking why I came into a set build ranting about nothing and making the set designer cry. When I looked up symptoms of lymphoma, the only good sign was that I wasn't tired *all* the time. Some days I didn't sleep at all. Some days it was just two or three hours in the early morning. This wasn't insomnia. I wasn't tired.

I considered other possibilities. Primary HIV infection. Multiple sclerosis. Several rare varieties of iron or protein or calcium buildup. I checked all of them. Advertising on my social media accounts very quickly consisted almost exclusively of targeted services for the chronically ill and dying. But I felt focused for the first time in months, perhaps in years. All the worries about other minds, about prophets, about conspiracies all left me. I had a tangible threat before me now, hiding under my skin. My head felt cool and clarified and focused.

I knew better than to just go to a doctor and say that I'd diagnosed myself with a terminal illness from the internet. That's how you get laughed out, or get *difficult* written in your chart, or get recommended to a psychiatrist who will recommend anxiety medication. I didn't want anxiety medication. I didn't feel anxious. I felt sick. I was certain I was sick, but I also knew that doctors don't respond well to patient confidence.

A few weeks after I found the lump, I booked an ordinary physical with a new doctor and prepared to appear shocked when he inevitably felt my neck or read my lab results and suggested—not to worry me too much, but—he wanted to run some extra tests. But then he didn't. He complimented me for having lost weight since last year. He told me to quit smoking. He said my vision was still good, but I might need glasses eventually. At the end of the appointment, I deviated from my own plan and motioned to the right side of my neck. I didn't want to sound terrified or like I had some idea already of what might be going on, so I said, *I think I felt some weird stuff in my neck the other day, around here?* The doctor said, *Yeah, there's all kinds of weird stuff in there. Don't press too hard.* Then he left.

Two weeks later I booked an appointment with another doctor, nearer to my apartment. I felt fainter every day; the morning I went in, I hadn't slept at all. I told them I was new in town and just trying to have a physical since I hadn't had one for a while, and I felt a little sick lately, but maybe it was the weather or just a cold? I had been squeezing the lump, and the skin on that side of my neck was red going on purple. Couldn't go unnoticed. The new doctor sounded like a public radio host. His office was covered in photographs of the sun rising, or alternatively, the sun setting, in what appeared to be Southeast Asian countries. After blood work, he told me that my triglycerides were too high. I should lose some weight, he said. Then he looked at the mark on my neck. *Do you know what that is?* he asked, and I pretended that I hadn't noticed it before. He scrutinized it. *Markings aren't right for a bite, but it might be worth a Lyme test,* he said. I agreed. He asked me if I had tried meditating at all. *I try to run a holistic practice,* he said. *Mental discipline can help with those triglyceride levels.* The Lyme test ultimately came back negative.

In March, I went home to Los Angeles for a week and booked an appointment with a doctor in my childhood neighborhood. When he came into the exam room, he looked at me like he recognized me from somewhere, but he didn't say anything about it. I had a different approach this time. *There's something in my neck,* I said. He felt around. In fact, he noticed, several of my lymph nodes were inflamed, all the way down to my shoulder. Persistent lymph node inflammation is a symptom of several cancers as well as blood toxicity and autoimmune disorder. (He didn't say that, but I knew it from online.)

Do you want to do any tests or anything? I asked. *No, no,* he said, *If I pulled fifty people off the street right now, twenty of them would have this. It's fine.*

I left, and on the flight back to Chicago, I passed out twice. Every moment for weeks that I was not entirely distracted, I was squeezing and needling and fingering the lump. Occasionally, God would remind me that nobody was going to help unless He let them.

Sometime in early April, I walked into the small bathroom off my bedroom to find it covered in chunks of food and blood. I thought that I'd thrown up, but I didn't remember. (I still don't remember now, either.) The first time I noticed it, the mess was dry already and stinking through the door. I started using my roommate's bathroom. I never cleaned mine. I spent a lot of time pacing on the corner of my street, so that if I lost consciousness, or started seizing, somebody would see me.

Later that month, I flew to Washington, DC, to interview for a job as a research assistant for a famous political writer who was working on a book that was never written. I slept on a college acquaintance's couch. When I arrived, he asked me if I had a cyst on my neck. He accepted *I think so?* as my answer before leaving to stay at his girlfriend's for the night. I sat on his couch alone for six or seven hours without standing up. I fingered the lump. I'd like to say I prayed, but it was more like listening. The Holy Ghost slurped and whispered at me for a while, which was happening more often those days, but he was also being un-usually cruel. I recall being self-conscious about my friend watching his surveillance footage later on; he'd see me mumbling to myself. I didn't want him to think I was weird.

Around 1:00 a.m., I had an epiphany. The Holy Ghost wasn't speaking into my head from heaven. He was inside the lump. He didn't tell me directly, but all of a sudden I knew it, like you know the unfamiliar hallway in a dream is your high school. The Ghost made a sound like sucking the end of a drink through a straw, which was the sound of him squeezing poison from the lump and into my veins and blood.

I found a toothpick somewhere in the apartment and put it into my neck. Then I tried a butter knife. Then my fingers. I put my dirty fingernails beneath my skin, tried to pull apart the places that I'd cut, to get a hold of something solid and not too slippery from blood and pus. I tried to reach the lump and take it out, but it was deeper than I thought it would be. I remained fixated for hours. I'd sit and wait then reach in and feel around again, telling myself it was smaller, realizing it was bigger, losing it, trying to find it, trying to squeeze it out. *From the very beginning of his illness*, writes Tolstoy in *The Death of Ivan Ilyich*, *life had been divided between two contrary and alternating moods: now it was despair and the expectation of this uncomprehended and terrible death, and now hope and an intently interested observation of the functioning of his organs.* I don't know when I fell asleep, but I did.

When I got back to Chicago, I noticed what looked like pellets on the carpet of my room. I thought it must have been rat poison, or at least my roommate, trying to frame me for a mess so he could kick me out. I had begun dating a girl named E. She was the first person I had seen seriously since college; the first person I loved, not with the juvenile infatuation of a teenager but the reliable affection of an adult. She was self-possessed and appeared to have a complete interior world; she didn't *need* me but wanted me and this was different from anything I had known before, and I was therefore determined not to fuck it up. I looked at whatever was on my floor for a while, then put my shoes back on and walked two miles to E.'s apartment. I didn't leave for over two weeks. I thought maybe it would be better to die there, where it was clean and there was light and it didn't smell like vomit.

I kept seeing doctors. In May, I called an ear, nose, and throat specialist downtown and told his assistant that my doctor had referred me for a lymph node abnormality. She said she hadn't received any referral yet, but she'd go ahead and put me on the schedule for next week and just confirm when the referral came in. I turned up to the appointment, and the ENT saw me, but after he spent a minute feeling my neck and staring down my throat with his flashlight, he asked, *What doctor referred you again?*

I told him I had been light-headed, that I had been throwing up, I thought maybe blood. That I'd ingested poison by mistake, I thought, on several occasions. I told him that I knew it was hard to see because

I'd been picking at it, but that there was something in my neck under the swelling and the scar, maybe an inflamed lymph node. The ENT was sixty or seventy years old, with the sort of patchwork beard that comes from not bothering anymore. He was otherwise bald.

He said, *It sounds like maybe you're sick, but you don't have lymphoma.*

Does it look like something else?

That has to do with your lymph nodes? No.

I asked what was in my neck and he shrugged. *Who knows? Nothing.*

I somehow put the word "biopsy" in a sentence.

I can give you a biopsy, he said, *but it's two thousand dollars and insurance won't cover it because it isn't necessary. It's an inpatient procedure, and it'll hurt like hell.*

I mean, if there's any chance it'll find—

He asked me what I did for a living. *Research assistant*, I said. *Okay*, he said. *My job is to look at people's ears and throats and determine if they have something to worry about, like cancer. You don't have anything to worry about. And what was the name of the doctor who referred you?*

In the waiting room on the way out, a nurse offered me antibiotic cream for my neck. The bottle was fake, and the cream was a nerve agent. I didn't fall for it. I didn't take it. I left.

In late May, I spent most of my time listening to a radio scan between the Holy Ghost, my own funeral, and the incoherent chatter of every mind around me, all while thinking about how ill I was. Imagine the *wa-wa-wa* of a ringing in your ear, then imagine you can hear words forming from the sound wave. Imagine static. It sounded like that.

I spoke maybe one hundred words per day, and largely the same ones. Every night E. and I ordered milkshakes from the same restaurant down the street. We watched an endless amount of television. I didn't speak very much. This was often the only time of day that I was eating. I think she was concerned, or maybe scared, and I am not sure if she was scared for me or of me or both, but I think I must have seemed callous, barely participating in conversations with somebody who was letting me freeload like that.

In June, I saw another doctor, this one on the north side of the city. Just looking to get checked out, first physical in a while, all the same lies. I told him all my symptoms, he said it certainly sounded like something was wrong, and he wanted to rule out the worst possibilities before proceeding. I thought, *Thank God I found a doctor They haven't gotten to yet.*

He ran tests for HIV, for blood markers of cancer, for genetic disorders, for anything else that might cause lymph inflammation and weight loss and vomiting and fear. He took several vials of blood and said he would call in a few days.

When he did call, I was alone in E.'s apartment. She had gone to work, I had not gone anywhere since the blood draw. I picked up the phone immediately.

He said, *Hey, how are you?*

I don't know how I am, man. Why don't you tell me? I didn't say that.

He said, *Your tests came back and*—overwhelming static. Couldn't hear anything. Cellphone interference. This really happened. The static sound was real.

What? I said.

Your tests, they—static static static. He hung up. I hung up. The line got disconnected somehow.

He called back: *Hello? EVERYTHING IS FINE.* He yelled that into the phone. The connection seemed bad, he said, so he wanted to lead with that. *EVERYTHING IS FINE. YOU'RE FINE.*

I wondered who had gotten to him in two days. Who had gotten to him in two days? Then I felt relief. I at least had to play along. I called E.: Great news, I'm fine! I went to Target. I bought a pink shirt. I began talking. A few weeks later, E. said, *It's nice to have you back.*

But you know where this is going. In a follow-up appointment, the doctor said that while I was physically healthy, I might want to consider seeing a specialist he knew. He made a referral. The specialist was a psychiatrist. I thought about not turning up, but at the last minute I decided to go, and it took, I think, less than an hour over two sessions to settle on an initial diagnosis. Everything was *all in my head*—and not. There was not a problem with the lymph nodes in my head, but there was a problem with my head. At the time, the psychiatrist used words like *mania* and *acute psychotic episode*. During our second appointment, he used a broader set of words: *bipolar disorder type one with psychotic features*. I was desperate to avoid a hospital, so I agreed to try medication and come back every week. He prescribed lithium. I took the lithium, but I didn't ever go back.

It is remarkable how quickly certain medications make the whole of your adult life stop making sense and start making sense all at once. It felt like, *I've been here all along*, but not quite. It's dream logic again: everything feels certainly real until you wake up, and then it's obvious—no, it wasn't real at all. But lying in bed, your body lags behind your thoughts. Your skin is still tense and your lungs are still clenching, and it takes months, or years, to settle down, not just a few minutes in the dark. I stopped seeing the psychiatrist, but I took the lithium and got it refilled. I felt slow but calm. I moved to a new apartment. Within a few months, I was hired for a full-time job. But my body lagged behind my thoughts, or my thoughts behind my body. I spent the next year thinking, How weird. How weird. How terribly, terribly weird.

Part II

Theories of the Forms

I

Our first cases of the insane, writes the historian Allen Thiher, *were probably the owners of those trepanned skulls frequently found in archaeological digs from the Stone Age.* This was the state of neurosurgery in 6,500 BC: the surgeon took a piece of stone and cut through hair and scalp and skull, exposing the brain to the air. *Madness has been localized in the head since time immemorial,* even if we didn't always know why.

Ancient Chinese doctors believed that madness was caused by an imbalance of bodily forces. Ancient Egyptians believed that madness came when organs shifted out of place. Ancient Greek and Romans believed that madness was caused by a misalignment of the stars. They all knew, like the ancient Persians and Hebrews and Americans knew, long before the birth of Freud, that the mad revealed themselves in their dreams. They all believed that no matter the proximate cause, madness was often a curse inflicted by angry Gods, or by an angry God, depending.

In the Gospel of Matthew, the disciples encountered a mad child whom they could not cure, but when Jesus came, he healed the child with ease. *Why could we not cast it out?* the disciples asked. Jesus rebuked them for their lack of expertise. *This kind does not go out except by prayer and fasting*, he said. Even Jesus Christ knew that madness came in different forms and called for different remedies. Even then, the power to treat the mad was bound up in the power to diagnose them.

II

For years, I believed I had a pretty clever joke prepared for when somebody inevitably asked me, *So, like, what's it like when a voice tells you to do something?*

Well, I'd say, *has your boss ever told you to do something? Your teacher? Your mom?*

Sure, they'd say.

I'd say, *It's just like that.*

I've had this joke ready for years, but it has never felt right to tell it. When you're asked a sincere but poorly worded question, it's rude to refuse to answer the question that they meant to ask. I don't want to be the schoolmarm saying, *I don't know, can you go to the bathroom?* Instead I say, *It's weird, it's not well understood.*

When a doctor finally tells you that you're *mentally ill*, you realize that you know—that you have known all along without knowing it—what it's *like* to be insane. But you do not therefore know what it is. Which is to say: *What's it like, when like, a voice tells you to do something?* It's like any voice you've ever heard. But what is this voice? Where does it come from? What chooses its words, what lips made its sound? Why can nobody else hear it? These questions are far more difficult to answer.

III

In the fifth century BC, the Greek physician Hippocrates proposed that the insane were neither possessed nor cursed, but sick, like a man with a cough or a cold. He believed that this illness, like physical illness, was caused by an imbalance between the four humors of the body. Different imbalances brought different afflictions, of which he identified three: mania, melancholia, and brain fever.

In the first century BC, the Roman physician Asclepiades believed that the mad were neither possessed nor cursed, nor sick, but suffering from the conditions of a difficult life. Madness, he said, was brought on by extraordinary episodes of grief or fear or rage.

Three hundred years later, the Greek physician Galen, who lived and worked in Rome, proposed a compromise. Madness could have physical and psychological origins, he said, among them shock, terror, alcoholism, blows to the head, changes in menstruation, and the disordered onset of adolescence. Which is to say: he believed that madness had many forms, and so could come from many causes, too. The search for those causes has continued along these same lines for millennia. A bad brain, a bad life, neither, or both.

It was Hippocrates's contemporary, Socrates, who first asked how it was possible to discover what you don't already know. How would you recognize it, even if you found it? How could you be sure? This question is central to Platonic epistemology; it leads, in several Socratic dialogues, to the theory of recollection, the idea that the world of things as we perceive them is only a world of instantiations and examples. Each child and rock and virtue is only a particular variation on the forms of children and virtues and rocks. The forms themselves, the Platonic rock in which all rocks participate, exist outside our world—in a place beyond heaven, Plato writes—where the soul learns them before being born. That's how we know. In life, we do not learn at all. We only recollect and recognize.

But for all the time spent in the Socratic dialogues trying to find out the forms of justice, virtue, knowledge, and truth, it is worth remembering that no definitive conclusions are ever really reached. Which is to say: it is possible that for all we may believe in our knowledge of the forms, we cannot remember anything at all.

IV

Medievals called madness *deofolseocnes*, devil-sickness. It drove men to *lepe* and *cryen* and *hyde themselves in preuy and secrete places*. The lunatic fell into *fulleuyll suspeccions* wrote Anglicus Bartholomeus in 1240 AD, and *therefore they hate & blame theyr frendes, and somtyme smite & slee them*. The fall of Man was responsible for this disease. Treatment required exorcism, flogging, prayer, or holy water. In some cases, beating, confinement, and hanging came after. In some cases, these patients were later canonized as saints.

If anyone is troubled by a devil, he may not touch the sacred mysteries, said the eighth-century Judgment of Clement. *If by the mercy of God and by fasting he is cleansed, he shall after ten years be received into the office of the clerics, not of the priests.* Even restored to sanity, you could never be made whole again. Such were the wages of the *wonderful passyons* that afflicted the mad *wyth suche a payne*, in *punishment of synne*.

In the seventeenth and eighteenth centuries, at the end of the Agrarian Age, most Europeans believed that madness came in some cases from a morbid humor, coloring the soul. In other cases, it came from a failure of the sanitary faculty of reason, or from an encounter— or absence of encounters—with the sublime. Its unifying symptom was the loss of reason, which is to say, the loss of the quality that separated men from other animals. In that time, the most influential manual on the treatment of madness was called *Two Discourses Concerning the Souls of Brutes*. Its author, the English physician Thomas Willis believed that having lost their reason, the mad must be compelled to regain it by the same methods used for breaking wild beasts.

By the nineteenth century, in the burgeoning city centers of the industrial revolution, many believed that madness came from a weakness of the nerves, a mechanical dysfunction of the brain or body. Society had failed to prepare its people for the stress of modern life. In that time, one of the most influential lectures on the treatment of madness was called *Brain and Soul* by Paul Emil Flechsig, director of the madhouse in Leipzig. Flechsig followed the industrial age, which ran from romanticism toward materialism, and believed that the brain was only so many electrical conductors, firing between themselves in a void. Madness came when these conductors malfunctioned, like a faulty light or factory machine or like a disjointed, derailing train.

V

As theories of the causes have shifted, taxonomies of the forms have grown. Near the end of the nineteenth century, the German biological psychiatrist Emil Kraepelin published his *Compendium der Psychiatrie*, a catalogue of human madness sufficient to fill a book. Kraepelin believed that madness was best classified by symptom clusters, each syndrome identified and differentiated by its presentation and prognosis. From these observations, he reverse-engineered from effect to cause: phenomena became names and things and forms, became an ontology that remains with us now. Like any taxonomy of obscure objects, the contents were liable to breed and meld and multiply. As in the early accounts of birds or medieval catalogues of saints, there are inevitably questions concerning where one thing ends and another begins, where one species is really two, where two saints were really one, whether or not we are getting ahead of ourselves or if we remain hopelessly behind. This too remains with us.

In 1840, the American government undertook its first effort to gather statistical information on the prevalence of insanity in the general population by adding a tick box to that year's census labeled "idiot/insane." A generation later, the 1880 census allowed for seven forms of madness: mania, melancholia, monomania, paresis, dementia, dipsomania, and epilepsy.

In 1854, at a conference of the Académie de Médecine in Paris, two eminent psychiatrists fought over the proper name of a new illness. The first was Jules Baillarger, a doctor already famous for his innovations in the treatment of depression. Baillarger had discovered a new form of madness. Despite some superficial similarities, this new malady was not merely a variation on the depressive personality, but a separate and far more severe condition. He called it *folie á double forme*, the double-form insanity. Baillarger believed that those suffering from double-form insanity could be identified by intense, alternating episodes of suicidal depression and manic lunacy. Unable to leave bed one day, they would the next day become grandiose, delusional, even violent, before inevitably turning back toward melancholia.

The other psychiatrist could not believe it. Jean-Pierre Falret had published his own paper just a few days prior on precisely the same condition: the circular insanity, *la folie circulaire*. Baillarger was a thief. Falret rushed to publish a new paper. Baillarger accused him of plagiarism. Falret pointed to his original paper. Baillarger scoffed—this first "paper" was scarcely more than clinical notes, no theory at all. He, not Falret, had found the form of this disease.

Baillarger believed the double-form insanity came from an irresolvable conflict between chained traumas in the patient's mind. Falret believed that the circular insanity was nothing more than a coincidence of unrelated, opposite episodes, and that each must be treated independently. Baillarger believed that this illness was incurable but manageable. Falret believed it led inevitably to dementia and death. Both psychiatrists ultimately confessed that the condition they were describing was already well documented by the time of their feud. The two men *were not without a little vainglory*, one contemporary observed. Kraepelin had a name for this form of madness, too: *manisch-depressives irresein*, the manic-depressive psychosis.

After the Second World War, the United States Army and Veterans Administration began to track the prevalence of insanity within its ranks. They developed their own taxonomy, adapted from the work of men like Kraepelin, which included psychophysiological, psychiatric, and personality disorders. It was this theory of the forms that was largely copied by the World Health Organization in their *International*

Classification of Diseases, sixth edition, as the global standard of mental health diagnostics. The *International Classification*, in turn, was re-imported to the United States by the American Psychiatric Association, who released it in 1952 as the first edition of the *Diagnostic and Statistical Manual of Mental Disorders* (*DSM*). Which is to say: the *DSM* is, through several fronts, a product of the American military.

The second edition of the *DSM* came out in 1968. The third edition, released in 1980, introduced *a number of important innovations*, including the reclassification of manic-depressive illness as bipolar disorder. Reformers believed this new name would reduce the stigma that had built up around the term manic depression. The *DSM-IV* (1994) and *DSM-5* (2013) went further. Both were the culmination of an effort *that involved more than 1,000 individuals and numerous professional organizations*, as the American Psychiatric Association later explained, including *the generation of hundreds of white papers, monographs, and journal articles*. The era of individual doctors tending their own gardens of the forms was over.

Among the reforms in *DSM-IV* and *5* was the discovery and classifications of several new forms of the double-form or circular or manic-depressive or bipolar madness. Now there were bipolar disorders type one, type two, and type three (called "cyclothymia"). Bipolar disorders with and without psychotic features. Bipolar disorders with or without delusions. Bipolar disorders mild, moderate, and severe. Bipolar disorders in partial remission or full remission or remission-state unspecified. Mania and hypomania and dysphoric episodes, called "mixed." Substance-induced, medication-induced, bipolar disorder due to another medical condition. Type not otherwise specified. Slow cycling. Intermittent cycling. Constant cycling. Rapid and ultra-rapid cycling. From a single genus of insanity came limitless species, diagnoses built up from appended limbs, more heft than weight, the kind it may take a full line in a spiral notebook to write out, no matter how small you make the letters (I've tried it), a name like: *bipolar disorder type one, rapid cycling with mixed episodes and associated psychosis*. Which is what that doctor in Chicago had said I had, in the spring of 2014, one year after the publication of *DSM-5* on the strength of two full-length assessment interviews and one two-page multiple choice survey.

So, okay, I thought. I'm bipolar. Nothing is new. I'm just learning the name for something that's been true for a long time.

VI

My mother has been taking medication for major depressive disorder for most of her adult life.

My uncle Joseph joined the Navy during Vietnam. He believed sincerely that in a past life he'd been Greg the Barbarian; he even went as far as having a broadsword custom made.

On the day Amy Winehouse died in London, my cousin Adam hanged himself in California.

My grandmother died hallucinating herself into the TV shows she watched; before medication, she hallucinated long-lost friends and sometimes Nazis tormenting her in her home.

My father is mentally healthy, although he has been medicated for acute anxiety since his fifties.

While it is commonly believed that serious forms of madness are hereditary in nature, efforts to locate genes linked to these diseases have proven mostly futile. Even twin studies have shown only limited predictive power. In the twentieth century, another generation of biological psychiatrists failed to identify the origins and causes of madness, which led a new generation of analysts to the psychogenic explanation—the curse of a bad life—mainly by attributing psychotic illness to bad mothers. The failure of these mothers might be inadequate affection. It might be too much affection. It might be an affection in proper proportion, but a faulty kind. These new psychiatrists differed in their theories. While this era is remembered poorly, its practitioners believed their approach was fundamentally kind. After all, a bad childhood might be cured. A patient born with a bad brain is hopeless.

Which is to say: the analysts and the biologists differ in the details, but they share the larger theory with the ancient faith in curses placed on bloodlines by an angry God—in one way or another, this is your parents' fault.

VII

Emil Kraepelin distinguished his manic-depressive psychosis from another psychotic illness: *dementia praecox*, a degenerative delusional and hallucinatory disorder often accompanied by paranoia, catatonia, and eventual senility. In the sixth edition of his *Lehrbuch der Psychiatrie*, Kraepelin made what is perhaps his most enduring contribution to the theories of the forms. Despite admitting that any serious psychiatric symptom may appear in any psychotic disorder, Kraepelin insisted that separate forms could nonetheless be identified by the pattern of symptom presentation. While manic depression might ultimately induce hallucinations, and dementia praecox might cause severe disturbances in the patient's mood, they nonetheless had distinct and independent origins. Manic depression was a disease of *affect*. Dementia Praecox was a disease of *cognition*. There is a difference. You cannot have both.

Kraepelin's divide between manic depression and dementia preaecox is known as the Kraepelinian dichotomy, and it remains the orthodox position of psychiatry today. But *dementia praecox* is long gone. When he was a child, the Swiss psychiatrist Eugen Bleuler watched his older sister descend into that disease, then watched as his parents had her taken away to an asylum. As an adult, he gave her condition a new name: *schizophrenia*, the emperor of our most feared forms of madness, the form most synonymous with the very idea of having gone insane.

Sigmund Freud did not treat schizophrenics. He had a private practice; schizophrenics were kept in asylums. Asylum patients could not be cured, only studied, in the hope that observation—or the eventual postmortem dissection of their brains—might finally find the origins of madness. *We cannot accept patients suffering from this disorder,* Freud wrote of schizophrenia. *Or at least cannot retain them for long, given that we set the prospect of therapeutic success as a precondition for our treatment.* But in 1911, on the recommendation of Carl Jung, he read a book published just eight years earlier in Germany: *Denkwürdigkeiten eines Nervenkranken,* a memoir of schizophrenia by the lunatic jurist Daniel Paul Schreber.

Later that same year, Freud published *Psycho-Analytic Notes on an Autobiographical Account of a Case of Paranoia (Dementia Paranoides).* In it, Freud revised his assessment of schizophrenia. The delusions of the schizophrenic could be interpreted because these delusions, Freud realized, were just another form of dreaming. Schizophrenia could be explained in the same manner as many other forms of madness; Schreber, in Freud's view, suffered from a particularly acute Oedipal complex, manifested in his relationship with his doctor, Paul Emil Flechsig, the author of *Brain and Soul.* Freud attributed this discovery to Schreber's remarkable insight, who he believed should have been made *professor of psychiatry and director of a mental hospital* himself. This was not so far-fetched. It was on the strength of his book that Daniel Schreber secured his release from the asylum. While evidently insane in a medical sense, the German court ruled that a man capable of producing and arranging for such a book was legally sane, clearly capable of managing his own affairs.

In the past century, more books and papers have been published concerning the case of Daniel Schreber than any other schizophrenic in the history of the world, each with its own theory about his madness. Freud believed the cause was Oedipal, of course. Jung believed that Schreber, like all schizophrenics, suffered from a biological illness, something genetic, or otherwise inherited through family lines. The Schreber case was the beginning of the end of the partnership between Freud and Jung. In late 1912, while speaking to an audience in New

York, Jung denounced Freud's psychogenic and sexually preoccupied approach to psychiatry, citing Schreber as a key example of Freud's error.

The French psychiatrist Jacques Lacan believed, like Freud, that Schreber's madness was sexual in origin. Michel Foucault believed Schreber was a kind of modern cipher, a replacement for Lancelot in the adventures of childhood. Another scholar called Schreber a vampire, a German Romantic resisting the impending mechanical and cosmopolitan age. Another argued that he was a preeminent legal theorist, indirectly constructing a uniform vision of the law. Scholars have blamed Schreber's schizophrenia on his father, on his wife, on his doctor, his country, his profession, his era, his failed bid for office. None of these theorists, including Freud, ever met Schreber. He became, as the journalist Robert Kolker called him, *the ideal psychiatric patient: one who cannot talk back.*

Schreber himself did not discuss his condition beyond his memoir. After the death of his mother, he went mad again. He went back into the asylum and never came out. But if the taxonomy of madness comes from its phenomenology, if we only guess at the ontology from there—if *what it's like* tells us *what it is,* and we do not really know beyond that; if all of this comes first from what the madman says is going on and what we see him do inside his madness, then perhaps it was not Bleuler or Kraepelin or Jung or Freud but Daniel Paul Schreber who invented schizophrenia after all.

Freud and Kraepelin were rough contemporaries. Both imagined themselves to be settling a single, urgent question: Is insanity an illness of the body, caused by a bad brain, or was it an illness of human experience, caught from a bad life? As in politics, the history of these two parties is the history of decades and centuries spent in cycles. One party comes to power and fails to deliver on the promise of permanent progress. It falls out of favor and cedes power back to the other.

The early twentieth century saw the rise of the "scientific" psychiatry of Kraepelin, which failed to make much progress at all. The middle of the twentieth century saw the rise of Freud and Jung and all the analysts who came after them, who failed to make much progress at all. The end of the twentieth century saw a "biological revolution," ushered in by breakthroughs in psychiatric pharmacology, restoring the heirs of Hippocrates and Kraepelin to power. They have failed to make much progress at all. No psychiatrist anywhere has been able to locate a definitive cause for any form of madness; genetic studies remain promising but inconclusive. The history of psychiatry is often told as the tale of a war between two theories of the forms of madness, two theories still warring today: the somatogenic—a bad brain—and the psychogenic—a bad life. Which is to say: the biologists and the analysts. Emil Kraepelin and Sigmund Freud. Hippocrates and Asclepiades.

Hippocrates was in vogue when I was born. Pharmaceutical corporations prefer it that way; *a chemical imbalance in the brain* is just a new way of saying *an imbalance of the four humors of the body*. Now, in the twenty-first century, we have become concerned about the over-prescription of psychiatric drugs and discovered once again how talk therapy of the kind pioneered by the Freudians produces better results in some patients than any known form of medication. The pendulum has begun to swing back the other way, back toward some new and yet unknown progeny of Asclepiades.

VIII

I believe that I am sitting on a table behind a building on a hill in Iowa, by the base of an oak tree where a single overlong blade of grass is smacking its limp head into the bark. It is 2018 and I have believed myself to be bipolar for four years.

I believe that the world is no larger than what I can see right now. The tree, the grass, the table, the road, curving up past the gas station and the supermarket, where it does not continue down the hill because the world stops.

I believe there is a man with a blanket over a birdcage about to pluck the blanket off. I am inside the cage. I am only looking at the drapery.

I believe there is no world at all.

I try to focus on the stupid, slapping grass strand on the tree. My doctor tells me that this is called derealization. If it worsens, I should call her straightaway. If it worsens, will I believe that she exists on the far side of the phone?

Contrary to the popular imagination, a bipolar mood episode is not a sudden attack. It is not a coughing fit. Which is to say: you are not feeling manic one day and then depressed the next. Such rapid oscillations, according to the prevailing theory of the forms, are more indicative of a borderline personality disorder. Even the episodes of a rapid cycling bipolar patient last weeks, or months—each building day by day until they reach their peak and crash, before receding into a stable, interstitial state. Which is to say: you wake up one day and realize, with creeping clarity, what's been happening for weeks beneath your notice.

After my initial diagnosis, I became dimly aware, over the course of many years, that I was getting worse. I began to notice, or my doctors began to notice, the presentation of certain symptoms—delusional thought patterns, ideas of reference, distortions in my ability to process words and faces—despite mood stabilizing medication and the apparent absence of severe mood symptoms. I had undergone, and am still undergoing, a variety of small changes in temperament and impulse and in the boundaries of my sense of what is reasonable.

These differences were nearly imperceptible in their slow progress; they grow like a gut or like hair. But over time they had come to constitute the far larger subsurface of my nervous illness. Bipolar disorder is not generally understood to entail these compounding losses in cognitive function. I did not appear to enter my ordinary period of remission between episodes anymore.

Not every change had come on slowly. The year before, after a period of intense exhaustion and stress, I had become very suddenly worse. I wasn't sleeping. I went to the hospital three times in as many months. I went to class and said nothing and then opened my mouth suddenly in the middle of a conversation and said things that did not make sense.

When I saw my doctor, he put me on antipsychotics in addition to my mood stabilizer. When this failed to entirely resolve my symptoms, he referred me to a specialist at a private practice on the edge of town for further examination.

In the *Theaetetus*, Socrates tells his interlocuter that he is not a philosopher, but a midwife like his mother. He is a midwife to men who are pregnant with ideas. He has never conceived an idea himself, but he knows the signs of somebody on the verge of birthing one. Or at least he thinks he does. The trouble is that every idea he's helped deliver has come out stillborn. He has spent so much time examining so many things but he still doesn't know anything at all.

IX

Twenty years after the advent of his dichotomy, Emil Kraepelin conceded that a *great number* of cases he encountered saw overlap between symptoms of schizophrenia and symptoms of bipolar disorder, even in his beloved pattern of presentation. Seven years after Kraepelin's death, the Russian psychiatrist Jacob Kasanin introduced the term *schizoaffective psychosis* to the field. Karl Kahlbaum, a German psychiatrist, identified the same condition; he called it *vesania typica circularis*, the circular insanity, again. The first edition of the *DSM* includes a small subtype of schizophrenia called schizoaffective disorder. The third edition of the *DSM* moved this condition to its own family: psychotic disorders not otherwise specified. The fourth edition of the *DSM* placed it under "Other Psychotic Disorders." Two subtypes were identified: depressive and bipolar.

On a bad afternoon in Iowa, under the green sky of a tornado watch, I saw the specialist that my doctor recommended, and he conducted a long interview, along with a series of verbal tests. He told me that the difference between schizoaffective disorder of the bipolar type and bipolar disorder with associated psychosis is defined as the presence of any psychotic symptoms for at least two weeks at any point in the patient's history that occurred in absence of the presence of a full manic or depressive episode. It is also believed that schizoaffective disorder, unlike most bipolar disorders, carries an elevated risk of ongoing cognitive decline.

It is, of course, very difficult to establish whether or not a patient has experienced symptoms of psychosis for two weeks or more in the absence of a severe mood episode. Severe mood episodes can induce psychosis; psychosis can induce extraordinary moods. It is difficult to convince yourself that thirteen days of psychosis in the absence of mania indicates one disorder, with its own origins and etiology and prognosis, while fifteen days indicates an entirely separate pathology. But then, a cough persisting a few weeks in presence of a fever is indicative of an upper respiratory infection. A cough persisting for weeks and months in the absence of any other pulmonary symptoms may be indicative of cancer.

Psychosis outside the presence of a mood episode is ordinarily established by patient history. The specialist asked me, in great detail, about my history of psychotic symptoms. He asked me about their chronology—Did they appear at the same time as manic episodes? Depressive episodes? Sometimes? All of the time? I tried to answer honestly: How would I know? I am not a trained psychiatrist. I do not know which moods are sane and which are not. How can I recognize what I don't know, even when I see it?

[The patient] suffers persistent problems with psychotic symptoms, the specialist wrote in his report. While orientation is currently *intact* and thought processes are mostly coherent, he *suffered delusions* and presented with a *flat affect. Following the interview, we discussed the differential diagnosis. I advised that most likely diagnoses are bipolar disorder with psychotic features versus schizoaffective disorder. I think schizoaffective*

disorder is the more likely diagnosis considering the long history of psychotic symptoms independent of mood episodes.

Regardless, he wrote, *I advised that the treatment would be similar.*

This diagnosis—*schizoaffective*—has followed me since then.

I didn't know then what this change meant. I did not know if it meant that I always "was" schizoaffective, or if I "was" bipolar, and then my condition became worse and changed. It is unclear, if a change occurred, what precipitated this change—Was it inevitable? A failure of my treatment? A shock to the system brought on by a particular episode, a particular moment of rage or fear? Would a different life have left me just bipolar? Would a different life have left me sane? Is there a life where I descended into schizophrenia entirely? Is that life still possible? I don't know that it matters very much. The treatment is largely *similar.*

In *Madness and Modernism,* the psychologist and critic Louis Sass writes that while manic depression and other mood disorders remain comprehensible extremes of ordinary human life, the schizophrenias have *often seemed like a limit-case or farthest borderland of human existence, something suggesting an almost unimaginable aberration.* The distinguishing feature of schizophrenia is not necessarily in its symptoms—which are each shared by other disorders—but in *the intense yet indescribable feelings of alienness such individuals can evoke.*

In the presence of normal people, as well as with patients of nearly every other psychiatric diagnosis, one feels an immediate sense of a shared humanity, whereas the schizophrenic seems to inhabit an entirely different universe, Sass explains, *he is someone from whom one feels separated by "a gulf which defies description."* European psychiatrists have labeled this reaction the "praecox feeling"—*the sense of encountering someone who seems "totally strange, puzzling, inconceivable, and uncanny . . . even to the point of being sinister and frightening."* The praecox feeling. Is that what my doctor felt with me? Is that why he sent me to the specialist? Did the specialist feel it, too?

For a long time, I told people it was terrible discovering that I was worse than I'd been told before, that I might continue to get worse throughout my whole life, but that's a lie. The truth is that it let me split the difference of my shame. For the first three years after my break in Chicago, I carried the name for my trouble like a bad memory to be suppressed. It was an issue now resolved that could be safely ignored. I told nobody but my parents and E. and a few other friends that I was ill. When a doctor declared me *schizoaffective* rather than *bipolar*, it did not change anything about my life. But now that I faced the specter of being something worse than manic-depressive, something more frightening and serious and potentially degenerative, it became easy to hide behind the old secret, to *open up* and say to everyone I knew, *Well, I'm bipolar! You caught me! I'm crazy! That's why I am the way I am! That's why I'm difficult. It's bad, but it could be worse! No need to speculate about anything more serious that might be going on at all.*

Maybe I was foolish to think that I could hide. Maybe everyone could feel that sinister, uncanny *praecox* on me, no matter what I said.

X

There are, of course, people (and more of them every day) who do not believe in our prevailing taxonomies, people who do not believe in the existence of madness in general.

They remind us, correctly, that while brain abnormalities exist in some psychiatric patients, there are no consistent organic "signs" of madness, nor any biological test for any psychiatric pathology.

They remind us that the origins of psychiatry are sadists, brain butchers, and Freudian perverts, and before that, theories of demonic possession.

They remind us that even our modern, scientific theories of the forms of madness are flimsy, unstable, and frequently ridiculous. They remind us of the early researchers, who relied on admitting patients to their asylums to dissect their brains, and of the gawkers, in the early days of the American Republic, who were charged four pence apiece to view the lunatics on the mad wing of Pennsylvania Hospital.

They remind us that centuries later, it is still the case that medicalized pain is individual pain, and that individual pain does not inspire political upheaval. It is more useful and more profitable to have a perpetual base of "patients" than it is to have the perpetual unrest of an unhappy polity. The official diagnostic criteria for *disability* and *recovery* in the modern world are based on productivity, on the patient's capacity to make money for somebody else. They remind us that, in this view, psychiatric diagnosis is little more than a form of discipline. They remind us that there is very little evidence at all, beside phenomena, that any of these pathologies exist at all.

It may be true, Mark Fisher wrote, that depression is a result of a serotonin deficiency in the brain. But how did that deficit come about? In an essay on depression and the politics of mental health, Mikkel Krause Frantzen says, *The importance of arriving at a political understanding of depression cannot be overstated. If the reader only takes one thing away from my text let it be this: depression has a set of causes and a concrete context that transcend any diagnostic manual, as well as the neoliberal ideology of focusing on subjects, not structures; personal responsibilities, not collective ones; chemistry, not capital.* Which is to say: if you lose your leg working in a coal mine, don't let the boss convince you that you were born with a leg disorder.

Psychiatry has long made a distinction between the forms of madness that have appeared in every society and at every point in history—the double-form insanities and circular insanities and schizophrenias—and those which are "culturally bound." But still, when does a taxonomy built on nothing but the testimony of the afflicted begin to turn upon itself? When does the snake begin to swallow its own tail? When do the afflicted, looking for a way to tell a doctor of some inchoate suffering, begin to imitate the doctor's language? Begin to believe what the doctors say the problem comes from, not because the doctors are persuasive, but because they have learned the only things you can believe if you want those doctors to help?

Still, I believe, and you believe, that some people are very clearly crazy, and that may be as specific as it is safe to go.

XI

The authors of the *DSM-5* worried that the schizoaffective diagnosis was a mistake. It has *poor predictive reliability*, they said. At a conference in the United States, a prominent psychiatrist told attendees that they *had hoped to get rid of the schizoaffective [disorder] as a diagnostic category because we don't think it's valid, and we don't think it's reliable*. But, he went on, the current state of diagnostics made it *absolutely indispensable to clinical practice*. A medical student on a now-defunct message board for trading psychiatric triage stories put it another way: schizoaffective disorder was *a lazy bucket diagnosis for overworked clinicians*.

In 2008, in the *Journal of Neuropsychiatry*, clinicians suggested a way to resolve the tension between the Kraepelinian dichotomy and the obviously inconsistent presentation of some patients by folding each one the forms of psychotic and mood disorders into an intersection of spectrums. On one axis, information processing, and on the other, emotional regulation. You mark where the patient falls on each and draw a line for diagnosis. *Studies of patients' symptoms, of the role of genes, of the course and outcome of illnesses over time, and of the response of symptoms to treatment, all point to similarities between schizophrenia and bipolar disorder rather than to differences*, argues an article in the *Mental Health Review Journal*. *In the last few years, researchers have argued that schizophrenia is a variant of bipolar disorder, the only true form of psychosis; that "bipolar disorder" is in fact the brain's own response to schizophrenia; and that a symptom-led approach, premised on the idea of a continuum in the frequency, severity and phenomenology of abnormal and normal experiences and behaviors, would enable us to move beyond diagnostic categories altogether*.

By the *DSM-VI*, the category of schizoaffective disorder may well be eliminated entirely. *Manic depression* and *dementia praecox* may collapse soon, too. My specialist still got his fee.

In "The Socratic Method and Psychoanalysis," the analyst and philosopher Jonathan Lear points out that at two separate points, both Phaedrus and Alcibiades said that Socrates is the strangest person who has ever lived. *The Greek word*, Lear writes, *is* atopotatos: *literally, the person most lacking a* topos—*a place.* Socrates appears lost. Lear is not the first to suggest, sometimes elliptically, sometimes explicitly, that Socrates suffered some form of madness.

But think of topos *in terms of pretense*, writes Lear. *The putting forth of a claim is precisely taking up a position in argumentative space. . . . Socrates has no such position, and this turns out to be the quintessence of human wisdom.*

Perhaps Socrates was mad. Perhaps he cured himself. He was executed by the people of Athens and Plato turned him into a saint. The trouble with knowing is that it is pretending, always. We cannot learn or even recollect anything at all.

XII

I believe my therapist when she says it is a kind of victory so long as I am not homeless, in prison, or dead. I believe my doctor when she says that my medication will prevent me from ever being that far gone. But I don't believe that I will remember to take my medication every day for the rest of my life.

I believe that there are patients who are far worse than I am, who disintegrate until the illness is the better part of their being, who are not worried about a *place* or *forms* or diagnostic history because they can barely speak a sentence at all. We do not know why some patients are resistant to medication. We do not know why some patients do not believe they need medication. We do not know why some patients, despite a positive reaction to medication, continue to degenerate in other ways.

I believe the paperwork I received upon discharge from a hospital in Chicago, several years ago: the patient is *having a mood problem*. I have a problem with my mood. I believe the paperwork I received upon discharge from a hospital in Iowa: *It looks like you've been having hallucinations and/or delusions. But a normal life is possible!*

I believe the journal article that my doctor sent me, where she highlighted *Reduction of time spent in a state of psychosis is important because active psychosis may indicate a period of disease progression. Psychotic relapse may cause positive symptoms to become increasingly refractory to antipsychotic medications, with failure to return to previous levels of functioning . . . recovery times subsequent to resumption of treatment following relapse became increasingly prolonged with each successive relapse.* Which is to say, I believe it is best to avoid the breaks, whatever they may really be.

But I am getting worse. I am so sensitive these days. I throw little tantrums and cry and pout at jokes because I do not understand that they are jokes. Even psychosis comes and goes without warning. I lose focus. I come back to the dinner table to a voice asking, *Where did you go?*

My doctor assures me that I am not schizophrenic, largely because of my level of function and because my periods of psychosis often—but don't always—come with episodes of mania or depression. But both my doctor and my therapist say, *when dealing with schizophrenia*, and *with schizophrenics*, and *in schizophrenia*, just before they say something that I should notice, or look out for, or be mindful of going forward.

XIII

For the lunatic Susanna Kaysen, the forms are simple. *Insanity comes in two basic varieties*, she wrote, *slow and fast.*

The common understanding of contemporary psychiatry is that after the reign of superstition, and then the reign of the analysts, a biological revolution took place, and that this scientific and medical approach made mental health, like physical health, into a scientific affair. But a scientific affair is an affair of phenomena, of observations and empiricism, not forms.

Psychiatrists believe they are scientists. They believe that their taxonomies reflect not just experience, but things. There is madness inside of the mad. We know the kinds, just not quite what they are. Some revolution, some analysis, some biological breakthrough will reveal the answer some day, perhaps through scans and tests, perhaps through talking, perhaps by drilling into skulls.

But literary criticism and psychiatry are not *merely analogous disciplines, adjacent series of assumptions and moves that parallel one another,* writes C. Barry Chabot. *All interpretation, whether of individual texts or of patients, is essentially a textual exercise; understanding strings of words, with their metaphors and their sequence, word-after-word, is the objective of both.* Perhaps psychiatrists are just close readers, like me. In the nineteenth century, psychiatry worked in largely the same way, but in that time, the signs were not found in the stories or the speech of patients, but in their faces, in the brows and skulls and eyes. In both cases, psychiatrists are critics, once of sculptures, now of words.

Perhaps the doctors are just disciplinarians, or animal breeders, or mystics, or cops, or cranks. Perhaps they are pretending, always. I've had more than one doctor say as much to me: *We don't really know what we're doing.* But, they inevitably say, *Does it matter what we know, so long as your medication is workings?* They think this admission and this question will gain my trust. It took twenty-four years for a doctor to tell me, *This is the kind of madness that you have.*

It only took four years for another to say, *No, that's wrong. It's this one.* Four years after that, and it is possible that this form of madness that they say I have will be removed from the garden of the forms entirely. I could blame all of this on doctors, on diagnostic quackery, but then: It took twenty-four years for me to go recognizably crazy. It only took four years to get worse, and I have gotten worse every year thereafter. There are two forms: *fast and slow*. But like Kraepelin's dichotomy, sometimes it can be both. We don't know why; not really. A bad brain, bad parents, bad humors, a bad life. A machine, a manual, a star, a garden, a form. The curse of an angry God, or angry Gods, depending.

Titration Diary

I take four different psychiatric medications twice per day, eight pills in total. I take some when I wake up and some just before I go to sleep. I take some during the day, too, but only if I need them.

This is the situation in the fall of 2019, at the beginning of my final year in the Midwest. But the situation changes often. I do not know what the average person believes psychiatric medication to be like, but before I took it, I thought of it as two states: *on your meds* and *off your meds*, like a drunk relative to the wagon. I had heard, as many people have no doubt heard, that *finding the right meds can take some time*, but I had not heard the truth: there is not some fixed but unknown combination of pills that will work for a given patient, *the right meds*, if only they could find them. Psychiatric medication is more like an aging ship. The weather changes, the wind shifts. Day turns to night. Course correction is inevitable. An old map helps. You can hire a navigator to help, but the captain is unstable. The captain is literally insane.

In the morning I take three hundred milligrams of extended-release lamotrigine. Lamotrigine was originally developed in the twentieth century as an epilepsy medication, but in the twenty-first, it was approved as a mood stabilizer, effective in delaying episodes of bipolar mania. *Treating the depression half,* one doctor told me, *is more of an art than a science.* Known side effects of lamotrigine include dizziness, drowsiness, headache, vision problems, nausea, stomach pain, difficulty sleeping, and, in rare cases, a condition called Stevens-Johnson syndrome, in which the skin begins to flake, and then peel, and then fall off of your body. I have never looked into whether this happens in patches or strips, all at once or slowly.

I take two hundred milligrams of Seroquel in the morning, and three hundred milligrams more at night. Seroquel is an atypical antipsychotic, sometimes called a second-generation antipsychotic; a replacement for the old antipsychotics that we associate with images of drooling, semi-conscious mental patients. I take Seroquel so I do not hear voices or believe things that are not true. Five hundred milligrams of Seroquel daily is near the maximum recommended dose. It wraps around my head like a thick, wet rag: nothing gets in, and very little comes out. The known side effects of Seroquel include drowsiness, dizziness, dry mouth, headache, fatigue, hunger, weight gain, blood sugar spikes, overheating, and a variety of movement disorders, including one called Parkinsonism, in which the medication interferes with dopamine transmission to such a degree that it causes dystonic tremors, similar to early-stage Parkinson's disease. Some research suggests that psychotic disorders are fundamentally disorders of dopamine transmission, an excess rather than a deficiency; a kind of inverse Parkinson's disease. After ten months on Seroquel, I developed Parkinsonism, and I take one-and-a-half milligrams of the Parkinson's medication benztropine.

Benztropine treats the tremor in my hands and the twitch in my face and the awkward, shuffling walk I've developed as a side effect of Seroquel. Benztropine has eliminated the face twitch and reduced the hand tremor, but I still walk oddly, and when I go to my local coffee shop and they hand me a mug, I still worry that I'll drop it. The known side effects of benztropine include drowsiness, dizziness, constipation, nausea, and vision problems.

Some days I take Ativan, a tranquilizer, used "as needed." I have taken as many as ten milligrams in a day, although this is neither safe nor necessary. There are weeks I need it every few hours, and weeks when I do not need it at all. The Ativan is a sleep aid, and a contingency plan when my other medication isn't working. Most medication works by reaching and maintaining a therapeutic level in the bloodstream over the course of days and weeks, but Ativan works immediately. I can take enough to knock myself out and recover some sanity while I'm down. So long as I have not stopped taking my medication entirely, a very long Ativan-induced nap is typically enough to get any incipient psychosis under control. The fall 2019 medication situation finds me mostly able to avoid taking Ativan at all.

I have been on this medication regimen for nearly two years. Together, these medications have been far more effective at keeping me stable and productive than previous combinations. The Seroquel, in particular, is less curative than it is an exchange of certain undesirable symptoms (hallucinations, delusions, catatonia, mania) for other undesirable symptoms (exhaustion, weight gain, blood sugar spikes, diminished cognitive function, my bootleg Parkinson's disease). By fall 2019, I have spent eighteen months telling my doctor at the University of Iowa that I do not like these side effects, but I have also been hospitalized twice in that time, and so he is reluctant to take chances. He told me it was better to feel tired and stupid and get fat than lose my mind. If I can go a full year without any psychotic symptoms, he will consider backing off the dose.

But in the spring of 2019, I finished my studies in Iowa and spent the summer in California. When I returned to Iowa in the fall to work as an adjunct instructor for the year, I discovered that I couldn't see my university doctor anymore. *In order to access student health, you must be a student*, the sensible appointment nurse told me on the telephone. My new position did not even come with health insurance, much less access to university medical personnel. I went on COBRA. I booked an appointment with a private psychiatrist in town.

Perhaps because this new doctor was younger, and therefore more up-to-date than my school doctor, or perhaps only because new doctors sometimes feel the need to do something new to demonstrate the new value they'll be bringing to your case, the doctor suggested, roughly half an hour into our first appointment, that the side effects of my Seroquel weren't worth it and that I might try switching to a different antipsychotic called Abilify.

Abilify is not a new drug. Like Seroquel, it is a second-generation antipsychotic. I'd known people who had taken it to mixed results. Some swore by it. Some reported an immediate return of psychotic symptoms, in one case joined by a weeks-long refusal to eat, broken only by the threat of immediate hospitalization.

But, my new doctor told me Abilify doesn't carry the same hunger and weight gain consequences as Seroquel. Abilify also rarely causes the degree of lethargy I've been feeling on Seroquel. Abilify is known to induce the same motor dysfunction I've gotten from the Seroquel, but every patient is different. We know what Seroquel does to your body. Perhaps Abilify won't do the same things. The worst-case scenario is no change. My doctor persuades me that even some improvement in some side effects is a good enough reason to switch, provided that the Abilify treats my psychiatric symptoms just as well. *It's a balancing act*, she said—and so has every doctor I've ever had at some point or another. Known side effects of Abilify include dizziness, drowsiness, nausea, excessive salivation, vision problems, and trouble sleeping.

Switching from one antipsychotic to another is not as simple as throwing out one bottle and picking up a new one. During our second session, after I agree to try the switch, my new doctor spends several long, silent minutes consulting a large manual on titration schedules before writing out a week-by-week guide. The goal is to get from five hundred milligrams daily of Seroquel to zero, without creating any dangerous break in the level of antipsychotic medication in my blood—

that is, without me losing my mind—while simultaneously going from zero to thirty milligrams daily of Abilify (the maximum recommended dose) in the increments necessary for the introduction of a powerful new drug. We must get two drivers, traveling in opposite directions at great speed, to toss my well-being from one car into the other without slowing down or swerving.

My doctor encouraged me to keep careful track of my symptoms and any other significant feelings over the course of the switch, if possible, she said, I should write them down in a diary.

FALL 2019, WEEK ONE: 400MG/SEROQUEL, 0MG/ABILIFY

TUESDAY: Before I can begin taking the Abilify, I have to begin coming off the Seroquel. This is partly to make room for the Abilify's therapeutic benefits, but it is also because coming off five hundred milligrams daily of Seroquel takes longer than scaling up to the new one on Abilify. If I taper off Seroquel too quickly, I might experience violent withdrawal symptoms. I experienced these symptoms the week my tremor started, when I could not get an appointment to see my psychiatrist right away, and so I stopped taking my medication cold turkey in a panic. I am not eager to repeat them. Seroquel withdrawal symptoms include nausea, vomiting, insomnia, dizziness, excessive sweating, and increased heart rate.

All of this is to say, if we do not give the Seroquel taper a head start before introducing the Abilify, I will throw up my medication, and there will be no way to tell whether or not it is working. I have been taking two one-hundred-milligram Seroquel tablets in the morning and one three-hundred-milligram tablet at night. This morning, I threw one of my morning tablets in the trash.

WEDNESDAY: About forty minutes after I take my morning medication, I feel my brain begin to clog. This may be a consequence of the lamotrigine, not the Seroquel. It's impossible to say. But the clog feels less total today than it did yesterday or the day before that or the week before. This may be a kind of reverse placebo effect. I am imagining myself cured by not taking a pill.

THURSDAY: At night, when I get into bed, my body feels very hot. But I fall asleep as easily as always.

FRIDAY: Never mind. I'm having trouble falling asleep. Ordinarily, this means that I'm preoccupied, but last night I just lay there for an hour or two and thought of nothing.

SATURDAY: I only got three hours of sleep. The truth is that I don't know what a normal amount of sleep is for me, how much I would sleep without pharmaceutical interference. I took a psych med for the first time five years ago. When that doctor in Chicago referred me to a psychiatrist and that psychiatrist decided I was bipolar, he prescribed lithium. Lithium was the first real mood stabilizer in modern medicine. Side effects of lithium include headache, nausea, dizziness, changes in appetite, hand tremors, dry mouth, increased thirst, increased urination, rashes, and hair loss. It is found mainly in rocks.

I filled my first prescription a few days after my diagnosis; a few weeks later, I was walking with a group of friends to the train station when I realized that I had forgotten to take my morning dose. I had the bottle in a laptop bag, which I had with me, and I lagged a few steps behind the group, took the bottle out, and dry-swallowed the capsule. One of my friends saw me and asked what it was. I said they were anxiety pills—I'd been feeling anxious lately—and that they made me nauseous. I never let anybody see those pills again. I kept the bottle in the back of my sock drawer, and when I had to take it with me, I put a sock or cotton balls inside the bottle to keep the pills from rattling. When I spent the night at E.'s apartment, I'd leave the bottle in my bag in the living room and wait until she was close to sleep and take them then. If she asked, I said I was thirsty or that I needed to use the bathroom. She must have thought I was terribly dehydrated most of the time for all the feverish drinking I had to do at night, but she seemed very glad that I was back to normal after the months of panic attacks, after the weeks of silence and milkshakes and doctors. She told me later that she'd been terrified by all that, that she knew I wasn't dying but that there didn't seem to be a way to talk me out of it. She confessed later that she'd even called my parents. She was more confused than scared. But that was over now. The moment at which you have solved a problem did not seem to me to be the moment when it was most urgent to worry somebody by telling them about the problem's real cause. So, for that first year on medication, my last year in Chicago, I sometimes took my lithium in the middle of the night.

SUNDAY: I slept through the night but spent two hours in the afternoon desperately afraid that I was about to get bad news. This may be a consequence of the dose reduction, but I am still on my mood stabilizer and tranquilizer and 80 percent of my Seroquel. This feeling comes sometimes, even at full doses. But I also feel as if I have more energy. Is this all in my head? Antipsychotics are all about blood serum levels. If I miss a dose, it isn't a big deal. But if I miss several doses, and my blood levels drop, and symptoms set in, getting stable is not as simple as taking the next pill on time. We're steering a big ship here. It turns slowly. I shouldn't expect much real change this week.

MONDAY: I am not sure that anything unusual is happening, except that I am waking up once or twice each night. On the full dose of Seroquel, I had a hard time getting up in the morning without a few tries. Now I can't stay asleep. Last night I woke up at 1:30 a.m., and then again at 4:00 a.m. But, I went the entire day forgetting that anything was unusual about my medication levels until I went to make this entry. Is this a good sign? I feel good. I may have felt good anyway.

FALL 2019, WEEK TWO: 300MG/SEROQUEL, 10MG/ABILIFY

TUESDAY: Seroquel, in higher doses, looks like what a child would draw if you asked them to draw a pill: oblong, round, and thick. Abilify is much smaller, pale pink or white and chalky, either a circle or triangle. The ten-milligram pills are particularly tiny, like my benztropine and

Ativan—if I take them with water, I'm sometimes unsure if I've swal-lowed them at all. On a few occasions, in the middle of the day, I have felt something against my gums and probed my tongue up to find a slivery pill, half dissolved and stuck above my tooth. It has started getting cold in Iowa. Last night I turned my heat on for the first time since last April, and the whole apartment rattled as the machine came to life. This morning, I took my first Abilify with great private cere-mony and waited.

WEDNESDAY: A few months after I began lithium, I moved into a new apartment in Chicago. I had new roommates, two different men I'd known in college. They both worked for a law firm downtown. I was unemployed. The lithium made me incredibly tired. I slept in until my roommates left, then on the advice of a new therapist, tried to keep the same routine each day. I ate breakfast at the same time, which was lunchtime. I walked the same mile route around a nearby park. I began to feel better. I wrote a bad play and managed some freelance writing.

E. stayed with me more than I stayed with her that year. I think that the effects of the lithium must have caused her to register some change in my personality, but I don't know. She didn't often say when I worried her, and I didn't often ask. I got fat, in a way particular to lithium. New driver's license and passport photos taken around that time preserve it: a puffed out, lazy, sagging face.

When my roommates came home, we drank, which you are not meant to do on lithium, or at all if you've been diagnosed with a serious psychiatric disorder. But for the first time in years, I did not feel either intensely powerful and important, or intensely afraid in company, and I wanted to spend time with my friends. On Sundays, E. slept in while the roommates and I walked two miles, rain or shine, to a restaurant where we began drinking around eight thirty in the morning and continued at home into the night.

I felt flat and foggy, like nothing was on the periphery that de-manded my attention. This was a very good feeling. I don't know if that is an unusual way to feel.

What I mean is: I want to tell you what lithium feels like, but I'm told lithium made me feel more like you do every day, or at least some approximation. Is that true? Of course, I can't say. I don't have a baseline for comparison.

I do know that after years of being unable to get or keep a job, and years unable to make friends easily, I was suddenly productive. By winter, I had begun to think of a career as a writer, and E. and I were almost popular as a couple. We went out a lot. I published at a decent clip. Things were very good.

I still hadn't told E., or anybody but my mom and dad, that I was taking medication. I loved E. More than that, I realized during that year that she might be the first person I could love; the first person who I could want through something other than the fog on mania. I felt safe with her, if not safe enough to tell her. I told myself that love—new, real, adult love—was an act of witness. I told myself that a lover is somebody who takes the discrete points of your life and weaves them into sense by watching. I told myself that I could trick my audience. I could be seen as I wanted to be seen, while omitting what I wanted from the tapestry. It wasn't all a lie. E. was seeing me become sane. She didn't need to know why. She would just be happier for it.

The next summer, a little over a year after I'd begun lithium, I accepted a job as a junior editor at a news website in Washington, DC. This would have been unimaginable a year prior. I quit smoking. I moved there in July.

Four years later, in Iowa, I am standing on my porch in the early winter cold smoking a second cigarette before I go back inside. I feel nothing, but it is a very active kind of nothing. There's energy in my stomach and my solar plexus. The energy is crouched and very still, not fidgeting or restless. It's knees-bent, ready-to-jump, waiting for some object to leap for. I go back inside. I've recently adopted a middle-aged black cat who possesses this same kind of energy because I was tired of living alone.

THURSDAY: The trouble with paying attention is that you notice things that were always there but that you did not see before. I suppose that's the point. I am on the lookout for an uptick in my symptoms and

I am waiting to find out what Abilify "feels like." I've spent the last half hour in a coffee shop, inexplicably afraid. But haven't I felt this way before? Don't I feel this way once or twice a week, every week, no matter what? I can't remember. I wasn't paying attention before.

I feel tired. Don't I always feel tired? I didn't feel so tired last week. Is this a new kind of tired? It feels like exhaustion, but not like I'd never woken up, which is how most meds feel. I've spent two years feeling like I never quite wake up at all. I don't spend this much time analyzing my energy level most of the time. What's signal and what's noise?

As it happens, this trouble is also the trouble of psychosis. You're paying too much attention to the white noise. You're finding patterns that are not there and assigning them a significance that they do not really possess. Last night, it was so hot in my apartment that I turned the heat off entirely; when I woke up this morning, I was freezing. Sensitivity to temperature can be a side effect of medication changes, but it is also a side effect of living alone in an old and poorly insulated house in the Midwest in the fall.

FRIDAY: For the first time in months, both of my hands are shaking.

SATURDAY: Both of my hands are shaking.

SUNDAY: Both of my hands are shaking. I've been on a trip this weekend. I've driven and taken a flight and then a train and then another train and then another flight and another drive. It was a nice trip, but it makes it hard to monitor symptoms for this journal. I feel uncomfortable away from home, although my trip was back to Washington, DC, where I have not been since the year that I lived there. When I made that move, in the summer of 2015, the moving company I'd hired didn't arrive for six weeks. I lived in a largely empty apartment with an air mattress and one chair. I didn't find a new doctor. I had lithium refills left, and for the first six months, I kept filling them. Lithium also requires regular blood tests, to measure patient blood serum level. I stopped getting those immediately.

I was working as an editor, and I was meant to be writing, too. But when I was home from the office, I was tired all the time. Perhaps it was just the consequence of a first experience with a regular job. I missed E., who visited sometimes, but who had left Chicago a few weeks after I did to go to graduate school in Ann Arbor. She was busier than she had been when we lived in the same place. We saw one another every six weeks, or seven, sometimes in one of our new homes, or in California, but most often in Chicago. My bus and her train converged there. We rented apartments for a few days at a time, often in converted attics or futtoned basements or the tops of newly gentrified towers. Once we stayed in a set of rooms owned by a piano teacher. She had a canopied bed and the sort of pea-green tiled bathroom that sends *House Hunters* into hysterics. In the living room there was a false bookshelf that swung open at the slightest accidental impact; it led to a secret storage hold filled with disused keyboards. There was a two-way mirror on the kitchen wall. We left a single unwashed plate in the sink. When we left, the piano teacher wrote us an angry letter about cleanliness.

I remember that trip because we had sex more than once. During the two years that we were ultimately long-distance, I had taken to skipping my medication for twenty-four hours before E. and I were meant to see each other, which worked well enough for that first day, but any visit longer than a weekend—like a nearly two-week trip through California we'd taken that spring I was in DC—saw me become completely apathetic to touch, avoiding possible sexual initiation in small ways: turns of the body, keeping us out until we were both exhausted, quickly turning out the lights to sleep. I think E. minded, but she never said anything. It might have caused an argument, and we never argued, I suspect because we were not particularly willing to tell one another the truth.

Alone in DC, I lay on my mattress surrounded by the Chinese food that I ordered nearly every day. I ate and ate until my gut was slick and swollen and felt like it might collapse into its own gravity. I had gained thirty or forty pounds. Sometimes I would look at what I was meant to be writing for a few minutes before shutting the computer again. My first assignment, meant to take two weeks, had taken two months. A second assignment, far more ambitious, was barely being written at all.

Around Christmas, I ran out of lithium refills and didn't find a new doctor to get more. By New Year's, the long, ambitious piece was finished, along with half a dozen more. By the end of the holidays, I had forgotten that I was doing something risky. Nobody knew I was meant to be on lithium. It was easy to let reality catch up to what I wanted everybody to believe. I quit eating meat. I started smoking cigarettes again. I told E. via text message; she wrote back that she was surprised I'd do that.

I don't know why I am thinking of this. I am on the lookout for an uptick in my symptoms and I am waiting to find out what Abilify "feels like." Well, just a small reduction in my Seroquel and my memories feel somatic. They feel vivid. They feel urgent. But then: I was also in DC for the first time in a long time. It is likely that this has nothing to do with my medication change at all. The trouble with my medication change is that both of my hands are shaking.

MONDAY: I was able to sleep in my own bed in Iowa City, thank God. I feel more at ease. On the advice of my new doctor, I've increased my benztropine dose to two milligrams daily. After just one day, the shaking in my hands has mostly stopped. Truthfully, it stopped the minute I got back to Iowa.

FALL 2019, WEEK THREE: 300MG/SEROQUEL, 10MG/ABILIFY

TUESDAY: There is no dose change this week, but that doesn't mean that nothing is happening. It is beginning to get colder outside. I get cold easily now; the wind wraps around the edges of my coat and sneaks under my shirt. I don't have laundry in my building, so I walk with a huge overstuffed black hamper bag across my back seven blocks to the laundromat at the edge of town. I feel nervous. I feel like something is wrong.

In Washington, after I stopped taking my lithium, nothing felt wrong for months. No medication at all, and I felt fine. I thought,

Thank God, the doctor was wrong. There was nothing wrong with me, I was just feeling weird for a few months. I didn't need this medication at all.

I lost weight. I got quite a bit of writing done. I did a lot of reading. I saw friends. I visited E. I drank. I did not read many emails or drafts for work. I did not feel like working at all; when I did work, I tore drafts to pieces, changed every other word, sent hostile emails to freelancers about entire books they might want to read before trying to write again. If I came to the office, I often stayed until 9:00 or 10:00 p.m., doing nothing but unable to move.

That spring, I took several commissions on essays from different writers and then forgot about their drafts for weeks and weeks. I told my immediate boss, during an argument over a long essay I'd written for the site, that her boss, who was the editor-in-chief, was engaged in a political conspiracy against my work. I threatened, repeatedly and for various reasons, to quit.

In summer, ten months after I moved to DC—and during the same long, manic night in which the editor-in-chief had already emailed me to ask that I stop tweeting that a well-known columnist and radio host was a beneficiary of nepotism—I sent a tweet that was taken to be advocating for riots in response to the Trump campaign. I was very publicly suspended from my job. I can't tell you if I believed what I said, even then—it's too long a digression. But I know that this was taken by some to be a heroic act, or at least reputation-validating, on my part. And I do know that it is not a coincidence that months without lithium provokes the sorts of public statements that are rewarded by the ecosystem of social media.

The week of my suspension corresponded with a long-planned visit from E. We took the unexpected free time to travel to New York, where one night we tried to sleep in an unbearably hot room, and I kicked a floor fan in the hallway until it broke.

After New York, I returned to DC and my job, but a week or two later, I spent a weekend in the hospital. The doctor there was the first to suggest that bipolar disorder was an insufficient diagnosis, but it didn't matter because I wouldn't see that doctor again. I told him that I wouldn't take lithium anymore, so he prescribed me lamotrigine and told me to call right away if a rash started around my mouth. It didn't and I never saw him again. I didn't see a doctor for nearly two years. I convinced the father of a friend, a psychiatrist, to write me refills for the lamotrigine without appointments. I bought the medication from the pharmacy in cash. I calmed down. I went back to work, but the next month I left my job to go back to school in Iowa. E. was happy for me. We'd still be long-distance, but we'd both be in the Midwest. Neither of us particularly liked Washington, DC, anyway.

WEDNESDAY: I took a walk this morning. It was still very cold but there were no clouds. It was very cold and very blue, grey sunlight on grey sidewalk. Half the leaves are still green. It hasn't snowed, but the city has begun to salt the roads and the salt rolled under my shoes, grinding and nibbling at the soles. I got a cup of coffee at a cafe. The clouds came while I was drinking it inside. On my way back, it began to rain. I stopped to wait under the awning at the side door of the redbrick Catholic hospital in my neighborhood. The psychiatric nurses there are known to be kinder than the ones at the university hospital.

The rain carried away the salt on the roads, then it stopped. I walked home. My hair was a little bit wet; it had begun to curl. I realized that I forgot to take my medication today.

THURSDAY: I remembered to take my medication today, but I find that I am forgetting a great number of little things. Why I walked into the kitchen, what time I'm meant to meet my friend, which streets in my small town are one-way. I don't believe this is a case of overeager pattern finding. I am getting lost, and I don't know if I am lost-in-thought or lost-in-nothing. When I snap out of it, it is like waking up without any memory of a dream.

FRIDAY: My hands are shaking again. My legs are very stiff. I'm making use of railings to keep steady. Still—I have more energy than I have had in years.

SATURDAY: Last night I woke up screaming. This isn't new. I have nightmares that look like nothing but feel like something right behind me, hands all over me and breathing. I wake up and don't remember precisely what was going on. I carry this feeling into the day. I had a long terror in the coffee shop again. I'm not trusting cars. They make the same turn right behind me for blocks. Why? People in public are talking about me but they get quiet when I walk by.

I realize that these are "symptomatic" feelings, and paradoxically this recognition—*insight*—is as good of a sign as any that they will not get out of control. I am meant to take Ativan when this is happening, even in the daytime.

Ativan is a benzo. It's like Xanax. It's meant to treat anxiety disorders. Understand this: a stable schizophrenic has the symptoms of what a liberal arts major considers their crippling anxiety disorder.

Ativan is addictive. I don't like taking it because before Seroquel and before lamotrigine and before lithium, the first drugs I took to treat myself were just drugs. I haven't taken a hard drug in years—but for years, when I couldn't finish during sex, I'd tell partners it was a consequence of old heroin use, because this I thought was more attractive than saying it was a consequence of powerful psychotropic medication.

I know that I drink too much. Over the last year, I have spent more than half the nights in any given week drinking by myself in bars. Half of my friends in Iowa are bartenders. Drinking hurts my mood; it makes my medication less effective. But it also blunts bad feelings and bad sounds. I am not sure if I don't want to take the Ativan because I do not want to be a drug addict again, or if I don't want to take it because when combined with too much alcohol, you could die. I don't want to worry about my drinking. I don't take the Ativan.

My sleep remains bad. Gregory Bateson once wrote about the *obscure dynamics* of the *curative nightmare*; the rare way in which the lunatic's mind may begin to repair itself in sleep. But I do not believe that is happening with me.

MONDAY: No shaking. For the first time in weeks, I slept completely through the night.

WINTER 2019, WEEK FOUR: 200MG/SEROQUEL, 20MG/ABILIFY

TUESDAY: It is possible that I have felt better because, while I have taken my morning medication every day since I forgot last week, including my Abilify, I have forgotten to take my nighttime medication—including the bulk of my Seroquel—for four days in a row. I only just noticed now. I only remembered because today is the day I change my doses again. In theory, my nighttime medication should help me sleep. The trouble is that it makes it difficult to wake up all day. I have not felt any symptoms of withdrawal.

WEDNESDAY: I am tired throughout the day, every day. The crouching energy is gone. I am not tired like I was tired on Seroquel. I am pretty sure I had been tired every day since I started Seroquel, although I do not have a good sense of an ordinary energy level anymore.

For two years after I went to the hospital in Washington, lamotrigine was enough on its own. I don't know why. I suppose it only appeared to be enough because I was doing well, or appeared to be: I had a job, then an offer from a graduate school; I had a girlfriend and friends. It wasn't until my second year in Iowa that I began seeing a psychiatrist again. That was the year E. finished school in Michigan and moved in with me. The spring before, around our fourth anniversary, we'd had an argument about an argument that devolved into a fight about how unfairly the other one was fighting and we didn't speak for over a week. When we did, on the phone, I told her for the first time that I was medicated. She neither asked about nor seemed to be bothered by my concealing it for so long.

When she moved in, E. brought bowls and pans and knives, a bed and several hundred books, two tables, posters (never unwrapped), a false Christmas tree, and a desire for our real relationship—the one that had been held off by a two-year long-distance interregnum—to begin. Our apartment filled up; it had the clutter of a home. I was so happy to see her. When we met, I was doing nothing and imagining a life I couldn't lead. When we met, she was waking up very early to stand on a street bridge in Chicago and watch the sun rise before going to work retail downtown. Now I was working, and she was working. With her new degree in public health, she got a job at a research lab in town. A few days after she arrived, we had drinks with a few of the friends I'd made in Iowa, and on the way home, she told me how nice it had been, how nice it was that we could do this sort of thing all the time from now on. I still kept my medication in a dresser drawer with my socks, but I went to see a doctor and I decided to quit smoking again.

With the Seroquel down and the Abilify up, I do not feel tired in the same way. I feel tired like I have been running too much. It's a physical exhaustion, not the cloud of smothering idiocy I've been working with for years. This new kind of tired feels better. I have not been running at all. My brain believes that I am *doing things* and need my rest, even when I am doing nothing at all. I am very behind on my work.

THURSDAY: Let me clarify that behind on my work means that I have not worked since my trip. I stare at open documents, and nothing happens with them. It doesn't feel hard; it feels like nothing.

FRIDAY: My hands are shaking just a little bit. My legs shuffle some days but not badly. I could live with this level of difficulty. You'd hardly notice half the time. I am traveling again, unexpectedly. Yesterday, I drove to Toronto to attend a last-minute wedding. I have had more time lately for friends.

SATURDAY: I filled Seroquel for the first time two months after E. came to Iowa City. She knew by then that I was ill, but I think the poison introduced by an important fact so long concealed was difficult to excise. Maybe we would have in time. But for all my desire to become sane and never tell anybody that anything had ever been wrong, the truth is that even medication cannot erase the self who needed it in the first place. I had made something of a name for myself as a writer,

and with prominence comes memory. All at once, I was engulfed in a
scandal, the sudden simultaneous outpouring of complaints, some true,
some merely opportunistic, all believable enough, concerning the various ways I had been abusive, cruel, irritating, aloof, difficult to work
with, impolite, prone to theft and threats of violence, impolitic, erratic,
unreliable and strange as a teenager. Because I had tried so hard to
conceal the fact of my illness, it was not generally known to anyone who
might have treated it as an explanation for my behavior. The damage
already done; it seemed cheap to raise the issue in response. I suppose
this was a kind of irony or punishment.

Over the course of the fall and winter, I lost all my work outside of
the university and most of my friends. I might have tried to stop it, but
with the stress came a new bout of psychosis and the beginning of the
Seroquel haze and the change to a schizoaffective diagnosis, and I gave
up without a fight. While E. stayed for a little while after that, I did
not. My medication dose went up and up, and I got fat. I slept a lot of
nights on the couch. I drank more than I did before and often did not
come home until E. was asleep. She left in the mornings on weekdays
before I could wake up. The Seroquel made me cloudy. I lived in the
same apartment as E. but that was all, and she lived with an incessant
source of shame and guilt and pain.

What does Seroquel feel like? It feels like the air-conditioning just
switched off. It feels like the white noise you didn't notice until it's
gone. I wonder how we know that any of these drugs are working. I am
told that Seroquel produces an *adaptive response* in the hippocampus
and that this, through some obscure and indirect mechanism, causes
me to regain a sense of what is the real world and what isn't. The word
"hippocampus" is Greek for horse-sea-monster, because that region of
the brain looks like a seahorse. My doctor said it was important to be
aggressive with the Seroquel until I was stable; until I was back to
normal and *feeling like myself again.*

Over the course of that fall, I became better acquainted with the
pharmacist downtown. Every time I went to the doctor, he increased

my dose, and I had to fill the new amount. The pharmacist said things to me like, *Last name? First name? Date of birth?* But he thought things like, *Hoooo boy. Hoooo howdy, they're upping his antipsychotic dose AGAIN? Oh boy.* They think that whenever I go to a pharmacy. It's all smiles and *How are you?* until they look at the names of the drugs they're filling.

I have thrown out my three-hundred-milligram capsules of Seroquel. The one-hundred-milligram bottle is running low. I'll never fill it again.

SUNDAY: There is a tremendous amount of bullshit concerning the "real you" who emerges from "the illness" (which is not you), but this is backward. The real you is the sick you. The real you is the one who scares people. The real you is the one who cannot keep a job or friends, cannot keep a relationship, treats people so poorly that nobody wants anything to do with you at all. The medicated you is only *better*. Faster. Stronger—at least in theory. The only certainty is the slow feeling on medication that you are becoming a different consciousness inside your body. The two people—the sick and the real. The truth is that you are an amalgamation of impressions and states: phenomenology, not ontology of being. I know this does not require medication to make clear. *We changed so much in so many little ways over the years that by the end we scarcely knew each other.* We have all heard this all the time, even among the sane. The medication is only a cipher for the literal. You notice your hair growing long, your gut getting fat—there are only two poles if you do not see yourself for a long while. How can you keep your subjectivities straight? How could you begin to ascertain which is the real one, which is best suited for apprehending the world as it really, objectively wants to be? Is that also the one who is the best behaved? There is not even a guarantee of improvement, a promise that the medication shrinks the tumor and reveals some uncorrupted soul. All lives and all selves, real and imaginary, may be wicked. The stable heart still sins. The new or true or false or better self does not, necessarily, improve upon the old. Why shouldn't he, just because he is sane? Is the drugged self more developed than the mad one, just because he comes after?

I suppose what I am trying to say is that in the same time I was burying my real self under Seroquel, I tried to have what was meant to be the real period of E.'s and my relationship. I would like to tell you what that real period was really like, but it never quite began.

One night, I walked to the next town over and checked into a motel room with cash, plotting to find my way to California the next day. E. found me, and I was coaxed, eventually with the help of the police, into going to that small brick Catholic hospital for an extra-large dose of tranquilizers. But for the most part, we were only very tired and very panicked, and when we did come up above the water, at dinner or while traveling or with the few friends we saw, and realized that we were having something like a good or normal time, it came immediately with the knowledge that this, which should be so usual, which we had waited several years to have each day, was so rare that there was rarely any pleasure in it at all.

Today, I went to mass at the cathedral in Toronto. No falling. No difficulty working. I have taken my medication and slept for the past few days without difficulty, despite the travel. I still feel as if I am spending my free time training for a title bout. My body hurts, but this is satisfying. It occurs to me that I am about two-thirds of the way into the titration. The worst-case scenario—total failure, loss of stability, a long recovery just to get the Seroquel working again—has not occurred and will not occur. Good. Good. Good.

MONDAY: I am back in Iowa City. I left the heat off while I was gone and so my apartment is very cold.

WINTER 2019, WEEK FIVE: 100MG/SEROQUEL, 30MG/ABILIFY

TUESDAY: I am now on thirty milligrams of Abilify, the target dose and the maximum recommended for this drug. Next week I will drop the Seroquel entirely. Then I will become somebody new again.

There's a bad assumption underlying how clinicians and patients and bystanders understand medication. The assumption is that without medication, you are seeing or hearing or feeling the world in error. Your subjectivity is misaligned with the objects it perceives. On medication, the error is corrected, like glasses for astigmatism. You see and feel and hear the objects as they really are.

I think we should be skeptical of these subject-object metaphysics. We're skeptical of them elsewhere in the human experience. Forget the permanence or facticity of the world; I don't even quite believe in this sick-and-sane model of the patient. I don't mean this politically. I am not a relativist. I am not saying that I believe my psychosis is as *valid* as my stability, nor that it is preferable. But there is no single "medicated" subject. There are a million medicated subjects. The subject on lamotrigine but no Seroquel, the subject on Seroquel but no Abilify, the subject a hundred milligrams north and a hundred milligrams south, the subject on the same dose in a different season, the subject under stress or living easy. There are psychiatric symptoms induced by medication and psychiatric symptoms alleviated by it; it is difficult to tell, after a while, where the lines are, what is medication and what is madness and what is neither, which subjectivity is which. Madness is an impairment of subjectivity itself. Medication can weld some of the fractures. But medication does not restore you to some prelapsarian state, to the subject as he might have been if he hadn't lost his mind. That man is gone. He never existed at all.

WEDNESDAY: I am listening to a so-so documentary podcast about the Seattle Supersonics while intermittently crying in my car. The sky has been a blank flat grey all week. I do not feel sad, although I think Seattle should have an NBA franchise again. I haven't seen anyone in days.

THURSDAY: My apartment is too big. I don't know what to do with the second bedroom. When E. broke up with me, she stayed in our apartment for several months after. It didn't make sense to break the lease. For those few months, we used both rooms. One of us was out most nights, and when we were both home, we didn't speak much. It was not so different from how it had been before she'd said she couldn't do this anymore. We lived in silence for a while.

At the end of that second year in Iowa, a year and a half before I began this diary, I made plans to go to California for the summer. On the last night we were in Iowa together, after a long time barely speaking, E. and I had dinner at a restaurant, and then we sat in our living room for a long time. She said, *We're being so adult about this.* I thought of saying that I was sorry that the real relationship had never started, or that I was sorry the Seroquel had taken me so out of life those last few months, or that I was sorry because she had spent two years waiting for an idea of me to come back, and when it became clear to her that it never would, she had spent several months in mourning and now the fact of my presence was an inconvenience to her grief.

She didn't leave me because of the Seroquel, anyway. She left, at least in part, because while it is one thing to live with an insane person, it is another to live with an insane person who is widely and perhaps rightly hated because some version of themselves—real or not—has crossed from the form of insanity in which you have a problem to the form in which you are a problem. It would have been fine if it had just been too much to be with a drugged-up lunatic. That's difficult. I struggle blaming people who leave spouses with cancer—you understand why they do something so cruel, at least—so how could I blame E.? I don't remember what I said. It was inoffensive. My mood was stable. She went to the bathroom to prepare for bed.

When she came out, she said, *Okay, I guess that's all then.* I asked if we were meant to hug. We did. I cried. She cried, and I was relieved. It would have been too shameful if it had just been me crying, if she'd been looking at her watch and wondering when it was no longer rude to get to bed. I said, *Nobody is dying.* She said, *Nobody is dying. Nobody is dying.*

It's a very peculiar and intense feeling of loss. I can feel her hand very lightly scratching the left side of my lower back when we hugged, can feel a kiss on the forehead, and a thumb on my hand between my thumb and index finger. What I mean is: on medication, you lose small parts of yourself in imperceptible bits. Here, in the same apartment where I am still living, I remember feeling that I'd lost half of myself in one hard rip.

FRIDAY: Both of my hands are shaking.

SATURDAY: My hands have calmed down. My walk is still shuffling. The new doctor says to give it time. It rained most of today. I don't trust people who say they like rain, but I like going out just after its stopped. The air feels present, and the world looks clean.

SUNDAY: I feel like I am forgetting who I am. I don't mean that I have amnesia; I am not forgetting my name. But I am losing a sense of linearity, and losing the ability, each morning, to spend a few minutes in bed remembering myself. I used to lay there and recall the facts of my life, recall what I was meant to be doing. It feels very vague now. This is not necessarily a bad thing. I hated this portion of the morning.

Lately, I have been feeling angry for the first time since I started Seroquel; I realize that I have felt frustrated and disappointed and ashamed, but I have not felt *angry* in years. I have felt wrapped up in cement, not plugged up but smothered from the outside. Now I feel good, like I could live a whole life this way. A little incoherent, a little day-by-day, no real memory of why. You can go this way for a long time. I like it more than feeling very little, which is how I've been feeling for years. I suppose this may be a consequence of living alone for so long now. I've been smoking indoors. It's gotten too cold to spend much time outside.

MONDAY: I'm sleeping through the night. I have begun to have a recurring dream, sometimes at night and sometimes half-awake in the daytime. In the dream, I am on a train, or in a car; in one version, I am on a train but it's an airplane, too. I need to get off. It's time to get off and I need to go. I have three or four bags I need to carry. But every time I pick one up, I notice that another one is missing. I am always missing something. I always set a bag down for just a minute so I can pick up another, and then I can't find the first bag. This isn't a panicked dream. I am not worried that I will miss my stop. But it's frustrating and tedious and boring. I didn't want to write this down. It feels like a lazy metaphor. But a lot of illness is a lazy metaphor. Go read about the stupid, boring, transparently plagiarized delusions that most psychotic patients have.

For the past few days I've had a stomachache. I've lost twenty pounds since I started this diary—the Seroquel hunger is gone. My apartment is clean. I cleaned it. I feel great. I'm awake. I slept all night. My cat slept next to me. I have energy. I have so much energy. This is better. This is so much better than it was before.

Asylum

Because there were no beds available in the psychiatric ward, I was once held in a bare storage room at the far end of the emergency wing of a hospital in Chicago, with nothing in it but a plastic-leather gurney and an empty locker, painted white. I paced for hours, alternatively talking to myself and crying. The nurse's station was just outside. The door was not locked, but I was told to call out if I needed to go down the hallway to the bathroom.

Like most patients, I do not have a good sense of this time—the order of events or their duration. In my memory, I jump from one scene to another and then jump back again, as if the whole experience happened out of order and at once, as in a dream. It was New Year's Eve, and the room was very bright.

The dream character of madness—writes Michel Foucault in *History of Madness*—*is one of the constant themes of the classical age*. Most cases of insanity, like most dreams, were understood to consist of little more than the reassembled phantasmagoria of the madman's memory and senses. But some cases, like some dreams, were believed to have the power of prophecy. In these cases, the madman gained the ability to *foretell the future, announce events, speak in tongues* and *to see things which are normally invisible*. What Foucault calls The Great Confinement began when civilization started to define mankind by the possession of reason, and madmen came to be regarded not as harmless, sometimes mystical figures, but as defective reasoners, *making a mistake.*

I'd abandoned E. in the apartment of a friend where we were staying and gone out bawling into the streets. I took the subway aimlessly for a few stops. When I got off, I thought I'd either check into the hospital or die. I told myself not to be so melodramatic. But I still walked several miles to the nearest emergency room and texted E. before I checked myself in. The nurses there took my phone and clothes and wallet and brought me to the empty room. One stayed behind and asked me questions: *What day is it? What year is it? What is the name of the president of the United States?* I don't remember how I answered. But afterward, the nurse left, and without my knowing, signed an order for my involuntary commitment. Without my knowing, the insurance card found in my wallet failed to go through, and so the same nurse requested an ambulance to transfer me to a public psychiatric hospital in downstate Illinois. No beds were currently available there, either. Without my knowing, I was taken off the waiting list for a room in the psych ward at the hospital, and I spent hours waiting for an opening downstate so that an ambulance could take me away.

In England and France, in the second half of the eighteenth century, when hospitals for the insane began to open, it was generally admitted that they should be looked after and treated by the guards rather than by the doctor, writes Foucault. It was not yet believed that the insane were any different from the vagrants, prostitutes, blasphemers, and other failures of reason and morality. It was only in the institutions, after lunatics were locked away from the world at large, that they came to the attention of doctors, only then that these doctors came to believe, like their classical predecessors, that the mad were not moral deviants, but poor, afflicted souls. Unlike their predecessors, they did not believe that the mad were prophets. They believed that they were sick, and like all sick men, perhaps they could be cured. This was the last of three stages in Foucault's history of madness. Once there had been conversation based in prophecy and wisdom. Then there was the advent of reason and the beginning of confinement. Only then did madness become a disease and an object of scientific inquiry. For Foucault, this was not the triumph of a more enlightened age, but only the latest contingent system of exclusion, well-suited to the prevailing mode of production, and ready to give way—as it did, indeed, give way, after Foucault's death—to the next ideology of insanity.

E. arrived at the hospital after a few hours and stayed with me in the bare room for a while. It was she, not I, who was told by a nurse that I was to be transferred to the public psychiatric hospital downstate, and it was she who insisted that I did have health insurance, that there was no need to move me. She spent hours coming in and out of my room, sitting with me before and after a large dose of tranquilizers put me in and out of sleep. Eventually, when the shift changed late at night, she found a new nurse who spent hours calling my insurance company and verifying, finally, that I was covered for this stay. But by then it was too late to transfer me upstairs, and it was too late to find a doctor who could override the hold order and release me that night. E. left me her large, wool scarf to use as a blanket. I lay on my side on the gurney for a while, hugging the scarf and smelling her on it until I fell asleep. Later, E. would tell me that a nurse chastised her for leaving the scarf. You cannot give somebody enough rope to hang himself in there.

In the morning, I woke up in a sedative haze. It was Sunday morning. The room stunk of my sleeping in it. I hadn't slept well. Two doors down the makeshift ward, an older patient had spent the night repeating, *tik . . . tik . . . tik . . . I'M THE BOMB!*, at which point he'd jump up and land again with a thud, then wait for a laugh that wasn't coming. I'd listened to two nurses and a hospital guard discussing whether this was a threat.

There is no common language . . . The constitution of madness as mental illness at the end of the eighteenth century bears witness to a rupture in dialogue, gives the separation as already enacted, and expels from the memory all those imperfect words, of no fixed syntax, spoken falteringly, in which the exchange between madness and reason was carried out, Foucault writes. The physical barrier becomes the conceptual barrier becomes the inability to communicate at all. The language of psychiatry is only a monologue by reason *about* madness, Foucault explains, spoken into the silent walls between the asylum and the outer world.

Sometime in the early afternoon, a psychiatrist was finally summoned who could ask me the legally required questions—*Do you intend to hurt yourself? Do you intend to hurt anybody else? Will you come back if you do?*—and to whom I could give the legally required answers: *No, no, and yes, of course I will. Of course.* E. came back from wherever she had spent the night and took me out of the hospital. It was the thirty-first of December. We went out into the bright, cold morning to wait for the new year.

• • •

Asylum comes to us from Greek, through Latin, and means more or less, "without the right of seizure." Churches were asylums once, places to take refuge when hunted by the law. An insane asylum protects a patient seizure, too, but having often been seized and brought there, and seized as often as not by the law, who is left for the lunatic to take refuge from inside?

In England, in 1774, Parliament brought doctors into the business of English madness by requiring a physician's certification before a patient could be committed. Between 1788 and 1820, the number of private insane asylums in the United Kingdom doubled. The asylum operators were often the same doctors making certifications of madness. They competed like any for-profit industry. One hospital operator offered a money-back guarantee for unsatisfied families if the patient was not cured within six months. Another, particularly adept at advertising gimmicks, operated two asylums, from which he made an estate worth nearly two hundred thousand pounds—nearly forty million dollars today.

Treatment in these asylums consisted mainly of cold-water shock, sleep deprivation, induced vomiting, bloodletting, nauseating motion devices, and burning caustic rubbed into open wounds. Nauseating a patient was considered far safer, and more humane, than bleeding him. The purpose of many of these treatments was to terrify the patient into sanity. Pain and terror, wrote one physician, caused the lunatic to *regain consciousness of his true self, to wake from his supersensual slumber, and to stay awake.* If the madman had lost his reason, he must be shocked back into it. The physicians who operated the early modern madhouses claimed that upward of 90 percent of lunatics could be cured by their methods.

The new asylum was the progeny of two motives: the old desire to confine undesirables, and the new ambition to cure the pitiable insane. The asylum came into its own when the trouble *of poverty, of incapacity for work, of inability to integrate with the group* became most pronounced, writes Foucault. This was *the moment when madness began to rank among the problems of the city.* Over time, the two motives lost their distinctiveness, and the asylum came to be understood only as sites of therapeutic treatment for the mad. But a motive hidden and forgotten is not a motive lost entirely.

Today even the specter of the asylum serves a therapeutic function. There is a way that my doctor says, *Do you think you need the hospital?* like the way I have heard cops say, *Do you need us to take you somewhere safe?* which activates a primal need to stay safe. This fear, on occasion, has proven powerful enough on its own to terrify me into remission, or at least good behavior. How much better I might be if I feared not just a night in a cold room, or three weeks in bland therapy, but bleeding, and vomiting, and unexpected drops into cold water? The early asylums are remembered as institutes of torture, but I would let these doctors torture me better if they could promise I'd be cured for good.

• • •

In 1790, a young Quaker named Hannah Mills died in an asylum in York. Members of her community suspected abuse by her asylum keepers.

Six years later, English Quakers founded a small asylum of their own. They called their asylum The Retreat. Patients were well fed and allowed outdoors; they were encouraged to read and write, to have parties and play chess. Among the more common treatments were warm baths of twenty minutes to an hour.

At the beginning of the nineteenth century, Quakers in the United States, following their English cousins, spearheaded what would come to be called the *moral reform* movement in American asylums. The journalist Robert Whitaker writes, *The blueprint for the moral-treatment asylum was fairly sharply defined . . . The facility was to be kept small, providing care to no more than 250 patients. It should be located in the country, the grounds graced by flowerbeds and gardens, where the mentally ill could take their fill of fresh air and find solace in tending to plants . . . Each day, a variety of activities would keep patients busy, which it was hoped would divert their thoughts from their obsessions and paranoid ideas.* These asylums, as a rule, did not employ doctors.

The humanitarians who operated the moral retreats believed that kindness alone might cure most madness. Throughout the nineteenth century, these institutions reported that between 60 and 80 percent of their patients *recovered*, which is to say, were able to return to their families and *function at an acceptable level*. Every doctor I have ever seen has talked to me about "function," measured my progress by my insight, by my employment, by the extent to which you would not know I was insane.

There is a reason, Foucault writes, that the mad were locked up with the vagrants and prostitutes and blasphemers in those early days. It was not that the state was cruel for its own sake. Rather, it was that the dawn of the age of reason was also the dawn of the age of capital, and such an age must have a way to deal with unruly and unwanted excesses in the labor force.

I would like nothing more than a long bath each day, twenty minutes to an hour. I would like a walk in the garden. I would like a meal, a party, a game of chess at night, and nothing else, not even sanity, expected of me at all. But a motive hidden and forgotten is not a motive lost entirely. Even under the sweet regime of kindly Quakers, we are after *a return to acceptable function* here. You cannot have long baths forever.

...

Dorothea Dix was the daughter of an itinerant alcoholic and a depressive invalid. She worked for a while as a governess, and then in Boston as the director of a school for girls, but following a breakdown in 1836 and a period of recuperation in England that brought her in contact with prominent Quaker philanthropists, Dix became the most voracious campaigner in American history for the transformation of lunatics in prison into patients in hospitals. On behalf of those poor souls *confined in cages, closets, cellars, stalls, pens! Chained naked, beaten with rods, and lashed into obedience*, she shamed nearly twenty states into building facilities for the insane. Dix lives in the American memory as the moral force behind our public asylums.

In 1860, the Calvinist minister Theophilus Packard had his wife, Elizabeth, committed to a Dix asylum in Jacksonville, Illinois. Elizabeth was not mad; the official cause of her commitment—*monomania*—stemmed from a combination of irregular religious belief and her husband's willingness to compensate the hospital generously for her care. After three years, with the help of her children, Elizabeth Packard was discharged from Jacksonville. When she returned home, her husband boarded her up in her room and tried to have her committed elsewhere; she escaped and a legal action ensued, where Packard was ultimately declared legally sane and set free. In the following years, Elizabeth formed the Anti-Insane Asylum Society and published several books, most famously *The Prisoners' Hidden Life, or Insane Asylums Unveiled*. The Society pressured Illinois into strengthening protections for the allegedly insane; over decades of campaigning, Packard shamed over a dozen states into releasing patients and tightening commitment standards. Her work inspired Nellie Bly, a journalist who in 1887 had herself committed to a madhouse in New York and reported on the horrifying conditions there. It was in Bly's famous report, *Ten Days in a Mad-House*, that I first read as a teenager about what might happen to me if I ever went insane.

Not every patient freed in the second half of the nineteenth century was misunderstood like Mrs. Packard. Many of those released from madhouses found themselves returned to prison after a little while; others were abandoned or even murdered by their families. The hospitals were glad to be rid of these kinds of patients. In his biannual reports to the Illinois state legislature, Jacksonville Superintendent Dr. Andrew McFarland argued that his institution was a hospital, where all patients must have hope for a cure. He wrote of the grave consideration that must be made when depriving a patient of their *personal liberty*, inveighed against the hostility that the odd but harmless madman faces in society, and even reported a visit from an aging Dorothea Dix herself. Like every director of a public service anywhere, he spent the bulk of his reports begging the state for money. Amid complaints of overcrowding, unfinished facilities, and delayed budgetary promises, he wrote that he would like to stop receiving patients from the local jails. *The subject reduces itself to the plain question*, he wrote. *Which is the more proper, to have a hospital attached to a penitentiary or to have a penitentiary attached to a hospital?*

Dix and Packard both believed that their efforts were a compassionate response to the plight of the insane. The cycle they began continued despite what any of them might have wanted. As the jails filled, authorities turned back to the asylums. In 1840, there were 2,561 lunatics in American hospitals. In 1890, there were 74,000 in public hospitals alone. By the 1870s, asylums became warehouses for hundreds of chronically and incurably mad patients. These new asylums blended new "moral" techniques with the old scientific approach, employing occasional bloodletting, morphine, and opium to sedate unruly patients. Water treatment, restraints, and confinement followed.

• • •

For a long time, I believed that I was lucky to go mad in a time when I would not be mistaken for a criminal but understood to be sick, to be told that I could not help my genes. The idea that genetics governed madness is a recent one. It was not until the twentieth century that a great deal of scientific and medical attention was paid to the genetic stock of the human race. But by the 1910s, eugenics was being offered as a science at Ivy League Universities; in 1914, a conference funded by cereal-magnate John Harvey Kellogg determined that the United States would need to sterilize just short of six million Americans by 1954 to attain an acceptable level of *subnormalcy*. In 1927, the Supreme Court ruled by a vote of eight to one that the involuntary sterilization of undesirables was perfectly constitutional. By 1932, thirty states had passed involuntary sterilization laws. On the basis of these laws, doctors sterilized more than 50,000 lunatics and other "mental deficients."

In 1900, there were 126,000 Americans confined in 131 public asylums. In 1903, there were 143,000. In the first half of the twentieth century, the average patient census grew from 962 to 2,316; some asylums held nearly 5,000 people. The state spent an average of one dollar per day per patient. Attendants in psychiatric facilities were paid less than half the wage of prison guards. At some of the new institutions, it took only a few years before the cheap brick used to build the walls began to crumble. It was these years that gave rise to our most enduring images of the madhouse: the padded room; the howling halls at night; the dazed, sedated patients drooling over greying breakfast mush; electroshock treatment and the prefrontal lobotomy, whose inventor, Dr. Egas Moniz, won the 1949 Nobel Prize in Medicine.

By then, doctors knew that madness was neither mysticism nor a moral failure, but a disease. But, they reasoned, there was no conflict between the *identification of an illness* and an *error*. It was only that the patient *was* the error now, and the asylum was the only way to keep his error quarantined, out of the blood of mankind. Perhaps, with a little public health intervention, it could be eradicated forever.

. . .

As I passed through some of Byberry's wards, writes Albert Deutsch in *The Shame of the States, I was reminded of the Nazi concentration camps at Belsen and Buchenwald. I entered buildings swarming with naked humans herded like cattle and treated with less concern, pervaded by a fetid odor so heavy, so nauseating, that the stench seemed to have almost a physical existence of its own. I saw hundreds of patients living under leaking roofs, surrounded by moldy, decaying walls, and sprawling on rotting floors for want of seats or benches.* Deutsch's exposé of American asylums was published in 1948. Belsen and Buchenwald were not yet old history.

Beginning in 1955, the Joint Commission on Mental Illness and Health held a series of public hearings to bolster support for a new federal mental health program to replace the horrors of the public hospitals in the states. On October 31, 1963, President John F. Kennedy signed the Mental Retardation Facilities and Community Mental Health Centers Construction Act; it was the last bill Kennedy signed in public before he died in Dallas. But the act, as the psychiatrist E. Fuller Torrey writes, had *no plan for the future funding of the mental health centers* and no realistic plan regarding what would happen to the discharged patients. It focused its resources on preventing insanity. But nobody knew how to prevent insanity yet.

The failed reform effort left a void, and the anti-psychiatry movement filled it. If the so-called hospitals could not be reformed, the activists argued, then they should be shuttered. In 1967, the psychiatric survivors movement achieved its greatest victory to date when Governor Ronald Reagan signed the Lanterman-Petris-Short Act (LPS), which closed nearly every state mental hospital in California while placing strict limits on the ability to commit patients against their will. To accommodate the newly freed ex-patients, the bill promised, like the federal program before it, to fund a network of community outpatient clinics with an army of social workers to service this more humane treatment regime. Each of the LPS Act's provisions reflected the concerns of a third of its coalition: well-intentioned liberals hoping to free a marginalized class, civil libertarians invested in the American right to be insane if you want to be, and Orange County Reaganite conservatives who believed, beneath paeans to responsibility and fiscal restraint, that psychiatry was Jewish horseshit.

Over the next several years, many states adopted their own version of LPS. The asylums closed but the community health centers often failed to materialize. In the 1970s, changes to the Social Security disability program incentivized states to release as much of their remaining asylum population as possible. Each discharged patient saved states an average of nine thousand dollars per year. In 1981, now-president Ronald Reagan block granted all remaining federal mental health funds back to the states. That same year, Reagan was shot by the paranoid schizophrenic John Hinckley Jr., who was then committed to a Dix mental hospital: St. Elizabeth's, in Washington, DC.

Deinstitutionalization, as this period is called, is still celebrated by mental health advocates as a great victory against the tyranny of the asylums. These activists do not celebrate Ronald Reagan, of course; many of them, at least, realized that many of their political allies were motivated by budgetary concerns and were unlikely to ever pay for the community clinics. But still, they'll tell you, it's better than what we had before. After deinstitutionalization, the insane, except in very narrow circumstances, could live free and die. Like the rich and the poor alike, they had the right to refuse medical care, to be tried in a court of law, and to sleep, if they wanted, on the wet stones beneath a bridge.

. . .

As a general rule, wrote the British psychiatrist Lionel Penrose, *if the prison services are extensive, the asylum population is relatively small and the reverse also tends to be true. The size of the prison population, furthermore, is closely related to the extent of the ascertained crime in a country.*

Somewhere between a quarter and fully half of all insane Americans will be jailed or incarcerated at some point in their lives.

In most American prisons, insane patients exceed the number of available beds for the insane.

In most American prisons, insane prisoners go weeks and months unable to see a doctor with any regularity.

The rate of suicide among insane prisoners is higher than any other group. Jobs for doctors in prison settings pay less than almost any equivalent position in the country.

A social worker once told me that the causation goes both ways. You would not believe, she said, how many patients tell me their first memory of a psychotic episode occurred in solitary confinement.

The prison system, already a system of gulags that differ from the Soviet model only inasmuch as they've been privatized and made profitable by American entrepreneurial ingenuity, are not designed to be asylums, too. To imagine the state of the prison hospital, imagine all the trouble of an American prison, and then graft an underfunded hospital onto its chest.

"Warden Figures Week in Solitary Ought to Teach Inmate Not to Be Schizophrenic," goes an Onion headline from April of 2018. In September of 2018, a schizophrenic prisoner held in solitary in Broward County Jail amputated his own penis and flushed it down a toilet. The jail had already come to the attention of the ACLU for two prior episodes in which schizophrenic prisoners were allowed to starve to death in solitary.

In her 2018 book, *Insane*, the journalist Alisa Roth writes that the Penrose Hypothesis *is seen by most experts as an oversimplification . . . As the number of people with mental illnesses in our jails and prisons has reached alarming levels, a story has emerged to explain how the crisis developed . . . The story begins with the failure of the state hospitals and the promise of community-based care. This led states to begin downsizing the hospitals and later closing them, which left hundreds of thousands of people without access to regular mental health care. Without proper treatment, their illness drove them to behavior that got them arrested until, over time, with ever-larger numbers of people with mental illness falling into criminal justice systems, jails and prisons became the new asylums.* But even at the height of the institutions, when 450,000 Americans lived in the asylums, they only constituted 1 percent of the American insane. Now, nearly 5 percent of our lunatics are in prison. Deinstitutionalization is estimated to have contributed only 4 to 7 percent of the overall rise in incarceration among the sane and insane alike. The cause remains unclear.

Every year in the United States, schizophrenics murder approximately the same number of people as policemen. It is unclear whose relative moral virtue is bolstered by this fact.

The largest de facto psychiatric hospital in the United States today is Los Angeles County Jail. I used to see it when I went to visit Marlon, a scattering of buildings visible from several points along the curve of the 101 freeway, hanging over downtown Los Angeles. I didn't know it was a jail then, or that 25 to 40 percent of its prisoners were believed to be insane, or that only a few could be housed in the special "High Observation Units" atop one of the jail's two "Twin Towers." I didn't know that the rest were below, waiting for beds, in overcrowded standard cells, some even held in common rooms, cuffed to cheap tables near social worker stations. I didn't know that more than 90 percent of the patients in California state psychiatric hospitals were sent there by the criminal-justice system.

Most of the lunatics in downtown Los Angeles are not in jail. They live just a little farther down the freeway on Skid Row. They ramble between tents, or sleep, or beg, waiting for the wave of gentrification to push them a few blocks farther south again. Some have come from county jail; others will be scooped up and sent there soon. When I go back to Los Angeles, I sometimes find myself driving down these streets, running red lights in case I linger too long and get caught. At other times, I linger; even get out and walk around for a while.

For many of us, the hospital was as much a refuge as it was a prison, writes Susanna Kaysen in *Girl, Interrupted. Though we were cut off from the world and all the trouble we enjoyed stirring up out there, we were also cut off from the demands and expectations that had driven us crazy.*

What could be expected of us now that we were stowed away in the loony bin? When I read this, I remember every time that I have looked at my medications and thought, if I stopped taking these, people would be disappointed. But if I kept not taking them, then soon enough nobody would expect anything of me at all.

• • •

Faced with prisons teeming with the insane, some have called for a return to the asylum. In 2015, the *Journal of the American Medical Association* ran an editorial titled in part "Bring Back the Asylum." This article was cited favorably by the *New York Times* and the *New York Review of Books.* In the 2010s, California spent $900,000,000 to build the largest forensic psychiatric hospital in the United States and announced plans for an inpatient psychiatric hospital at the California Men's Colony. In 2019, the Kamala Harris campaign for president of the United States advocated a set of policies that would have increased funding for psychiatric facilities and made it easier for doctors and family members to institutionalize patients against their will.

This plan was met with widespread condemnation by patients and their allies in the press. *If you cannot imagine schizophrenic or bipolar or otherwise ill people who are happy, stable, loved, loving, and productive members of their communities, your "solutions" are going to look more like "storage" because you don't think there's a better option for their lives,* wrote one prominent essayist. The same writer responded to a tweet where somebody pointed out how *most people are just not equipped to care for a family member with severe mental illness over several years, no matter how much they love them or want to do this for them* by saying that, *FIRST OF ALL,* they *distrust any conversation that frames mental illness first and foremost as a burden on family members.*

But if your son is insane and homeless and refusing meds and violent; if your daughter is self-medicating with heroin and stealing your money and refusing to come home; if your mother keeps flushing her pills and drinking and saying there's a demon in you that she's going to get out, and you can't stand to put her out on the street but you can't afford a hospital or a home and you've called doctors and called the police but they can't do anything because your mother refuses treatment and the definition of an "imminent threat" is so narrow these days; if you just feel helpless and don't know what to do and are wondering, in some dark and unspeakable moments, whether it might not be better to kill your insane relative while they're not looking—just put them out of their misery for everybody's sake; this really happens—then really *any* plan, *any* solution is better than being scolded again for perpetuating stigma and failing to center the right people and generally having bad thoughts for which you oughta be ashamed. You're ashamed already.

• • •

For Foucault, the asylum was the child of the prison, it carried on its blood. The turn from prison to asylum to prison to asylum lives on like all genealogies: as strands in the genetic structure of the institutions, baked into their logic and practice, reproducing and mutating and carrying forward unconsciously and inevitably by every succeeding generation. But what else can we do?

The insane are not like other marginal people; we are not all shackled where we might otherwise prosper. Many of us are inevitably dependent on others for care. The trouble is that the institutions designed to care for us were prisons—are prisons—and when they have failed, real prisons have taken their place. There are movements of Reformers, to fix the asylums, and movements of Survivors, against the asylums, back and forth for three hundred years, and both movements are right and wrong and desperate and myopic. The asylum can become a weapon against the dissident sane. The asylum can become a weapon against the insane. Prisons provoke outrage provoke asylums provoke outrage provoke freedom provoke prisons provoke outrage provoke the asylum. The asylums *were the product of a blending of two motives*, curing the mad and confining the mad for the protection of society. It is easy enough to find partisans for either motive, but the trouble is that both motives are justified, and both motives give way to torture, then reform, then torture, then reform; freedom then dependence then freedom then dependence, again and again.

From the ages of twelve to twenty-four, I contracted strep throat nearly every spring or summer. For days, it would hurt to swallow, and for days, I would long for the symptoms to inevitably worsen—for constant pain and swelling and fever—because this would mean a visit to the doctor. I longed for the doctor because his intervention would mean the end of my disease. The year I was diagnosed with manic depression was the first year I did not get strep throat, and I have not gotten it once since.

I don't long for doctors anymore. They are the jury of the mad; every meeting carries the risk that I'll be sent away. But there are times that I have longed for my symptoms to worsen—for mood swings and hallucinations and delusions—because then the doctor would have to send me somewhere safe. The trouble is that the mad need something that often hurts us. What I mean is we are in love with the asylum, even when we are not.

The year after my titration diary, I move to New York City with a girl named J. We live above a laundromat in Queens. I changed antipsychotics again, added lithium back, changed doses of everything else. I am more stable than ever before. But still, sometimes the steady sound of the machines and the way they gently roll my floorboards has convinced me that I am a captive in an asylum out at sea. I can smell the sea air sometimes; on cloudy days, I believe that I can see where the immense false city built on the upper deck gives way to the grey ocean. My medication makes me forget when I was seized and brought here; my books, my cats, J.—all of them are in a scheme to keep me from wandering too far out, from escaping this asylum.

I sometimes believe this for days, but what keeps me from trying to run is not the fact that I do not know if I could escape—do not know if

I could even swim from the edge of this great hospital ship back to the real world—but the fear that if I did run away, or fought back, or even howled too much in protest, then the doctors supervising this elaborate cell will give in and let me go. That outside of this asylum on the ocean, I will find myself homeless, or in prison, in a world I do not understand and cannot survive. To be inside the asylum is to be held, and sometimes hurt. To be outside the asylum is to be abandoned, and sometimes left for dead.

For all its seven hundred pages, Foucault's *History of Madness* is a simple story. Since its release in 1961, two generations of critics have pointed out that it is riddled with factual inaccuracies and dubious historical conjecture. Even Foucault did not believe it was definitive. The book should *recopy, fragment, repeat, simulate and replicate itself, and finally disappear without the person who happened to produce it ever being able to claim the right to be its master*, he wrote in the preface to the 1972 edition. But there is no real consensus yet on whether Foucault's fragmented, replicating, and simulating text was simply a litany of false starts, like a bad and half-remembered dream, or whether by gathering and sifting through the flotsam and jetsam of the history of madness, it became that other, rarer kind of dream: the kind that sees *strange things, which are normally invisible*, the kind that though it may *speak in tongues*, has the power to predict the future.

Insight

J. tells me that I smell bad. Almost anybody who has met me in the past ten or fifteen years could tell you that, but almost nobody but J. would tell me. She has a particular sense of order, a just-so vision of her surroundings: the placement of furniture, the arrangement of closets, the scents of the hand soap and the dish soap and me. I forget to shower. I forget to put deodorant on. I forget to brush my teeth. I remember at an inconvenient time; it feels impossible. I forget to do laundry and wind up searching the bottom of the hamper for the underwear and shirts I only wore once, back when I was optimistic that I'd do laundry before I ran out of clean clothes. I wear the same clothes every day. I own the same item several times over. I am unable to imagine myself in different clothes.

I met J. years ago in Chicago. But I lived in Iowa, and she was weeks away from moving to France to work as an English teacher in a school near Paris. I visited her there on New Year's, a year after my last stay in the hospital. She is funny and unpretentious and unembarrassed by her own convictions, which is a rare thing these days. Two years passed before we moved in together in New York. I was excited to be living with J. I tried to be honest with her from the beginning; when we sat outside a bar in Paris and she asked me if we could be together, I told her how difficult it might be. *I'm sick*, I said. *I take medication; I can keep it together on short visits, but it won't be like that when we live in the same place.* While I was saying it, I thought, *This is a mistake*, but it wasn't. I was *honest with her*—every cliché will tell you that's what you ought to do. In turn, she was honest with me: I smell bad.

It's a kind of sweating, stale, sour stink most of the time. I don't smell like organic waste; it isn't quite that bad, but I don't shower very often, so I smell like somebody who hasn't taken a shower in a while. I used to smoke, which covered up the smell with a different stench. Nicotine is one of the few drugs known to suppress both the positive and negative symptoms of psychotic disorders; it is the most popular medication on Earth among the mad. But J. made me quit, and now J. and I live together in an apartment, and every few days she summons up the lack of tact required to tell me that I smell bad. Sometimes I shower but sometimes I forget, and J. asks me why I didn't shower when I said I would. I shower every few days when we are together, which is far more often than I showered before.

J. tells me that I've forgotten other things, too. I've forgotten that I said I'd call my father; I've forgotten that we already had lunch. I've forgotten where the oven mitts are, whether we even have oven mitts or if I should use dishrags instead to take our lunch out of the oven (*They're hanging right there on the fridge*, J. says). I've forgotten faces. If you gave me the name of any student that I've ever had, I could tell you about their work, but I wouldn't recognize a single one of them on the street. I remember the name of every Roman Emperor from Caesar Augustus to Romulus Augustus, although I am shaky, sometimes, during the Crisis of the Third Century. The damage to my memory is chaotic and seemingly random, although it appears to be centered in the short and medium term, and on anything committed to long-term memory after my first psychotic episode.

I forget words while I'm speaking. When this first began, around the time my form was reclassified *schizoaffective*, not *bipolar*, I would shake my head back and forth and start probing syllables before inventing some compound noun to compensate. Now I've learned to speak slowly and take long pauses.

The forgetting isn't the reason I don't shower, but there are times I feel that I could summon the will to turn the shower on—and I mean to just as soon as I've finished what I'm doing, but then I forget. Sometimes I tell J. that I'll shower without her even asking me, but then I forget, and I worry she thinks I've changed my mind to spite her. I am aware, most of the time, that there is a memory there, beyond my reach, like I am aware, most of the time, that there is a shower I am meant to take, dishes I am meant to clean, trash that I need to take out. But there are blanks between them, like spots rubbed out on a map. Between the impulse and the act, there is a trembling fear in a solar plexus, like a dream where you realize that you have forgotten how to walk.

A few weeks ago, J. and I bought furniture, and while most of it came together just fine, I'd had to improvise a few steps in the assembly of our new desk, and I hadn't yet gotten around to fixing one of the drawers or installing the front door of the storage cabinet below. J. told me that I said I'd do this today, but I'd forgotten.

The desk was in a room right off the small living room in the center of our apartment and I'd been sitting on the new couch all day, forgetting to fix the drawer. J. came in and asked if that's something I'll be able to do today, and I said sure, forgetting that this is not the first time that she's asked.

• • •

In between the positive exclamations of a psychotic disorder—bouts of delusion, mania, hallucinatory experience, and everything associated with the lunatic—are the dull murmurs of what are called negative symptoms. The variety and the intensity of these negative symptoms vary by patient and between the forms of the spectrum of sensory and mood disorders, but generally include a blunt affect, social isolation, difficulty feeling pleasure, a lack of willpower, and poverty of speech.

My negative symptoms are not so pervasive or complete as they are in some patients, but I have had them all, and some—like poverty of speech, called alogia—have gotten worse with time. Medication does not treat negative symptoms, and so even in the patient whose madness is controlled completely by mood stabilizers and antipsychotics, these symptoms persist. Which is to say there are many people who are schizophrenic, or schizoaffective, or bipolar, but not insane. No longer crazy but still unwell.

I am grossly disorganized. I did not begin to keep a calendar until I was twenty-eight years old and even that calendar is not maintained correctly. I fill it in bursts, only to neglect what I've written. I have always been a poor student. I used to compensate for the chaos of my thoughts and notes with an active memory, but now I've lost that, too. I forget about work. I design organization systems for my books, make schedules, and then lose their organizing principles halfway through. I have tried, at various times, to compensate for these deficiencies through scrupulous notetaking, but my notes are filled with haphazard interjections and half-completed sentences, spread out over two laptop applications, the note function on my phone, emails to myself, hand-written reminders on paper, on receipts and scraps, on the whiteboard I keep next to my desk. Often I cannot remember where I've written down the note I need.

J.'s and my apartment has a sensible layout. The entryway leads into the kitchen and the hallway, which leads to the bedroom and the living room. To reach the kitchen in the morning, I must pass the bathroom. My toothpaste is on the counter to remind me to brush my teeth, but my toothbrush is in the medicine cabinet, to remind me to find my razor to shave. My razor sits across the tops of my pill bottles, to remind me to take my medicine. My therapist says these are "activation triggers" that will prompt me to do what is simple for other people to do without prompting. Still, I often forget to brush my teeth and go a few days between bouts of energy sufficient to shave. Seeing the razor helps me remember, but memory is not the same as will. I have purchased and filled several seven-day medicine holders. But as often as not, I take my dose straight from the bottle and forget where I left off in the week. I forget to take my medication more than I should.

Past the bedroom and the bathroom and the kitchen is the living room. I wish it weren't there; it's easy to get waylaid going through it. On the far side of the living room are the doors to the small second bedroom we use as an office. I must pass through the living room to get there. There is only one direction that means "go to work"; unlike J., who can work in bed, or at her vanity, or on the couch, I can only work in the office. My books and notes are already scattered there; I can't move what I need without making the mess into something irredeemable and setting myself back weeks. The apartment is set up to direct me toward tasks, but I have also spent many days sitting at my desk, collating and reformulating notes and lists of tasks before getting up and walking back the other way, to the living room or the kitchen or the bedroom or out the door. The office leads to the living room leads to the rest of the apartment; there is only one direction that means "I've wandered away from work, again." I'll try again tomorrow.

I arrange my laptop like the apartment. Before I go to bed, I arrange the tabs and windows as prompts when I open my laptop in the morning. My notepad is on top, opened to one of my schedules; my word processor is under that—documents I need to work on open, documents I need to reference minimized but there. If I need particular websites, they're open in their own window. There is something at work here other than procrastination or excuses or sloth. There is a blank. All the technical terms for negative symptoms—avolition, anhedonia, asociality, alogia—are blanks, absences, or negations.

The desk was still broken, uneven and without usable shelves, at any rate. I remembered that J. had asked me to fix them. I went to add it to one of my lists, only to discover that I'd already written it down for yesterday.

I walked from the bedroom past the bathroom through the living room across the office, open my computer. I played online chess for hours. While I was playing chess, J. looked over from the couch and asked if I was going to have a chance to fix the desk today. I told her that I already said I would, that it's on my list.

• • •

I am rude. I do not mean to be, but rudeness is an absence, too. Absence of anticipation, context, patience, grace. I let silence linger. I don't respond, or respond methodically, with the same word to every sentence. I talk over other people. I speak too quickly, or too slowly, my intonation implying connotations that do not exist. I go blank. I do not make eye contact; I never have. When I spoke better, I came off as imperious; now, I come off as aloof. I am far more fluid in writing than I am in speech these days, but even my emails and texts and letters can be disordered, excessive, or blunt—too much or not enough; I learn weeks or years after the fact that somebody believes I've given them the brush-off, or that I was suspiciously eager to talk—that I am up to something creepy—by which point no correction can undo the impression that has solidified in their sense of me.

Every other symptom compounds this one. A mood stabilizer is not foolproof; I am more irritable, more easily frustrated and discouraged and confused than I was before. An antipsychotic is not foolproof; it can take hours of an argument for it to become clear that I am operating from a set of delusional assumptions. I show up late, unshowered, poorly dressed. I forget the names of significant others; forget what I said I would bring.

I had to break off writing just now; J. called from the kitchen: *Aren't you going to help me?* We'd gotten groceries and I'd walked to the office straightaway. I'd meant to help her unpack our bags, but when I sat down at my desk, the thought was lost. My capacity to become distracted, to lose context, to watch a train of thought derail over a cliff and vanish forever is so total that I can't properly protest that I am not inconsiderate. I have lost a great deal of my capacity to consider.

I can't read tone anymore. This is often the trouble with J. She likes jokes and I like jokes, but I am unable to tell if she is joking and I am unable to control my reaction to what I am not taking to be a joke. We sit on the couch and our cat joins us. I pay attention to the cat. *Are you going to leave me for her?* J. asks, and I say, *What? What do you mean? Why would I do that? She's a cat.* It comes out in a pathetic, quiet voice. She says, *I'm joking,* I say, *Okay.* She asks if I'm all right. I say, *I'm fine,* because, by this point, I am feeling defensive. I believe J. is annoyed with me more often than she is. I say, *What? What's wrong?* And she says, *Nothing.* Then, *Nothing!* Now I've actually annoyed her.

I was out in the living room when J. asked again, *Do you think you'll fix the desk today?* I said that it may not be fixable. It's a cheap desk, from IKEA. Some of the nails went in wrong, and once the particle board starts to crack, there's not much that can be done. I'd installed one of the drawers, but it's shaky. It may never go in straight. *The desk still works, as a desk,* I said. It's a flat surface. J. said, *Well, if it's unfixable, we should get a new one.* She meant, *Try to fix it, but we can look into something else if you can't.* But I heard, *The desk is unfixable, and we should get a new one.* I thought, *There'll need to be room for a new one.* I thought, *Okay, she doesn't like this desk.* Which is to say: I am rude, and unable to read tone, and impulsive and forgetful and disorganized, and beneath all that, I was feeling, in an unreasonable but sane way, a little spiteful, so I walked into the office with a hammer and took the desk completely apart. I carried a section into the living room; when I dropped it on the floor, it exploded into pieces. J. looked up from the couch and asked what the fuck I was doing.

• • •

Medication does not control negative symptoms, but there are ways to treat them. The prompting order of my apartment helps. So does sleep. There is therapy designed to help me focus my speech, training for retaining some attention span. Exercise, maintaining a predictable routine, not exposing myself to overwhelming stimulation—many of these are the same tasks that help to control positive symptoms, too. I am not meant to take drugs, and I don't. I am not meant to drink, but I do. I am meant to avoid stimulants, including caffeine, but caffeine is all that I have to counteract the sedative power of my medication, so I drink coffee, and tea, and novelty teas, and soda. The first thing J. and I bought for our apartment was a machine that can make four different kinds of coffee.

I don't know how my self-maintenance, my *self-care*, stacks up against the typical patient. I could try harder. I would recommend trying harder to anyone who asked: get sleep, don't drink, keep a limited life. But self-awareness is not the same as action; as often as not, it's an alibi. I can tell you that I could live a better life. But saying, *I should avoid caffeine* does not negate the effect of caffeine on my body. It is possible that if I stopped drinking caffeine, it would have almost no effect at all. There are limits to these habits, diminishing returns. It is possible I have already exceeded them. I might drink more and be fine. I only know I have to keep up my sleep. One day without sleep and I am wrecked for a day. Two days and it will be a week. The last time I did not sleep for three days, I wound up in the hospital. I have slept the past few days, but J. and I have two cats now and they've been playing or fighting in the night. Sometimes that's all it takes.

The desk is a major casualty of a misunderstanding, of my inability to understand anything but literal speech on bad days. But it is only a misunderstanding, which is to say, it should have been resolved quickly, which, of course, it was not. An important habit for avoiding both negative symptoms and positive symptoms is avoiding stressful situations, but I am very easily frustrated, and it is difficult, when I am frustrated, not to begin to spiral into anguish. It is difficult for J. to avoid frustration when I have taken apart our desk and left it in pieces on the living room floor.

I was beginning to suspect, very rapidly, that J. had tricked me on purpose. This was some sort of disciplinary test, related, in some way, to the possibility that I was undergoing treatment here in the apartment, which was, I think, on a large ship. I could smell the seawater in the distance. Did J. come with me? Or was she part of the staff? Why couldn't I remember? When I am beginning to spiral, I am meant to try any number of therapeutic tricks to calm myself down. Sitting still is a good beginning, followed by *cognitive defusion*, a process by which you try to separate your thoughts into manageable portions. I am told this works well if you are otherwise sane; I find that it works for me sometimes, but not that time. I sat down on the couch, then lay down on it. I was not wearing socks or shoes and the bottoms of my feet were black from the dust and detritus of our apartment and our cats. J. reminded me not to put my dirty feet up on the couch and all hope of defusion was lost and then there was yelling and crying and pacing and my things shoved into my bag to escape.

. . .

You can read about more troubling cases. Open any message board for the friends and family of the insane. The son who put his father in a sling for six weeks this time. The daughter who refused to leave home, or eat that poisoned food, or take her medication, like she refuses every time. The wife who covers the mirrors and hides in the closet and refuses to come out until it's "safe." The grandmother who tells her caretaker every day that she's a monster, a jailer, demands to know why she's keeping her drugged up in this place *At this point*, the caretaker writes, *I find myself just agreeing with her, on all the terrible things she says about me, just so she'll calm down.* I am not usually so bad but once I did hide in the closet, refusing to come out where one of the cats could see me. Once I did wrap myself up on the bathroom floor and only agree to come to bed with a blanket covering my face for safety. When J. woke up in the morning and tried to lift it off my face, I screamed.

But that time, with the desk, I was just angry. I did not want to be reminded about the couch, did not want to be reminded about the desk, did not want to be told to shower, to brush my teeth, to be minded and monitored like this. She said, *I'm just trying to help you build better habits*. She reminded me that I asked her to help me with these things. I resented her saying so. I am like anybody else in that way: I resent being reminded how much I rely on other people. So she was crying and I was crying, a meltdown that would embarrass even a child. I said, *I want to get off the boat.* I said, *Is this them punishing me?* J. does not even bother, at this point, to try to make sense of what I mean.

· · ·

The trouble is that all the habits, all the prompts and tricks and routines, all this *self-care*, has diminishing returns. Medication helps, of course, but so does care, not self-care. It helps to be cared for. For years, I kept my illness a secret from most people. I told J. before we started dating. I told her, the night she asked me to be with her, that it might be more trouble than it's worth, that there is a difference between saying to yourself, *Yes, of course I'll help this person who I love*, and staying after you've been screamed at for doing just that. It helps to be cared for, but I resent being handled. J. resents my resenting her care. I resent needing to be cared for. She resents that whatever the reason, whatever my doctor's note says, it is still annoying, particularly when you are as conscientious as J. is, as dedicated to cleanliness and order as she is, to be living with a man who has an absence where there was once a need to shower and who asks to be reminded but hates the reminder he gets.

So I was crying and going very quickly from confusion and shame about the desk to shame and anger about the couch, to the general principle of my helplessness and my resentment, to the suspicion—as negative symptoms become positive ones—that all of this was some elaborate trap. I paced back and forth between the bedroom and the living room and office for a while, unsure of where I was being directed to go. J. said something, I don't remember what. I said, *You're right, it isn't!* (I remember that more clearly than any other part of this, although I don't remember what "it" is) and took my bag and walked out of the door onto the street.

...

Self-care was once a very literal term, but Americans do not frequently hear it used in this way anymore. The years in which I began to hear so much about self-care from doctors were the same years that *self-care* began to enter the mainstream as a broad lifestyle aspiration for the sane. For a while I noticed it incessantly: in magazine stories and Facebook posts and Instagram captions and tweets and even dropped into ordinary conversation. I didn't think much about the differences between that self-care and my own. For a long time, I imagined that this was only over-recognition; the way that after buying a new car, one sees that make and model everywhere. For a long time, I was only curious about the apparent enthusiasm of all these sane self-carers, as I imagined them tending to their sleep hygiene and defusing their cognition. It was like the friends with what I would describe as ordinary levels of stress and relationship dysfunction who nonetheless sought out and reported excitement at the prospect of private therapy. Who is so keen to do their homework? Whenever someone asks me if they should go to therapy, I say no. I do not want to go to therapy. It is tedious and difficult and dull. I go because I have to. But the sort of person who goes because they want to is the real lunatic, the real victim of some hitherto undetected personality disorder.

But self-care, as it exists in the mainstream, is not homework. Go online, or go to a university, or simply google the right combination of terms, or say the right words in earshot of your smart device, and wait for your advertising stream to adjust: self-care, as it's encountered now, is something else, or several somethings, somewhere between a vaguely left-leaning political ideology and a consumer fad. It has arrived in this decade as a moral alibi for liberal-minded strivers. What I mean is that our own worst impulses, our laziness and selfishness and self-deception, like nothing more than to disguise themselves as brave acts. A great deal of the history of human effort has been expended trying to align feeling good with being good, to figuring out how to narrow the gap between what we'd like to do and what we ought to. It is easy to desire goodness and difficult to be good; difficult to desire selfishness but easy to be selfish. We want to feel and know that we are doing the righteous thing, while giving ourselves license to do what comes naturally and easily to us. *Self-care* is only the new term of art for this old habit.

I suppose it's a coincidence that the name for all of this is the same as the name of the rationale for why I'm not meant to stay out late, or smoke a joint, or have too much coffee ever again. And I suppose it is a coincidence that I am most sympathetic to this line of thinking when I am trying to resent J. taking care of me, when I am trying to resent anybody suggesting that I cannot always take care of myself.

I drove for a while. I don't remember how long. I was looking for the edge of the ship. There is water in every direction in New York. I saw the East River. I saw the sea just past LaGuardia. I wondered if these were just canals in the hull. I worried that if I went back home I would be punished. I don't know if I believe all of this. I took a desk apart. I thought that's what J. wanted. I thought: *Maybe she tricked me.* I thought: *Maybe she didn't, and I am only stupid and ashamed.* I imagined a whole life with J. hovering over my shoulder, telling me to pick this up and throw that out and watch where I sit and fix the desk. I remembered a time months ago, in Iowa, when I believed that J. had fooled me into thinking that I was *mentally ill* at all, how I'd resisted taking a tranquilizer: it would make me stupid, make me forget what I'd figured out. Eventually I'd calmed down and thought, *No, you're being crazy. Take the pill, it'll help,* and I'd fallen asleep after, but now I was thinking, *Was I right after all? Did that pill make me forget, and just now I'm beginning to remember?* I thought, *No, you are insane, but this is not insane. It's normal to take apart the desk like that. It's normal to mind being minded.*

When I moved in with J., she cleared a whole shelf in the bathroom cabinet for my medication. She is patient even when I lose my mind. I told her what was wrong with me before we got together. While I was saying it, I thought *This is a mistake,* but it wasn't. Sometimes, if I am feeling poorly, and I am confused or upset or I cry, I retreat to my bed and she brings me an Ativan and then holds me for a while and does not feel the need to tell me lies like, *It'll be okay* or *It's fine.* When I say I'm sorry, she says, *It's just hard,* and this sometimes calms me better than the Ativan does. I think: *What a trick, what a performance.*

By this point, I was driving somewhere on Long Island.

I decided to drive to the IKEA there. There may be a new desk. J. and I went to this IKEA before. They were out of stock, so we'd ordered our furniture online. But perhaps the stock has been replenished in the intervening weeks. I drive half an hour to the strip mall parking lot in the suburbs. I walk the whole maze of display rooms before reaching the warehouse full of boxes. The desk is at the end of a long aisle.

There is no desk there. They are still out of stock. There is another IKEA in Brooklyn and I thought, *I should drive there.* I thought, *If I drive, I will not need to think about what I'm doing.* An hour later, I found the store by the docks. I walked through the display rooms, to the warehouse, where I found once again that all the desks were out of stock. I went back to Queens. I tried two other stores. No desks. I don't know what I really thought about. Captivity at sea. Nothing at all. I sat in my car in a parking lot in Queens for a long time.

J. had called twice and texted a few times. I wrote back. I huff and puff about self-determination, Needing Space, I can't be minded, I'm an adult, you're so critical, this isn't about my illness, et cetera, et cetera; which is to say, I texted J. about minding my *self-care* in the modern way. But I am worried, really, that J. will decide it is too much to keep taking care of me at all.

• • •

One of the greatest predictors of patient prognosis in the case of psychotic disorders is the degree of patient insight, which is to say, the degree to which the patient is aware of their disorder. Lack of insight is called *anosognosia,* another absence. Anosognosiatic patients—comprising, in some estimates, roughly half of schizophrenic and schizoaffective patients—do not often recover for very long. If you cannot believe that you are ill, then you are unlikely to take your medication. If you do not take your medication, your condition will worsen. If your condition worsens, you are no more likely to take your medication, no more likely to engage in the tedium of self-care. Even if an anosognosiatic patient manages to live an ordinary life, you are unlikely to hear from them. Patients who do not believe they are ill, as a rule, are unlikely to write or speak about their experience of illness. Because anosognosia is not random—it is correlated, in various accounts, with a mental defect in the right hemisphere of the brain, with frontal lobe impairment, and, to a lesser extent, with measurable IQ—the patients you are likely to hear from are necessarily a nonrepresentative sample of the insane. Which is to say, remember, whenever you hear from one of us, that you are hearing from the relatively fortunate, from the relatively stable, and from those relatively likely to be invested in shedding the embarrassment of our madness and persuading you that we are merely misunderstood, respectable, and safe.

I do not always possess insight. Almost no patient does. To be without anosognosia is only to be without the absence, without the impossibility of insight. I have insight most days. Self-care, like medication, encourages insight. They compound one another, and they decay together. But they are not impregnable. When I am lost, I lose my insight, too. When my insight slips, it can be piecemeal. My psychiatrist once told me about a patient with a high degree of insight—capable, she said, of recounting his first psychotic episode, capable of taking his medication, of recognizing the warning signs of an incipient meltdown—but who believed, and who would tell you anytime you spoke to him, that he was running for president, and he hoped he had your vote. Insight is not a switch turned on and off. I have been trained to identify irrational thoughts, but even putting it that way is an effort on my part to explain to you objectively what is happening to me, how I might see it clearly in another person. My subject experience, even of delusion, is of thoughts as rational as any others. Resisting them is a matter of the intellect resisting intuition, the process of learning to subordinate your own judgment to the judgment of consensus reality. This does not come easily, at least to me.

I wondered again if this was a test. I tried a *reality check*, a trick where the patient tries to locate an objective marker against which to test the reliability of possibly delusional thoughts. A reality check is just a way to ask yourself—what do you really know? This works sometimes. But that time, like many times, it occurred to me that the number of things I could say that I *know* surely, particularly from my car in a parking lot in Queens, are very few things at all. So I froze for a while. I stopped texting, stopped driving, stopped thinking about desks.

I don't know how long I froze. I must have been thinking but I don't know about what. Maybe I thought of everything I'd said before about self-care. Maybe I thought, *Where am I going to sleep tonight?* Maybe I thought, *J. is going to give up one day, and not even for the poor, contemporary self-care reasons, but for the very good reason that I need to be taken care of, and this is difficult work, and I refuse to be taken care of so often that it is pointless work, too.*

• • •

The best story that I've ever heard about self-care is the Greek myth of Arachne. Arachne was a weaver, unparalleled among mortals, who boasted that her talents exceeded even those of Athena. Athena, hearing of this boast, challenged Arachne to a contest of skill. Arachne accepted. In several versions, Athena gave Arachne a chance to forfeit, but she refused. In Ovid's telling, Arachne not only refused, but her entry into the contest was a particularly savage quilt, depicting the Gods engaged in all their greatest hits of misbehavior. In every version, Arachne wins. After being defeated, the humiliated Athena turned Arachne into a spider. If she liked weaving so much, she could weave forever. She could weave for her life.

I like this story because unlike most victims of Olympian wrath, Arachne's punishment serves no particular purpose. She is not Atlas, holding up the world. She is not Narcissus, serving as a heavy-handed warning against pride. She is not even Prometheus, nutrition assistance for one fortunate eagle. Arachne could stop weaving. No version of this story says that Athena forces her to make a web. It's only that if Arachne stops, then she'll have no home, catch no food, and die. That's what it is to be a spider. But that's all. Arachne teaches no lessons and bears no great responsibility. If she quits, and starves, and dies, then it is doubtful that anyone, except perhaps the unlucky Athenian who has to clean up the dead spider on his floor, would notice the death of the great, boastful weaver at all.

I went back home in the evening. It's more a matter of inertia than of will. I sat in the parking lot for a long time and could not remember anywhere else I might go. The sun started going down. I wasn't so far from home, and it only took a few minutes to drive there. J. was glad to see me. She was confused, of course, and upset, because what had seemed to me to be a catastrophic break was to her a source of confusion. Or rather, she was worried and angry at once; angry over the desk and over my escalation and unkindness, and worried over what all of that—and what my subsequent disappearance, the incoherence of my texts, and my manner when I returned—indicated about my stability.

• • •

There are times when I am angry and unkind in ways that have nothing to do with madness at all. There are times when madness makes me difficult and strange in ways that can resemble anger but is not. Often the line is not so clear. Anger becomes stress becomes a destabilizing effect; rational emotion gives way to irrational emotion and by the end of a long day, the two are intertwined and inseparable. I think this is difficult for J. She does not want to blame me for what I cannot control, and to mistake illness for offense. But she doesn't want to excuse any cruelty because it may be madness, or, in either case, to suppress the fact that even unintended hurt is hurt. She's usually charitable to me.

Her worry and compassion overtake her anger easily. This is good for me, but I'm not sure if it's always fair to her.

When I came home, she was sitting on the couch and relieved to see me. I took two Ativan and went to sleep and apologized in the morning.

Unfortunately, writes Virginia Woolf of writing memoirs, *one only remembers what is exceptional.* But as an account of a life, the exceptional events can be misleading. I am telling you this because it is relevant, because I am meant to be revealing something about the lives of the insane, or this life, at least, because I think it is connected to larger contemporary tendencies in how many of us think of *love* and *care*, but it is not what I care about, nor what I love. I care that J. and I are equally stubborn about being fucked over by utility companies. I love that when J. hears me coming into rooms, she hides and tries to scare me, but if she does scare me, she says *I'm sorry!* even though she's laughing. These are unexceptional things, but I remember them.

The day after I came home, we bought a new desk from a nearby store. They delivered it in one piece, no assembly required. I spent a few days off-balance. J. and I spent most of them sitting on the couch. I kept my feet on the floor. I made sure to sleep, and to keep to my routines, to mind the tedium with particular attention. Still, I felt unbalanced for the better part of the week. I didn't decide that I was wrong about the hospital ship, but the idea began to melt and recede and disappear. I have a poor memory. I forget.

• • •

And this is it then: more than hospitals or drugs or enormous psychiatric events, more than Madness in its full expression. It is this life of small panics, of low, simmering paranoia; of the times I am aloof, forgetful, rude, and quiet; of haziness, a half-incorporeal life, the utter disappearance of routine ability, fields of lost and foggy time. I still forget to shower but *forget* is not the right word and *choose* is not the right word, either—the knowledge, at bottom, that it could be worse and is not guaranteed to be better. The knowledge that most days I do not leave, do not misunderstand, do not take a desk apart, do not hallucinate—most days are calm and quiet and *unexceptional* for anyone but J. and me. Some days are still paranoia, still waking up unmoored, descending into suspicion, anger, absence, confusing nights spent crumpled on the floor. Beneath all of this, of course, are still the ordinary difficulties of love, even among the sane. Just this week we had a small fight over the proper peeling of an egg.

I worry that there is no compassion, no *understanding* that can overcome the fits and hurt and confusion and shame; the inevitability and cyclicality of being near me every day. It can change a person over time, even if they don't want it to change them. I worry sometimes that I am making J. cold, and she is so warm and her warmth is the better part of what I love about her. Sometimes, when I know that I am making her life hell, I say something about how I shouldn't be around other people, it isn't fair to them, and I suppose this is a kind of self-pity but I say it because I am very worried that its true.

Maybe this is insight, too: to see what you cannot know and cannot solve. Without it there would be no apartment, no J., no life beyond the slow slide toward the street or the asylum. But with it, there is still the knowing that this is not the last time this will happen. There is still J. knowing that this is not the last time this will happen, too. And there is the decision, every day, by both of us, to live with what we must live with so that we can have what we still want: each other. I love J. more than anyone I have ever known. I worry sometimes that she will stop loving me, but I love her, in part, because I don't believe she will. The other parts are her voice and her hair and her eyes; how she is firm in her convictions; how she is funny, even when I have given her no reason to laugh at all. Insight is knowing what you want, and I want this and her.

While I was gone, J. carried the pieces of the desk down to the curbside and left them for the city. For several mornings, I saw the pieces sitting there when I went outside. But one hot morning, I went down and outside, and they were gone.

Part III

Disability Studies

Who are we speaking of when we speak of the insane? A trick question. We don't speak of the insane at all, anymore. We speak of the *mentally ill.*

Who are the *mentally ill?* The political and academic fashions of the past fifty years have given us two answers. The first answer is: *nobody.* The second answer is: *everybody. Maybe even you!*

Madness, they say, is culturally bound and specious, an insidious means of *social oppression* designed to discredit, confine, shame, and stigmatize undesirables. It is quackery. It's torture. It's fraud. Then they say: *20 percent of Americans are currently struggling with their mental health. If you need help, talk to your doctor today.*

Nobody

Antipsychiatry has never had a better ally than psychiatry itself. It would be enough if psychiatry was merely a young science, still caught up in the inevitable errors and uncertainties of youth, but for most of its brief history, psychiatric practice has insisted on being incompetent, corrupt, and brutal too. We could forgive the nineteenth-century alienist for believing odd religious views to be evidence of "monomania," or the analyst of the 1960s for believing cold mothers produce schizophrenic sons. But it is difficult to believe that any doctor thought so many political dissidents just happened to be lunatics, or that it was a mere coincidence how many rich men had managed to marry women who turned out to be insane. Perhaps many doctors really did believe that you could torture a madman better, but I doubt that many of them were convinced by sound scientific evidence that large doses of bribery, graft, and land speculation were an essential part of the cure. Perhaps it was inevitable that eugenicists would get into the asylum business, but it is suspicious how quickly the doctors opened the doors, how eagerly they assisted in sterilizing procedures. The history of psychiatry has oscillated so regularly from stupidity to sadism and back again that it should be no surprise when the exposure of so many brutal analysts became, for many people, *analysts: all brutes.* When the frequently abusive asylum became the asylum: intrinsically abusive. When the malpractice of psychiatry became psychiatry: a malicious practice.

The failures of psychiatry have bred generations of critics who are as varied as schools of psychiatry. Outright rejection is common. But there are also critics who believe in psychiatric difficulties but not in their cures. They believe that modern medicine, with its rigidity and desire to pathologize, is ill suited to "cure" anyone. The cause of madness, in their view, might be "stress" or "trauma" or some other vaguely psychiatric condition, but its best left to social workers and graduates of liberal arts colleges to attend to. There are critics who believe there may be such a thing as madness, or there may not be, but in either case, a little more *mindfulness* is all the cure anybody needs. There are critics who believe all so-called patients are merely misunderstood—a million Jack Nicholsons flying over the cuckoo's nest, hanging too loose for the stern quacks. There are Scientologists who are not so much against totalizing systems for assessing and directing human behavior but who are ruthless when it comes to brand competitors. Many of these critics lack much particular criticism, but they possess a vague sense that doctors are up to something. Maybe the medicine is the *real* disease.

There are critics who reject any kind of psychiatric or therapeutic work on the basis that *any* "psychiatric difficulty" is not simply a mistake, but a smokescreen for other failures. When the critic is reactionary, the failures are personal. When the critic is liberal, the failures are social. If the critic is not especially political, or just not thinking of politics at the moment, the source of the failures depends upon whether they like the lunatic in question. Thomas Szasz, perhaps the twentieth century's most famous anti-psychiatrist, called mental illness a *name for problems in living*, but showing the sort of dexterity required to become one of the most prominent psychiatric critics of his time, he conceded that both social *and* personal failures could be blamed. Living, he wrote, is an arduous process, particularly in modern times. Some have a great deal of difficulty adjusting. He also believed that insanity pleas ought to be abolished because criminals were malingerers and liars, looking for a way out. You might as well call the priest to testify about the state of the defendant's soul.

Some strains of anti-psychiatry are more robust than others. Szasz, no matter his other views, urged compassion for those battling a difficult life. The Scottish psychiatrist R. D. Laing rejected the label of *anti-psychiatry* but nonetheless opposed medical interventions; he did not believe, at bottom, that the mad were inalterably broken. Among today's academic classes, there are many who freely admit the existence of psychiatric *symptoms*—depressions, manias, psychoses—but who will remind you that nobody has ever located the "chemical imbalance" in any brain, and who are curious why we don't ask whether or not, as the madman famously says, it's the *world* that's crazy, not him. The truth is that my heart is with these skeptics, but I am more cynical still: It is one thing to invent a disease and sell a "cure." It is another, far more ambitious kind of racket, to identify a real disease and treat it exclusively on an arduous subscription model.

Defenders of psychiatry might gesture at some ideal form of their practice, free from all these mistakes and bigotries, but critics need only remind them that this ideal does not exist. *Psychoanalysis is like the*

Russian Revolution, write Gilles Deleuze and Félix Guattari. *We don't know when it started going bad. We have to keep going back further.* There have been so many un-ideal cases—so many whose certification relied only on mildly eccentric behavior or mildly eccentric opinion, or even ordinary opinion, or race, or sexuality, run afoul of a father or a husband or a state—that it is difficult to remain confident in the minority of cases where psychiatric diagnosis is appropriate. From there it is not too difficult to assert that the ideal *cannot* exist at all. It would be easier to defend psychiatry if psychiatry could provide a satisfactory explanation for why some two or three percent of the population is insane. It would be easier if, lacking an explanation, the psychiatrists could at least avoid engaging in the sort of quackery and railroading which makes it very easy to imagine all psychiatric practice is hopelessly corrupt. Perhaps real psychiatry has never been tried, but the history of actually existing psychiatry has been a history of abuse and failure.

In this century, many of these competing critical tendencies have found their way from loose networks of "psychiatric survivors" and particular iconoclast thinkers into the safer and more formal organizational pastures of the academic humanities. The field of mad studies, an obscure corner of disability studies (itself a minor subdivision of the humanities) is the consequence of this migration, particularly in the decades since early material and Marxist conceptions of disability were largely replaced by more identity-based critiques copied and pasted from feminist studies, queer studies, and other essentialist disciplines. This is often explicit: in her seminal 1997 book *Extraordinary Bodies*—the book often credited with inventing disability studies—scholar Rosemarie Garland-Thomson wrote that her aim was to *move disability from the realm of medicine into that of political minorities, to recast it from a form of pathology to a form of ethnicity.*

In 2018, another prominent humanities scholar summed up this turn by worrying about the dominating influence of the *medical gaze* in understanding madness. He located his own project in an effort to *claim control* of the study of *cognitive disability* from the *health and medical sciences.* He did not say, precisely, what would happen should this scholar-activist model win that struggle. Perhaps humanities professors would take over the management of my medication regimen. Perhaps they would merely supervise my doctors, to make sure they weren't being led too far astray by their gaze. For other critics, even this does not go far enough. A faction of mad studies scholars argue that to include the insane among the ranks of the disabled is only a gentler form of stigma. Psychiatry is a colonizing force, they say. There is nothing wrong with the insane but the abuse they have suffered from their doctors.

While these critics vary in their willingness to believe in the existence of genuine psychiatric symptoms—some concede, some do not, that under any regime we might still see two to three percent of the population apparently struck by "madness"—what is remarkable is how little these varied beliefs matter to the field's near-uniform commitment to relentlessly and exclusively emphasizing the *social oppression* of the mad, both by psychiatry and by a confused and fearful society. The existence or nonexistence of madness somehow renders no effect on the proposed solutions, which always consist of abolishing the regime established by the psychiatrists and their "diagnosis-treatment-cure" ideology, and replacing it with a new regime, centered around "centering" the self-conception of the mad, considering our "subaltern perspectives," *fighting stigma*, and doing anything else that comes to mind, so long as it takes madness, real or not, to be first and always an area of social and ideological struggle.

The mad studies scholars publish paper after paper calling on one another to *resist* the co-option of "mad culture" by psychiatrists. They go on, sometimes for dozens of pages, on the most fitting name for the mad; *psychobiosocialpoliticalbodymind impaired* is a serious candidate these days. A great deal of time is dedicated to documenting the obscene abuse of psychiatric practice against black people and queer people and women, and while this is a history well worth documenting, these efforts rarely get around to saying what ought to be done with actual psychiatric patients once all the falsely accused have been freed. A great deal of time is given over to talks and papers on the proper manners for the organization of disability studies conferences, which tells you something about which lunatics these scholars believe must be considered first. Friendly fire is common. In 2020, an academic paper argued that the Hearing Voices Movement, already a site of radical anti-psychiatry, might nonetheless marginalize those whose madness was not defined by the rigid barrier of palpable psychosis, particularly those who have *queered madness* through self-diagnosis of multiple personality disorder. A neurodiversity studies perspective, they chided, might help bring the movement *into the twenty-first century*. The cynic says that psychiatrists have a professional interest in never seeing their patients cured. So much the same for the activists.

But a curious thing has happened over the past generation of American life. At the dawn of the twenty-first century, it appeared that the anti-psychiatrists had won the war. Their condemnations of the asylum prevailed with deinstitutionalization; their skepticism regarding "diagnosis" and "treatment" became the common sense of our intellectual culture. Everybody knew how terrible the *stigma* against the mad could be; everybody lamented the ignorance and cruelty of our efforts to treat them with padded rooms and electricity. But despite all of this, psychiatry itself—its diagnoses, its medications, its therapy sessions, and its billable hours—has never been more prominent in public life. Psychiatry, so thoroughly defeated, is everywhere.

Everybody

In the early twenty-first century, at precisely the same moment that *madness* was in the process of being abolished by university professors, *mental illness* began to afflict every member of Western society, or at least those with access to health insurance. Among the striver classes, *stigma* was thoroughly defeated. Living in that culture, you might even believe that—having done away with the barriers to *opening up*—we had revealed a hitherto unseen epidemic of mood disorders. Everywhere, otherwise well-functioning and successful professionals were attesting to crippling anxiety; otherwise-comfortable people told us they were struggling—always *struggling*—with depression. Half of the creative class claimed to have post-traumatic stress disorder—always *severe* post-traumatic stress disorder, one wonders where all the merely *moderate* cases have gone—and the other half claimed to have somehow only dated the tiny sliver of living people with narcissistic personality disorders. Everyone was terribly busy attending to their *mental illness*, to maximizing their *mental health*.

These new mentally ill are not like the mad. They are not lunatics, psychos, or *crazy*. Where the mad are terrifying, disorganized, crippled, and degenerating; the *mentally ill* are just having a hard time. They're suffering a deficit in their attention. They're anxious and depressed. Like the mad, the mentally ill can be *misunderstood*, even *stigmatized*, but unlike the mad, to understand the *mentally ill* would not be to appreciate the depth and seriousness of a lifelong disease. It would be only to appreciate the depth and seriousness with which every difficult feeling they have can be attributed to a multiplying selection of diagnoses and treated at out-of-network provider rates. A Harvard Medical School study finds that 46 percent of the population *qualifies as neurodivergent*. Five more percent and they will be the majority, and then the sane will be the weird ones.

If there is a single point on which every critic agrees, it is in the capaciousness and failure of the *DSM*. For the anti-psychiatrist, it is a manual of oppression, a constructor of illness rather than a description. But for the most strident defenders of psychiatry, it is a joke as it expands relentlessly to include so many dubious pathologies. Reactionary defender of the asylum E. Fuller Torrey has lamented the profitable turn of psychiatry services toward the *wealthy and worried well*. For skeptics and zealots alike, one scholar observed, *mental illness is— discursively speaking—at once everywhere and nowhere.*

I've seen a graphic floating around social media with a picture labeled THE ADHD ICEBERG. Above the water—what people think ADHD is— are "trouble focusing" and "fidgeting." Beneath the water, occupying roughly three-quarters of the scene, are over two dozen additional symptoms, including "difficulty maintaining relationships," "auditory processing disorder," "poor impulse control," "mood swings," "forgetting to eat, sleep, go to the bathroom," and rejection sensitive dysphoria (rendered as "rejective sensitive disorder" in the graphic), a condition which makes it clinically difficult to be disliked. Incidentally, these are also the symptoms associated with nearly every other mental illness on earth, as well as the known side effects of amphetamines, a common treatment for ADHD. Incidentally, there are nearly identical graphics for "anxiety" and "depression" and half a dozen other distinct forms of *mental illness.*

The effect of these graphics is never to effect any change in the diagnosis or treatment of these illnesses, nor to indicate any skepticism regarding the cause of such diverse symptoms. Instead, these memes exist to communicate a social argument with an online audience: *My condition ought to afford me more credit as a heroic subject than it does.* The stigma that *mental illness* culture of this kind is fighting is not *against* the illness—not against the notion that the disordered are not as frightening or deranged as culture might lead you to believe—but against the idea that the disorder is relatively manageable and limited in scope. IF PEOPLE KNEW HOW MUCH OCD MAKES YOU DESPISE YOURSELF IN EVERY SINGLE WAY, I DON'T THINK PEOPLE WOULD JOKE ABOUT IT ANYMORE, reads another meme, in full. If the original anti-stigma campaigns emerged to help the mad convince the world that they aren't so different from everybody else, the anti-stigma campaigns of the *mentally ill* exist to convince the world that they are different, interestingly different, *having a harder time* different, more credible and pitiable and brave than you were led to believe. Like so much contemporary personal writing, they are somehow self-abasing and self-aggrandizing all at once. Perhaps their authors really do suffer from rejection sensitivity dysphoria.

There is a term—disease mongering—which refers to the phenomenon wherein the diagnostic boundaries of some illness are aggressively expanded at the same moment that "awareness" of that malady is promoted to the public. More people come to know that they may have this disease, and more people meet its qualifications. It's a good situation for drug companies. If you turn on your television right now and see an "Ask your doctor about . . ." ad for some new drug, promising to treat some vague, new sort of illness, that's disease mongering in action.

In the age of opening up and fighting stigma, insanity has been a disease mongered so thoroughly that there are perhaps more people in the United States taking psychiatric medication despite being entirely sane than there are people with serious psychiatric disorders. Roughly 3 percent of the population is bipolar. Another 2 percent or so are schizophrenic. A few more major depressives, a few serious obsessive-compulsives— we are still talking about one in twenty or thirty Americans. Now consider how many of us, and particularly how many strivers, are medicated for anxiety. Consider how many take stimulants for ADHD.

Unlike the mad, the *mentally ill* really do face primarily *social* problems, not medical or economic problems. They are, in this way, the imagined object of both disability studies and anti-psychiatric skepticism, summoned into existence post hoc by the logic of expanding markets. Advertisements for serious psychiatric medication—mood stabilizers and antipsychotics—air on lowbrow daytime television. Advertisements for anti-depressants, anxiety medications, and talk therapy air with prestige dramas. This is not a mistake. The *mentally ill* are a marketing invention, constituting *as many as 20 percent of Americans at any given time!* This is before we even reach the *empaths, covert narcissists, sex addicts*, and other victims—or beneficiaries—of pseudo-psychiatric conditions popularized by television and the internet.

It is also not a mistake that the emperor of fashionable maladies is *trauma*, which is a kind of madness caused by social life. Trauma may come from a singular past event, or from a continuous life of difficult experiences. It may even come epigenetically, through the difficult experiences of one's distant relatives. That some holders of this view likely also suffer from a clinically significant psychological trauma is merely incidental: trauma in this configuration is a rhetorical stance, a claimed status; like many of the newly recognized *mentally ill*, it is nearly indistinguishable in its practical deployment from astrology. The medical aesthetic is only that: a sort of dress-up. Its purpose is to define the speaker by giving them archetypal characteristics, to stake out who they are in easy-to-remember contrasts in a world of overwhelming social connection and overlap. This does not require cynicism on the part of the "patient" any more than astrology requires cynicism from the seeker. Being *such a Leo* doesn't just tell other people who you are, it helps you tell yourself who you are, too. It becomes the foundation of a stable sense of self, a thing otherwise so elusive in Western postmodernity. If you self-describe in that way, you probably believe it, or very badly want to. Unlike astrology, *mental illness* of this kind is available primarily to those who can afford largely private, non-emergency psychiatric care from an indulgent doctor or those willing to self-diagnose.

The patients themselves are hardly to blame. The Anxious and Depressed, Deeply Traumatized with a Deficit in their Attention: they are, I am sure, feeling very poorly. They are not doctors, nor God—how do they know that their sadness is not Depression? How do they know that their discomfort is not Anxiety? When they spend a whole day in nervousness and agitation and worry, who is to say that isn't a panic attack? It might very well be; they don't know any better. They don't feel well! This is more comforting than the alternative, the possibility that there really is something outside of your own head worth panicking about. The possibility that while many people may find themselves *mentally ill*, it is the world that's gone crazy. This would not be the first time that a civilization has displaced responsibility for its own depravity onto the inability of its citizens to put up with such conditions.

Of course, in an age governed by the false security of *facts* and *science*, the clinic is only the latest specialized idiom to be vulgarized by a public discourse searching for stable ground. We have seen it already with evolutionary biology, with critical race theory, Marxism, constitutional law—why not let the psychiatrists have a turn watching their discipline recapitulated as a broad explanatory framework for human suffering by a terminally insecure professional class? These new patients have *difficulties in living*, and they are reaching for the idiom at hand. That many of these new patients are among the most insistent activist-critics of psychiatry is hardly even a contradiction. Like the rash of contemporary bourgeoise Catholic converts who become sedevacantists at the very moment of their first communion, the self-identified *mentally ill* only reveal the tension that motivates their original distress: in modernity, institutions and their discourses retain all of their power but none of their potency. A Catholic without a heresy is only a credulous normie. A mental patient without psychiatry is only sad. The twentieth-century revelation of social reality as mere *discourse* did not generate an alternative to discourse as the basis of a coherent and intelligible social existence. What's left to do? You have to take the poison in order to throw it up and feeling sick is better than feeling nothing.

The line between a real psychiatric condition and a mere *problem of living* can be difficult to find, particularly when the symptoms fall short of spectacular madness. When do feelings of anxiety indicate a pathology, and when do they indicate an emotional reaction to ordinary life? The answer is cause, and failing that, degree, but lacking a proven theory of the cause of madness, we are left to render a judgment, and that judgment has generally followed profit before it follows probability. The allure of psychiatric language and diagnosis corresponds perfectly to broadening awareness of psychiatric dysfunction and a real reduction in stigma. It is seized upon at the very moment that it serves a useful purpose in moral reasoning by people who are expanding the definition of *mental illness* to include, in some sense, all their bad feelings. Widening "awareness" plus widening diagnostic boundaries: disease mongering in action. Bad feelings become "trauma" and not just "pain" precisely because trauma is clinical, and rare, and scientifically verified and therefore can do the credibility enhancing work that mere bad feelings can't. Trauma is the pain of ordinary life declared extraordinary, with a doctor's note to prove it. Even the unfolding nightmare of history is only an input for a targeted ad, a means of comparing all hitherto existing society to an inventory of your personal bad feelings and finding the diagnosis that's *right for you*. Often this is just a matter of expanding the customer base. Perhaps your inability to drain spot-up jumpers and pad your college application with a varsity jacket may be a sign of clinically poor hand-eye coordination. Ask your doctor if Wellshootrin may be right for you. The side effects are similar to the Adderall you're already taking to enhance your performance on the SAT.

This expanding market for psychiatric services, sold at upmarket rates to the sane, should not come as a surprise. It is beyond a cliché to say that the world has become at once more luxurious and threadbare; that where precarity recedes, *anxiety* appears. There are as many causes as there are feeds to refresh. Therapy becomes more worthwhile the more it reflects a growing trouble in ordinary life. A corollary of a world in which success for these new strivers is dependent on acquiring security and precarious resources through the cultivation of a personal brand is the inevitability of a world in which any part of your person can undermine or destroy that brand, and with it your career or security. This puts a good deal of pressure on the strivers to present a sympathetic persona to the world, but it also pressures them to never see that persona compromised. Most of it is granular. For the strivers who can count themselves a member in good standing of the public-facing professional class, even friendship is nothing more than a collaboration, based on contract law and subject to termination at will. If even one's closest peers and colleagues and friends—and what is the difference, anymore, between these things?—must be treated with a certain kind of cultivated paranoia, then what room is left for genuine ambivalence, negativity, poor behavior, or even unfavorable impressions?

Because the strivers, regardless of their alleged politics, have no politics anymore, just variations on brand cultivation, and because one must cultivate a brand to survive in this market at all, marketing is all that's left. It is impossible or at least dangerous to talk through your shit with somebody you aren't paying and who isn't bound by law to keep your confidence. The great relief that so many strivers feel during therapy is the relief of finally being able to speak honestly with somebody they can trust. In the nineteenth century, it was widely believed that the pace and stress of urban life precipitated an epidemic of psychiatric collapse in otherwise sane people. Now, it is relaxing to get off the internet and put your phone away and just walk around for a while in the loud, fast city streets.

The steady transformation of *madness* and its intense, specific difficulties into *mental illness* and its diffuse unhappiness and attendant social struggles has borne an additional, ironic consequence: there are so many more *people suffering from mental illness* than there are madmen that when the two are grouped together under the single rubric of psychiatric attention, the *mentally ill* become the typical case. Their particular situation is taken to be the average situation of the whole, vindicating the anti-psychiatrist who believes madness is generally a cover for individual difficulty with an arduous life. Their particular needs are taken to be the average needs of the whole, validating the activist and scholar who believes the mentally ill primarily face *social* difficulties. Their particular respectability—struggling, perhaps, but ultimately capable of attaining prestige employment—becomes the presumed respectability of the whole. The mad, with their frequent dysfunction, troubling affects, bizarre and even terrifying behavior, are once again subject to the old stigmas but now for politically correct reasons. Their madness is no longer taken to be the cause of their difficulties because their difficulties are statistical outliers among the *mentally ill*. After all, as many as 20 percent of Americans struggle with mental illness, and you don't see them screaming or losing their jobs or living on the street or going to prison. That's just a few rotten souls, whose condition is *not an excuse*.

Somebodies

In *The Power and the Glory*, Graham Greene's whisky priest arrives in a small village in the middle of the night. The village has not had a clergyman for years. After hiding him in a hut, a villager asks the whisky priest if he will stay up and hear the confessions of the villagers before he goes to sleep. The whisky priest is tired and wants to wait until morning, but the villager is worried that the police will come before then and it will be too late. Why not be safe and hear confessions now? The whisky priest, exhausted and frustrated and dreading the prospect of hearing hours of tedious confession in the middle of the night, bursts into tears.

The villager leaves him. He goes to another hut and invites the others to confess. *It's late*, they say. *Can't we wait until morning?* The villager scolds them: *What do you think the priest has come here for?* he asks. *Would you insult him? He is a very holy father. There he is in my hut now, weeping for our sins.*

As my condition became worse and it became impossible to avoid telling people that I was ill, I found that my confession provoked frequent counter-confessions. Some were straightforward: a schizophrenic father or a bipolar sibling—perhaps I could relate. But many of the people I spoke to wanted to speak about their own difficulties, their assumptions or suspicions regarding their own madness. Were they depressed? Were they delusional? Should they go to therapy? They had heard that as many as *20 percent of Americans are struggling with mental illness* and began to wonder if their own odd thoughts and feelings were signs. When they saw that I was not screaming or weeping or frothing at the mouth, not talking to myself or evidently floridly psychotic, they began to imagine that how they felt might be something like how I feel—after all, we were both sitting there, *having trouble*.

I tried to remind them, as often as I could, that I am not a psychologist or a psychiatrist. I am not an expert. I don't know. In any case, I tried to avoid saying out loud that I have no desire to know. I have met people who assume I've considered a career in social work—wouldn't I like to *help people like me?* Perhaps people who have less insight, who are less stable, who are having a harder time?—but I am exhausted enough dealing with myself. I am not in my hut, *weeping for the sins* of all the other poor lunatics. I love them, in the way one loves any imagined confederate, but I don't want to be a priest.

In the first years after my diagnosis, when I began to tell the people closest to me—my parents, E., a few friends—they did not react poorly. They hardly reacted at all. My mother said, *Okay.* E. said, *Yeah okay, that makes sense.* Neither mentioned it again without my prompting. I liked it better that way.

For a long time, I believed that I had been born into a crossroads in the ideologies of madness. From the east came the old vestigial stigmas: the frothing maniacs, the madwomen in their attics, the wackos and psychos and lunatic caricatures on TV. From the west, the scholars, preaching kinder language and *gazes* making their long march against *stigma* through the halls of the institutions. From the north came the *mentally ill,* the dupes and status-seekers and strivers and rubes, all far too eager to be mad. From the south, the anti-psychiatrists, calling all this confusion, oppression, and lies. None, I thought, could quite be blamed. Each could see its opposite marching in to take the high ground. None could afford to stand down. But after a while, I began to ask myself why these roads were crossing here at all. What lay at this intersection? What force of history had called all these factions here at once? The answer is that they are all marching in their own way under the banner of austerity.

The insane, the truly insane, are a small group. The estimated rate of schizophrenia and manic depression combined constitute slightly less than 5 percent of the population; with the addition of the schizo-affective, acutely borderline, severely obsessive-compulsive, and other species of serious psychiatric condition, the mad still number fewer than six of every hundred people. Of that small number, those who cannot live an ordinary life, or whose ordinary lives are propped up only by incessant medical and social intervention are a smaller number still. But even these few are time-consuming, difficult, and expensive. They are difficult to care for even when they want to be cared for; they are doubly difficult because a frequent symptom of their difficulty is a hostile refusal of help. When they are treated, their treatment is costly and tedious and rarely guaranteed to work. I am not among the worst cases. My mood symptoms are typically moderate, occasionally severe. My psychosis is intermittent and it emerged later on, a good sign for my prognosis. I respond well to medication; I can work and live on my own. Still, my treatment costs tens of thousands of dollars every year, even before occasional and inevitable emergency expenses. I am a cheap case, as far as the mad go, but even I am a loss on my insurer's balance sheet. Even the good cases are a costly pain.

The mad have fallen under the auspices of public welfare for nearly two hundred years in the West. Public asylums, assisted living, home-care, medication programs, disability payments, and specialized legal protections have all been marshaled in various efforts to contain and assist a population that is unlikely to ever produce commensurate value. Some can, and do, of course, but many can't, and this is contrary to the logic of capital, even the logic of a capitalist welfare state. Most forms of assistance aren't like this. Poverty assistance in general, socialized medicine in general, even programs of racial reparation in general, are premised on the implicit understanding that once state assistance has made the beneficiary whole, they will get back to productivity—be *lifted out of poverty* or *given a full stake in the American dream* and become a part of the mass labor and consumption force. But many of the mad will never do this, at least not in the aggregate. Some, like me, will regain the better part of their senses. Some will just survive. Some—many, even—will become permanent wards of the state, unable to function on their own. This is a problem for any social order premised on efficiency and self-dependence, on the presumption that individuals are rational economic agents who must—either through assistance, if you are liberal, or peril, if you are conservative—be directed toward productivity. In an effort to correct this problem, any such ideological order necessarily tries to justify the easiest possible solution: just cut society's losses and stop helping.

Every presently fashionable theory of the mad contributes to this cause. What *stigmatizers* still exist make the case explicitly: we should feel contempt, not pity, for frothing lunatics and dangerous madmen. The obvious end of the logic of anti-psychiatry, even the sympathetic kind, is identical: we should dismantle both psychiatric services justified by the so-called existence of biological madness. Either we're squandering resources on malingerers or helping avaricious witch doctors railroad unwitting victims.

For those who cannot be persuaded to hate or disbelieve in madness, the identity scholars and language reformers offer a miserly alternative, disguised as political enlightenment: even if the mad exist, they say, their trouble is primarily *social*. We should help them, of course, but the solution must be social, too, concerned first and foremost with etiquette and *awareness*. It is far cheaper to censure *stigma* than to furnish potentially unlimited quantities of financial and medical assistance to a dependent population. Better to suggest that calling them *dependent* is offensive.

The growing ranks of the *mentally ill*, meanwhile, do their part to offset losses in the psychiatric services sector. Persuaded that *mental health* requires diligent prophylaxis, they redirect existing psychiatric services toward a population that can afford to pay: themselves. And each time they pay, they give good fodder to the skeptics and activists alike by standing in as the dubiously diagnosed, primarily *oppressed* "patients" that the skeptics and activists are speaking of. *See*, the critics say, gesturing at the anxious and depressed striver, *this is what we're talking about, right here*. Like many enemies, all these camps are co-dependent: they need one another to go on.

These factions work in concert, some deliberately, some accidentally, to transform the question of whether society is morally obliged to help a small population that is unlikely to ever repay society for its help into a debate over whether that population exists at all, and if it does exist, whether it really needs *material* assistance or if a little symbolic recognition would suffice. For all the talk of *ableism* and *fighting stigma* and concern for *liberating* the mad from their marginalization, the history of Western insanity in the twentieth and twenty-first centuries is the history of a particularly brutal case of service depletion, inflicted by liberal austerity regimes, on a population which, even in a *stigma-free* world, would still rely disproportionately on state care. Meanwhile, the dupe-servants of privatization and atomization encourage the mad to realign their expectations toward inclusion in the new sensitivity training regimes. When that fails, the police are called to discipline this wasted, unused, and unusable labor force. The mad constitute less than 5 percent of the population. They are between 25 percent and 50 percent of the victims of state-sanctioned murder by law enforcement each year. So services are cut and cut and cut, with so many flavors of justification that anyone might find at least one reason agreeable to their politics. What's left of the infrastructure is privatized and resold to as many as *20 percent of all Americans* for a tidy profit: neoliberal ingenuity in action.

Audre Lorde writes in her *Cancer Journals, it is easier to demand happiness than to clean up the environment.* So now the same with *anxiety*. Meanwhile the mad, who are after all such a small number of people, cannot stop any of this. Some can afford to take care of themselves, or they are taken care of by friends and families who can afford it. Some muddle on, as they always have. Some, more every year, do not.

Austerity measures can be accomplished without the consent of its objects and even over their visible protest—ask food stamp recipients, or public university professors, or residents of low-income housing— but it is easier if the victims are co-opted, too. The insane, no matter their present state of affliction, are no more immune than anybody else to the influence of ideology. If the mad themselves begin to believe that they are the victims of a con, if we indulge in the ego-satisfying belief that our psychiatric problems are primarily social and that they can be solved with better manners alone, then the work of austerity meets little resistance at all. *After all*, says the vulture as he strips and sells the asylum for parts, as he closes the outpatient clinic, as he denies SSDI checks and prescription assistance, *I've listened to the scholars. I've listened to the activists. I'm subscribed to all the radical journals and newsletters and zines. I'm tearing down an instrument of oppression here!* he says. *You want to prop it up? I'm giving these people—these misunderstood geniuses, these radicals, these poor oppressed who I would never stigmatize at all—the liberation that they've needed all along. But hey, if that makes you uneasy, don't worry. I can get you something for that. Just hand me your insurance card and give me the co-pay up front. I take cash or check or card.*

The Lunatic Fringe

On August 10, 2016, a thirty-two-year-old trucking executive named Tony Timpa picked up a phone in a parking lot in Dallas and dialed 911. He told the dispatcher that he had schizophrenia but hadn't taken his medication. He needed help. While Timpa waited, he was handcuffed by a security guard. The police arrived, and within twenty minutes, he was dead.

Officers told Timpa's mother that Tony had suffered a heart attack at a local bar and died. After it came out that Timpa had in fact died in police custody, the cops insisted that Timpa had been aggressive when they found him. He was dangerously unstable and high—he'd told the dispatcher that he'd taken drugs—and when they arrived, they had to restrain him. They'd had to zip tie his hands and hold him down to prevent him from rolling into the street. When he passed out, they assumed it was the drugs. When he died, they figured it was an overdose.

But in July 2019, bodycam footage of the incident became public. In it, you can hear Timpa asking for help. You can hear him say, *You're going to kill me! You're going to kill me!* before he passes out. The police hold Timpa's face down for nearly fifteen minutes. They joke about him staying down. *Tony, time for school!* one of them says; *I don't want to go to school! Five more minutes, Mom!* shouts another. The cops push

Tony's limp body around, but they don't check for a pulse. Later, an autopsy found that Tony Timpa suffered sudden cardiac death, brought on in part by *the stress associated with physical restraint*. Tony Timpa was killed by Texas cops who thought it was hilarious.

Police kill the insane at extraordinary rates. The mad are some sixteen times more likely than the average person to be murdered during an encounter with law enforcement, and this is the worst rate—by far—of any subcategory of the general population. I have written so much about the violence that the mad inflict on one another, on the street and in hospitals and in life, about the ways so many of us become both the perpetrators and victims of brutality, but despite all of that, I still feel safer, and the numbers say I should feel safer, with an unmedicated lunatic than I do with an armed American cop.

· · ·

The ordinary line from mainstream mental health advocacy organizations is that police must be trained in *de-escalation tactics*. The police need to recognize the difference between a violent threat and a man in the midst of a mental health crisis, as if these are always different things. Better yet, social workers ought to be sent in lieu of police officers, although this requires that the 911 caller or the dispatcher be able to *recognize a mental health crisis*, too. This is an excellent situation for educational consultants. Soon everybody will need to complete a course in recognizing the signs of a crisis. Everybody will be deputized into this kinder, gentler police force for the mad.

The de-escalation advocates imagine that the typical encounter between the officer and the madman is a story about confusion. They imagine the madman acting in a way that isn't—but could be interpreted as—erratic or dangerous. They imagine a cop who doesn't want to kill a civilian, but who sincerely believes that they're dealing with a dangerous person that they must stop. They draw their gun. They issue commands. The commands are ignored. They yell louder. Still nothing. The madman makes a sudden move. The cops open fire. *If only they knew how to recognize the signs of a mental health crisis!* the activists lament.

I do not believe that most meetings between lunatics and cops go this way at all. American police routinely open fire when their lives are not in any reasonable danger. Even when there's no danger at all. If they want to shoot, they shoot; de-escalation would just get in the way. They don't even need to believe that they are protecting anybody or dealing with a threat to public peace. The police didn't find Tony Timpa on their own. Nobody saw him acting strangely and called 911. He called himself. He told dispatchers where he was. The police arrived. They weren't afraid of him, but they still killed him. They didn't even use a gun.

Officers arrive on the scene: the lunatic isn't dangerous but he's weird and loud. He doesn't respond to police instructions. The cops try to de-escalate—they've had the training, they know there's a mental health crisis happening, they try—but the madman won't cooperate. He swings. Or he runs. Or he scares the nice parkgoers. He threatens to run into traffic. He needs to be restrained. The cops grab the madman and wrestle him to the ground and something happens—a crack, a thud, too much time spent kneeling on the madman's back. Who knows? But now there's no pulse. He's dead. What is the training for that, even if the officer was acting in good faith?

And what if the madman really is dangerous? He's menacing somebody. Civilians are afraid. He's too far gone to *de-escalate*. Does the officer now have a license to kill? How dangerous do they need to be? I suspect many of these encounters begin when police are summoned to a sidewalk, bench, or doorframe, where some lunatic is sleeping. The cops wake the head case up and tell him to move along. If the madman—exhausted and surprised and not-all-together at all—wakes up screaming or spitting or swinging, is that enough to pull the trigger? When has someone exhausted their right to understanding?

I don't want to conflate the narrow question of police murder with the broad political situation of the American insane. But in the presence of frequent extrajudicial execution, it is difficult to remember questions of housing, healthcare, work, or welfare, much less the tertiary questions of social propriety that so consume the *mental illness* high culture. At any rate, it is the easiest question. *Should the police murder unarmed schizophrenics who call for help from a parking lot?* After that, we have to confront the bosses, then the doctors, then the families, and the answers become murkier the further in you go. *A madman comes to the door of the law.* He is immediately shot. Why bother with the rest of the story? Less Kafka; more Mickey Spillane.

· · ·

I've been picked up by police before. As a teenager and in my early twenties, as my symptoms first began to manifest, I was picked up more than once for disorderly conduct—yelling in the streets, or sleeping on a patch of grass by the sidewalk, or crashing my car. I've been stopped, picked up, and questioned more than a dozen times since. I get lost. I act strangely. I know the look in an officer's eyes when he's trying to remember the signs of a mental health crisis: when one hand is trying to remember his de-escalation training, while the other hand slides down toward his holster.

That night in Iowa—when I left my apartment convinced that I had to go to California and walked twelve miles to the next town over and checked into a hotel under a fake name and waited for the morning bus to come—E. and two other friends managed to find me. When I wouldn't acknowledge them or come with them or even stay in one place, they called the police. I wasn't threatening them or even yelling. I just kept trying to walk or run away. I barely recognized them. I was gone.

They did everything right: They explained to the police that I was having a *mental health issue.* They said I wasn't armed and wasn't dangerous. The police came and confronted me, but it took hours for me to calm down and agree to go to the hospital. I didn't make a scene—psychosis isn't like that all the time—but I ran across a freeway onramp in the dark into a ditch to escape the officers. I played hide-and-seek with them in a parking structure. When they managed to corner me, I told them I had something important to do. I said, *Am I breaking the law? I'm just walking. I'm just walking. I'm just walking,* over and over until they gave up. They didn't help at all. I went back to my motel room and E. sat outside the door and eventually she persuaded me to go to the hospital.

What if different cops had come? What if they'd gotten out of their squad car, guns drawn, and I'd made the wrong move? What if they'd cornered me, and I'd tried to push past them, or hit one of them, and they'd shot me? What if, as I ran across the onramp, they'd pursued and tackled me and in the process of restraining me, I'd died on the ground? What if they'd laughed about it? What if they'd thought it was funny to roll me into the road and pretend I was asleep after I said, *You're gonna kill me! You're gonna kill me!*?

I am absolutely certain that I will have another encounter with the police someday. I will probably have many. I am too small, too white, too neurotic and slow to terrify a police officer. I don't worry that those police officers won't be trained in de-escalation. Many cops are even patient and kind. I worry that there'll be a scuffle and something will go wrong. I worry I'll run into traffic. I worry that one cop—and in my whole life it will only ever take one cop—will be the kind who can recognize the signs of a mental health crisis but who just doesn't care. He gets out of his squad car, gun already drawn and ready.

• • •

The ableism is particularly awful again today, some holy woke poster tweets. *Instead of "stupid," "dumb," "insane," or "crazy" how about we be accurate?* The poster lists alternative phrases, including "foolish." Several hours later, they follow up: *It's been brought to my attention that "foolish" is also ableist, please avoid that term as well!* Oh well. I had rather be any kind o' thing than a Fool. And yet I would not be thee.

These sorts of PSAs are cheap and common and constitute a great deal of the existing "political activism" around madness in the United States. I do not know what the politics of the mad ought to be, but they cannot be this. Even the arcane critical confusion of the bio-politics scholars is too ambitious for these people. All the marches against stigma and national awareness days, all the National Alliance on Mental Illness messaging and the "fight against ableism"; all of it is just conjuring up a new class to be "advocated for" who need "activists" and "allies," the collapse of every kind of idiocy, lunacy, and madness into a single new ascriptive concern, equipped with its own special intersectional needs. Even the needs don't get much attention—the whole project simply insists that there is a group with needs, and that group needs representation, and we are that representation, so why not set up a recurring donation? It's all magic and conjuring in service of a grift: the notion that there are "mental health causes" sectioned off in their own special corner of the world, with a special metaphysical status, requiring special kinds of spells, atomized and totally disconnected from (frankly insulted by your attempt to "reduce" them to, in fact!) any shared political struggle for socialized housing or socialized medicine or criminal justice reform. Again, please donate to our organization. For a small annual contribution, we'll invite you to the march and the gala and keep disciplining the bad-word users, keep Doing the Work, keep asking very, very nicely if everybody else will please be nice to you head cases. Who knows? Perhaps one day it'll work.

I don't care about magic words one way or the other. I am barely more comforted by the radical who says the madman is uniquely hurt by capitalism, as if capitalism were the first great horror of human history. Are our present Marxists any better? There has been an immense influx of new and particularly young people into the so-called American left over the past decade. But while they've come over to the "right team" in the sense that they can correctly identify the broad contending classes of a materialist left account of the world, they are still basically liberal in their sense of how that conflict takes place. They still have a Manichaean view of morality, where there are Good People and Bad People, and what kind of person you are in some way reflects your individual choices about the state of your soul. They tend to believe bankers and landlords are Bad People, rather than believing that rent-seeking is an inevitable and brutal consequence of land enclosure. They claim to hate the defensive "a few bad apples" theory of racist cops, but they only seem to take issue with the words "a few," instead believing like all utopian anarchists that the *kinds of people who become cops*, and indeed anybody interested in enforcing state power, are all bad apples. They claim to believe in the politics of class and structures of power but act as if a class is merely a quorum of individually Good or Bad individuals with the Right or the Wrong ideas, as if changing structure simply means eliminating all the wrong kinds of people. What can they do for the mad? Defund the asylums? It's already been tried.

The truth is that the insane are a problem for every mode of production: for the agrarian, the imperial, the feudal, the bourgeois. We take up more resources than we consume. We have Special Needs, as they say. The ideology of every hitherto existing economic regime has found a way to justify hating that inefficiency, of locking us up in institutions or leaving us on the street or killing us, not because people have too much stigma in their hearts, but because what else are you going to do with us when you're busy trying to run an economy? No byzantine striver language game will change that. Let us leap forward into the great socialist future. From each according to their ability, to each according to their needs. We will need to work out what to do in the case of those whose abilities are limited, whose needs are great, and who are perhaps too addled by delusion to ascertain their own abilities or express their own needs.

I am not an activist nor an organizer, nor any kind of political representative for the insane. But when I think of how the mad might seek justice, I don't think of activism or organizing at all. I don't think of marches or campaigns or legislation; I think of terrorism. I think: liberate Los Angeles County Jail. I think: bomb the old site of Pilgrim State Hospital. I think: hold the DA's children hostage until every insanity plea is not met with tough talk about how the family needs the justice of another schizophrenic in solitary confinement or the electric chair.

I sometimes imagine writing a speculative novel about a planet where 95 percent of the population has schizophrenia; the action starts when their science advances to the point that they discover that the voices they all hear are not an empirical phenomenon or the whispers of their God, but a widely shared sensory disorder. But the real question is: How could such a society even reach that level of technology? What I mean is that even if I wanted to be a terrorist, it is difficult enough to organize one wing of a psychiatric hospital. It is difficult enough to organize the sane into a disciplined and dedicated cell. An Al-Qaeda of the Mad isn't even far-fetched; it's the premise of a bad skit for the long-term care ward's biannual talent show. In 1971, a group of German lunatics did form the Sozialistisches Patientenkollektiv—the Socialist Patients' Collective—and in 1978, when a member was arrested crossing illegally from Canada into Vermont, the FBI identified her as a terrorist, but the joke was on the FBI. Even the West German authorities clarified in a statement to a newspaper that the group was *fairly harmless*.

...

The truth is that the mad do not need to occupy a building to be thought of as terrorists; we are already imagined that way. This is ordinarily taken to be a kind of stigma, but it may be true. The National Alliance on Mental Illness says on their website that the association of schizophrenia and violence is a dangerous myth. Actually, they say, the majority of violent crimes aren't committed by schizophrenics.

And that's true. Schizophrenics make up less than 2 percent of the population. They are not committing 51 percent of the violent crimes.

Do the mad commit violent acts more often than the sane? It is difficult to say. The best studies suggest that we do, although substance abuse is often the accelerant required for the fire. It is unclear who is being counted among the *mentally ill* in the first place. Do they mean any mental illness, regardless of severity, including the moderately depressed, the anxious, the Adderall-addled millennial striver "speaking out" about his "struggles with mental health"? Do they mean only severe mental illness, like bipolar disorder? Do they mean what most people imagine when discussing the criminally mad, which is to say, do they mean schizophrenia?

What does it mean to "become violent"? We do not track the number of shoves and punches and thankfully empty threats carried out by the paranoid or manic or suicidal every year. Do we only mean the violence that ends with a police report? Only the violence that police officers become aware of? Do we only mean felonious batteries? Only murders? Attempted murders? Do misdemeanors count? Do we count fights between the homeless, or in bars, or in private homes, far from the eyes of anybody running a statistical analysis? Do we just mean physical violence? Or is it physical violence plus the threat of physical violence? Both, plus the nonviolent acts rhetorically refigured as "violence" by humanities graduate faculties? We are talking about terrorism. Is it enough to terrify? To make the sane uncomfortable, threatened, to get them feeling unsafe?

Are the rates based on patient reports? Police reports? Only when charges are filed? When an indictment is secured? Where a conviction was obtained? If a schizophrenic proffers a defense of not guilty by reason of insanity, and this plea is rejected, not because the defendant is a malingerer but because their illness doesn't satisfy the strict legal boundaries of insanity for the purposes of criminal law, does their crime count as one committed by the mentally ill, or—reflecting the court's view—is this another crime for the sane criminal pile? If a criminal is diagnosed only after they enter the prison system and are, perhaps for the first time in their life, able to see a psychiatrist at all: Are the statistics updated? Are we sure that they ought to be? After all, it may have been the extraordinary stress of prison itself that brought on the first episode.

We are told that the mad are far more likely to be the victims of a violent crime than the perpetrator, and it's true, but only because the mad are many times more likely than the average person to be the victim of an assault. The mad terrorize. The mad are terrorized. Perhaps we are not the inexplicable object of police brutality, but the targets of an undeclared and righteous war on terror. How dangerous are the mad? What liberties may the state take to contain us?

• • •

During the 2020 presidential campaign season, I fantasized a great deal about a man-in-the-street interview series I wished somebody would make. In this series, the interviewer would ask Elizabeth Warren voters why they supported her. When the subjects invariably said, *because she has a plan for that!* the interviewer would ask the voter to describe any of those plans in any detail beyond their headline promises.

I never meant this as a dig on Warren herself, who presumably knew the details of her own platform, but as a dig on the type of voter who is enthusiastic about the idea of detailed plans but uninterested in the details themselves. It's a strange phenomenon, because the selling point for these voters—the existence of specific, complex details—is transformed, in practice, into its opposite: a general claim to competence, in which the particulars are not the point but merely the evidence for the abstract claim. It's similar to the central premise of the 2016 Clinton campaign: vote for the person with a broad ability to get things done. Don't worry terribly much about what precisely will get done, about what this competence will competently do. I call this tendency the Specifics General.

Homework-energy presidential campaigns are not the only place where calls for particulars become vague. Consider the common rejoinder to "cancel culture" in which critics describe a situation, person, or people in general as "complex." It's certainly true that almost all situations, or people, are more complex than their old racist tweet, and it is even true that in many cases, reckoning with this complexity would force us to make more humane, or just accurate, judgments than we ordinarily see in those cases. But "examining the complexity" requires precisely that: looking, often for a long time, at an intricate set of facts, checking the validity of those facts, weighing them against context and history and contrary evidence. It requires being uncertain, and making difficult decisions about what to do with imperfect knowledge, and even what to do with the knowledge we can be sure of. It creates discomfort, ambiguity, even ambivalence. You do sometimes see this happen with "calls for complexity," but quite a lot of the time, the people calling for complexity are a lot like the people who were terribly excited about Warren's plan buffet: a general desire for nuance does not come with an actual willingness to examine those nuances. The call for complexity is a vague hand wave toward the idea of complexity in general. In those cases, it's rightly called a kind of bullshit dodge.

Because Western psychiatrists are forbidden from classing mainstream religious beliefs as delusional or psychotic thoughts. I am a Roman Catholic. I am thinking of a Sunday in ordinary time, with a gospel reading from the Sermon on the Mount. I am thinking of the best-known passage of that sermon:

> "You have heard that it was said, 'Eye for eye, and tooth for tooth.' But I tell you, do not resist an evil person. If anyone slaps you on the right cheek, turn to them the other cheek also. And if anyone wants to sue you and take your shirt, hand over your coat as well. If anyone forces you to go one mile, go with them two miles. Give to the one who asks you, and do not turn away from the one who wants to borrow from you.

*"You have heard that it was said, 'Love your neighbor and hate your enemy.'
But I tell you, love your enemies and pray for those who persecute you, that
you may be children of your Father in heaven. He causes his sun to rise on
the evil and the good, and sends rain on the righteous and the unrighteous.
If you love those who love you, what reward will you get? Are not even the
tax collectors doing that? And if you greet only your own people, what are
you doing more than others? Do not even pagans do that?"*

I have never in my life heard a homily that takes this proposi-
tion seriously. Instead, the parish hears the common paraphrase: It is
Christian to forgive your enemies. Turn the other cheek. Often, this
is explicated to the parish in terms of small-bore problems—*end that
feud with your brother-in-law; be nicer to your awful coworker; life's too
short!*—and if the difficulty is touched on at all, it is only touched on
in general. *This is a difficult teaching*, a priest or a deacon might say.

Catholics everywhere acknowledge, in general, the profundity and
difficulty of the Sermon on the Mount. But very few are willing to
deal in the specifics: a command to allow yourself to be destroyed and
humiliated. Being told, specifically, that it is not enough to be good
to your family and friends. No sermon that I have ever heard on this
passage says, specifically, what it plainly says: if somebody murders your
child in front of you, enjoyed it, and isn't sorry, you are commanded
by God to love that person, and pray for them, and offer up your other
child, if they ask for them. It is better to let yourself be brutalized than
to fight back. That is what Christ is saying here. But it is treated, so
often, as yet another opportunity for the specifics general, an enthusiasm for the gloss and a refusal to look directly at the details. What
would they tell us? Should the mad allow themselves to be destroyed?
If the lobotomist takes one hemisphere of your failing brain, turn to
him the other also?

We see the specifics general in the politics of madness, too. Whenever mental illness enters the American discourse, it is accompanied by
calls for complexity. Mental illness is a complex problem. Its patients

have complex needs. The relationship between the mad and the police, the mad and the prisons, is incredibly complicated; the relationship between insanity and homelessness and joblessness is complicated, too. Institutions were violent, abusive places. Abolishing them has left hundreds of thousands of crazy people helpless on the streets. The best treatment for lunatics is to get them to take their medication, but many insane people refuse medication. It is important for the dignity of the insane to have agency in their own life, but making them accept care will often take away their agency. Medication comes with many side effects. Some of these side effects are worse, on a day-to-day basis, than the symptoms of untreated insanity. It may take a long time to find the right balance of pills and therapies for any given patient, if that balance can be found at all. Medication and hospital care and therapy are expensive. The insane are capable of working sometimes, but not all of us and not reliably. A society exclusively of the insane could not pay for its own care. What is to be done?

Nobody will say. We hear endlessly about the *complexity*. We hear about the *pain of families* and the *failure of communities*. When the mad are mentioned at all in political life, it is in an endless stream of *acknowledgments*, the endless galas and marches and panels, the politicians who *see us* and *care for us*, who promise to *center* us in special ceremonies, but we hear very little in the way of any program. What program could suffice? Even that question is too far down the road. *Sorry, we couldn't win the election! Sorry, we couldn't get the bill passed! Sorry, we don't really want to pursue any kind of health care system; have fun running around all day trying to find medication you can afford. Really sorry about that! But listen, don't worry, I've got something even better. You want to be centered, right? I'm going to center the hell out of you. Every year, in a special televised ceremony in the Rose Garden, I'm gonna read the name of every schizophrenic and manic-depressive and poor sad-sack brain-broken son of a bitch murdered by the police in the last year. I'm going to read them slow and solemn, as serious as anything you've ever heard. And if you're really lucky—and at the rate things are going, you will be—then one day, when you aren't able to get your meds, and you aren't able to get to the hospital, and you kill yourself, or get killed by a cop, or get lost in a blizzard and lay down and freeze somewhere in the empty heartless Midwest, then you can look down as you float up to heaven, and spot the Rose Garden from way up there in the clouds, and see me at that podium once again, affirming that your thing is the only thing, by reading your sad dead name out, too.*

I sat down to write this essay with a one-line summary of my intentions—some unifying thoughts re: a way forward for confronting not just the politeness and stigma and respectability issues, but the real hungry, hard, and violent political situation of the insane—but I have nothing new. I find myself like so many of the desperate, impotently fantasizing about the cheap satisfaction of a terrorist's revenge. Occupy the odd federal building, wave the odd gun around, and demand—not ask, demand—not nicer language, or more rigorous critiques, but an unlimited supply of free antipsychotics and an easier time obtaining disability benefits. Free medicine, free housing, good jobs. Just don't call the housing—the specialized housing for the mad—an institution. Found a new NAMI based on that. Make John Hinckley Jr. the president. He was an activist. He had teeth. They let him out a few years ago; he's free.

• • •

In *Unspeakable Conversations*, Harriet McBryde Johnson recounts an invitation to debate the philosopher Peter Singer at Princeton. Singer is an advocate of selective infanticide, the effort to purge the human race of lives too crippled to be worth living at all. Johnson is an attorney and disability rights activist; because of a neuromuscular illness, she relies on a motor wheelchair and a bedpan and an attendant to live. Singer would like to debate Johnson in front of his undergraduate lecture. *He insists he doesn't want to kill me,* Johnson writes. *He simply thinks it would have been better, all things considered, to have given my parents the option of killing the baby I once was, and to let other parents kill similar babies as they come along and thereby avoid the suffering that comes with lives like mine.*

The essay revolves around the unexpected ways that Singer and Johnson relate to one another. He is exceptionally polite, friendly, even helpful, without embarrassing Johnson. She likes him, a bit, and goes to Princeton despite the approbation of her activist community, who feel it is a betrayal for Johnson to legitimize Singer by debating him at all. When I read it, I can't help giving the same answers to Johnson's allies as Johnson gives Singer: no matter what we might prefer, no matter the outcome of any debate, we both exist. But Johnson goes further than recognizing the reality of a world inhabited by the disabled. She accepts Singer's premise that lives must be proved worth living and argues, with him and with the reader, for the undeniable reality of disabled lives well lived.

This is common enough among the crippled, physically and mentally alike. *Although I would joyfully accept a cure if it were offered me, I do not need a cure and I do not regret having become ill,* writes the disability scholar Susan Wendell. *Disabled lives have value in themselves. They create different ways of being that give valuable perspectives on life and the world, different ways of being human.* I admire this kind of defiance, but I don't share it. I would give almost anything to be cured. I regret going mad, if one can regret acts of God.

I agree with Singer. It would be better if people like me weren't born at all. That's the rational position. But must we be rational? I want to live. I have an irrational desire to live, to go on living. I am irrationally happy I was born. Those are my politics. I want to go on living, even mad and shamed. Even if the medicine stops working, even when I'm delirious, crippled, and confused, even when I'm in danger, even when I'm dangerous, I want to live.

Art Therapy

Virginia Woolf found that her frequent bouts of debilitating illness were *partly mystical. How shall I express it? . . . Something happens in my mind.* She preferred poetry to prose when she was sick and could do without sympathy, too. *We do not know our own souls, let alone the souls of others,* she wrote. *Human beings do not go hand in hand the whole stretch of the way. There is a virgin forest in each; a snowfield where even the print of birds' feet is unknown. Here we go alone, and like it better so. Always to have sympathy, always to be accompanied, always to be understood would be intolerable.*

In 1941, Woolf drowned herself in River Ouse at Lewes. The precise nature of her illness remains unknown. She sought an explanation all her life and never got one. She suffered physical symptoms—exhaustion, fainting, difficulty moving and breathing—but she reported hearing voices, too. *I have fought against it, but I can't any longer,* she wrote to her sister. She told her husband, Leonard, that she was *going mad again.* In her suicide note she told him: *I shan't recover this time.*

...

I've been thinking lately about Kanye West. His reputation has suffered the past few years, in part because his most recent albums are among his worst, but mainly because he is unstable. How crazy is Kanye? Is he on medication right now? How much of his behavior can be attributed to his manic depression, and how much to his poor personality? Does his madness explain his stranger moves, or is it an excuse? Is he *brave*— like Carrie Fisher was *brave*, or David Harbour is *brave*—for *opening up* about his *mental illness*—or do his antics leave him in the company of Mel Gibson and Brian Wilson, those morally suspect and off-putting "troubled geniuses" who are rapidly going out of style? Pete Davidson gets up on SNL and says, *One crazy person to another, being mentally ill is not an excuse to act like a jackass*, and I wonder if what Pete means is, *If you use this excuse, they might not let me use it anymore*. Pete has a borderline personality disorder, and it will never, ever not come up in a profile. Kanye West's madness is a staple of his coverage, too, but as he descends further and further into ignominy—as his marriage collapses and his tweets become more dire, as he books more appearances on Tucker Carlson and lashes out more frequently and more aggressively against his enemies in the liberal intellectual class, as he descends into the paranoia and career-ruining hinterlands of anti-Semitic conspiracy theories—we are told over and over that Kanye's madness is unrelated to his behavior. He's just an increasingly unstable, erratic, and grandiose man acting out in public who happens to have a mood disorder characterized in part by erratic, grandiose, and offensive behavior. It's just a coincidence. To say otherwise is *stigmatizing*. It's giving him an *excuse*.

West is sometimes taken to be insulated from the consequences of insanity by his celebrity and wealth, but wealth and celebrity are not conducive to recovery. The truth of Kanye's talents make it hard to combat grandiose delusions. As he says, he really is a *musical genius*. The money exacerbates manic possibilities: when he wants to act out, he can really act out. The fame is even more dangerous. When ordinary manic patients demand to see the president—they've got some great ideas he really needs to hear—nobody takes them to the White House. But Kanye West really is as powerful as the manic patient believes himself to be. He can go to the White House. He can tell the president that he isn't bipolar at all—he was just sleep deprived—and then spend an hour sharing his great ideas for the country. He can run for president himself. The papers will take him seriously.

Cultural critics love mentally ill celebrities, love to celebrate them, but they don't want celebrities with any of the troubling symptoms of mental illness. Depressives are ideal; they suffer quietly. The best madness is pure *pathos*, something to overcome but nothing more. Kanye engenders no such sympathy. He provokes backlash from manic-depressives, too. *He's so embarrassing,* they say. Or worse: *I worry sometimes that's how bad it could be for me.* But how well it could be going for so many of us! To just be rich and successful and famous and controversial; to be down but never out. To have a job and a house and friends and children. So many lunatics could do worse, are doing worse, than Kanye West.

Kanye, stop embarrassing us! But that's what madness does.

• • •

I didn't write about madness for a long time. I hated the idea of being a *Mad Artist,* even more the idea of writing about madness itself. When I wrote about my own case, if I wrote about it at all, I was elliptical: an essay on the hypochondria and hallucinatory terror that beset me in my early twenties; an essay on my time in the wilderness, characterized as drug rehab; an essay on Freud and guilt, without any particular explanation of my own interest. Mainly I wrote about anything else. I wanted so badly to have my sanity remain unquestioned that for years and years when I melted down, I refused to explain why, no matter how damaging the consequences. I would have rather been thought of as wicked than sick.

In the years following my diagnosis, personal essays were in vogue. So was the language of the clinic. The *personal essay about mental health* was doubly popular, but tedious. I rolled my eyes at author after author confessing to this or that psychiatric difficulty, detailing their *struggle* like notes for a seminar. They all seemed very cloying. So many read as a gambit for being called brave—*I am so afraid to be telling you this!* they said, and I thought, *So why are you?*

But here I am. I have been desperate for a long time not to be somebody who is *about* insanity, to be something other than *the madness guy*. But that was just another way of imagining *the illness* as some possessing ghost, rather than me, as much of me as my hands or hair or eyes. What else is there but this? I set out to write my first essay about being mad after I had been taking medication for four years. I felt, for perhaps the first time, that I had attained sufficient distance from my diagnosis to speak about it as something that *had happened* to me, rather than as something that was *happening*. But I was wrong.

• • •

In the sixteenth-century poem *Orlando Furioso*, Charlemagne's great paladin goes mad when he sees his lover run away with another man. He rampages across the Western world in a murderous rage. Another knight, Astolfo, commissions a flaming chariot and rides it to the moon, where he finds Orlando's sanity. He bottles it up and returns to Earth. When Orlando inhales from the bottle, he is cured.

In the nineteenth-century poem "Maud," Alfred, Lord Tennyson's hero cures herself of madness. *It is time, O passionate heart and morbid eye/That old hysterical mock-disease should die.* It's as easy as that. Two lines.

In the twenty-first-century television show, *The Leftovers*, the old sheriff Kevin Garvey Sr. sees two percent of the world's population disappear, and he goes mad. He is committed to a lunatic asylum, but he escapes and rampages across Australia in search of a ritual song to save the world. He does not find the song or save the world and is last seen sitting on a roof with his son after the great flood turns out to be a brief night of heavy rain. He was cured, he said, when he simply agreed to do what the voices told him to.

• • •

The mad have long suffered in American media from a *problem of representation*. A study says that 38 percent of characters with mental health conditions are disparaged by other characters on TV; in film, it's nearly half. *The erroneous belief that individuals with mental health conditions are largely "dangerous" to society is one that is being reinforced in media depictions*, the study says. I have been hearing of this *representation problem* my whole life. What I have seen, for my whole life, are books and films and TV shows in which characters discuss this problem. In small press masterpieces and low-brow movies, in primetime dramas and daytime made-for-TV films, I am always hearing what a shame it is how all the other movies and books and TV shows are disparaging the *mentally ill*.

The first time I really wrote about madness, I wrote about someone else. I began writing letters to a schizophrenic murderer who had been imprisoned for many years. I wanted to write about him, to go to California and interview him if I could. But I'd encountered a dilemma as I began to write. The man was not on medication; while his condition had stabilized some over the years, his letters were ridiculous, unfocused, written in awkward grammar, irregular casing and punctuation, accompanied by weird drawings. I worried that paraphrasing or "translating" them might be patronizing, but that if I simply let him speak for himself without proper context, he'd come off as a joke, exploited by an opportunistic writer. I asked a group of other writers for ideas about how I could avoid these traps while maintaining the integrity of the piece.

Many had good suggestions, but one of them was more concerned with my project in general. *I hope you're writing the man and not the disease*, she said, *because there's a lot of stigma around mentally ill people. I don't know if you know this but people with schizophrenia can lead perfectly normal lives, and they're more likely to be murdered than to murder someone else.* I didn't say much. *Thanks* and *Yeah, I know that, but still . . .*

In the days that followed I found myself returning to the exchange in my head. I got angry sometimes. I fantasized about saying, *Yeah, I agree there's a lot of stigma out there.* I fantasized about saying, *For example, there are all these well-intentioned humanities graduates who think we should be more sensitive to the poor, stigmatized schizophrenics, who are so exploited by writers, and by art, these defenseless souls, who are so maligned, and so pitiable, that they could never, for example, turn up largely functional in a room full of writers, asking you for advice.*

Some weeks later, I sat down with an older, far more successful writer to ask for his advice. In the course of the conversation, he told me that he'd coached a bipolar teenager on a basketball team. One day, the teen had started yelling about how they shouldn't bother dribbling the ball and instead just throw it down the court on every rebound. Then, he took off all his clothing piece by piece. Later, he'd gone to jail for a while, then gotten out, then assaulted somebody, and the writer wasn't sure where he was now. And then I thought that we do have a *representation problem.* You could never put that teenager on TV or let him write about what going mad had felt like. It might provoke more stigma. The mad have got to be respectable these days.

•••

In his *Mirror Poems,* John Lydgate says of the coming apocalypse that men shall run about like drunks, deadly pale and devoid of blood, unable to speak to one another, *as witless people of reason and of mind* and mad.

In *The Book of the Knight of La Tour-Landry,* religious pilgrims gather in a hermit's chapel, where the hermit prays that they will know their sins. The pilgrims begin to pull apart their clothing; *all they that iangeled beganne to cry like wode folke oute of her mynde.* They are only restored to sanity when they confess in earnest.

Sometime between 1416 and 1420, the English poet Hoccleve went mad. After a few years, he recovered, and in a poem titled "My Compleinte" he details his symptoms: depression, memory loss, bizarre public behavior. But Hoccleve's madness is not the real subject of the poem. *For boug that my wit were hoom come agein*, Hoccleve goes on.

> *Men wolde it not so vndirstonde or take*
> *With me to dele hadden they disdein*
> *A riteous persone I was and forake*
> *Min oolde friendship was al ouershake*
> *No wigt with me list make daliaunce*
> *The world me made a straunge countinaunce*
> *Wich bat myn herte son gan to tourment.*

This may be the first work of literature ever written about the shame of going mad, even after your sanity comes back.

• • •

Because it was the beneficiary of the most potent Streisand Effect in recent memory, I went to see 2019's *Joker* in theaters with a firm sense of what the movie would be. It would be a paean to empty nihilism, as one magazine told me, or a gratuitous mess, as another suggested, not nearly *as edgy as it thinks*. It would glorify white supremacy or toxic masculinity or the Proud Boys; it would be a rallying cry for incels, with a sexless, entitled, and resentful protagonist. It would be the probable cause of a mass shooting—presumably because the Joker would commit one and inspire copycats. In truth, I didn't really believe it would be like any of those things, but I was curious to see what kind of movie had transformed so many good millennial liberals into the very Tipper Gores who had once persuaded their parents not to let them buy Eminem records in the 1990s. Mainly, I expected it to be a superhero movie, which is to say, I expected it to be fine as far as an eight dollar ticket on a cold night in Iowa goes.

Aside from roughly twenty minutes devoted to Batman mythos, the actual plot of *Joker* is as follows: In early 1980s New York City, at the tail end of deinstitutionalization, a schizophrenic man is released from a psychiatric hospital and goes to live with his ailing mother. His mother is also ill, and she had abused the man as a child. The two get along well enough these days. The man has a social worker and access to a variety of psych meds. He has dreams of becoming a standup comic but only manages to hold down a job as a party clown. The man doesn't have many friends. He's awkward and unnerving. While his medication and therapy keeps him stable, he's still off in some difficult-to-describe way and struggles with ordinary social interactions. People on the street peg him as a sickly creep. He's hassled and yelled at and beat up and robbed with the numbing frequency common to the poor and sick. Even his coworkers, who are professional clowns, think he's kind of a freak. He doesn't seem dangerous, but the people around him react the way people always react to people like him: by keeping their distance, because, *I don't know, man, there's something wrong with that guy. He's weird. He makes me nervous.*

Austerity is coming. The city is in the middle of a garbage strike. The subways are filthy. Crime is up. The city makes deep budget cuts, and the man loses his caseworker. He no longer gets therapy; worse, he can no longer afford his medication. Over the course of a few weeks, the man destabilizes. He becomes more awkward, more inappropriate, more *grossly disorganized*, as a doctor might say. He sleeps less, then stops sleeping. His behavior becomes increasingly erratic. He begins acting out and ultimately loses his job. Soon after, his delusions come back. He experiences increasingly consuming bouts of hallucinatory psychosis and oscillates between mania and catatonia. He begins exhibiting strong suicidal ideation. Ultimately, he turns violent. After a brief crime spree, he is arrested and remanded to a forensic psychiatric hospital for the criminally insane. *Joker* may be a superhero movie, but apart from the segments dedicated to reminding the audience that they are learning about the iconic foil of a comic book IP, it is also a true story, one which has played out thousands of times, perhaps tens of thousands of times, in this country over the past fifty years.

I spent a while thinking about why the *Joker* that actually appears on screens was so different from the Joker I'd read about, the one about an incel who commits hate crimes. Part of the reason is obvious: many, many thousands of words, in posts, and articles, and tweets, were written before the release of *Joker* by culture-industry writers who had not actually seen the film. They saw a trailer, which had all the tedious indicators of a self-serious *twisted* comic book movie and guessed what it would be about. But even after the film's release, critics kept after it. Even some of the respectable "mentally ill" weighed in on the movie, mainly to remind everybody that they have Anxiety and Depression and they've never killed anybody. The trouble was that even if the *Joker* was "crazy," this was bad, stigmatizing representation.

The problem of the "representation" of the mad has arisen in an era animated by the increasing expectation that American art be explicitly didactic. We expect our cultural products—from our lyric essay collections to our Marvel movies—to provide moral instruction, and those products are assessed largely by the extent to which they can be mined for morally pleasing content. For the striver set that dominates mainstream cultural criticism, the moral content in question is frequently no deeper than representation and recognizable culture war aesthetics. But worse than any application of this school of criticism is the way in which the didactic style has become the default lens of the liberal-minded American viewer. All movies, all novels, all musicals and poems and television shows are taken to possess an internal, coherent, and deliberate politics. The game of critical consumption is to work out what those politics are, then decide whether they're *good* or *shit*. The mad Joker must "represent" some cultural tendency, and we are meant to figure out whether we are on "his side" (and therefore the movie's "side") or not.

This is made difficult by the fact that Joaquin Phoenix's Joker is an unstable lunatic whose escalating delusions lead him to felonious violence. What are his ideological commitments? In general, mentally unstable people do not possess a coherent ideology. Late in the movie,

Joker goes on an extended, uncomfortable rant about being down-trodden, and how the rich are awful, and how all the people who pissed on him are going to "get what they deserve," and I suppose you can read reactionary resentment into that, or even righteous class-antagonism, and interpret its moral valence accordingly, but you can also see it for what it is: a deranged, aggressive, semi-lucid tirade assembled awkwardly from unsophisticated clichés by a very ill man who has cobbled together a theory of his own unhappiness and fear. He's digested bits of "reasons" from the decaying world around them and vomited them back up in a kind of pathetic rage. Do critics imagine that the unstable schizophrenics in our psychiatric hospitals are giving eloquent, nuanced speeches about shame and stigma when they try to articulate their discontent?

When his social worker tells him that the city has cut funding for her department and they won't be able to see each other anymore, Phoenix's Joker asks what he is supposed to do. Where should he get his medication? The social worker tells him that the people in charge don't really give a shit about people like him. *They don't give a shit about people like me, either*, she adds. They didn't. They still don't.

• • •

In *Clans of the Alphane Moon*, Philip K. Dick imagines a world populated by psychiatric patients. They divide themselves into a functional clan system along diagnostic lines. The critic and novelist Sandra Newman called this conceit ridiculous and offensive.

The novel *Zeno's Conscience* is framed as a diary, written by the titular character but published by his psychoanalyst after Zeno stops coming to therapy. The plot has Zeno briefly institutionalized to overcome a cigarette addiction, but there is no evidence that he is mad. Near the middle of the book, he even procures a certificate from a doctor to prove to his ailing father that he is sane. But, the analyst warns readers in his introduction, the book is full of lies.

In Sophocles, the Greek warrior Ajax is denied the armor of the great Achilles. In revenge, he sets out to murder Agamemnon and Menelaus, but Athena intervenes and drives him mad, so he goes and murders the Greek herdsmen and their cattle instead. Ajax recovers, and filled with shame, he impales himself upon his sword.

. . .

Charlotte Brontë's Bertha is the Madwoman in the Attic, the best remembered character in *Jane Eyre*. Afraid of scandal, her husband, Mr. Rochester, does not keep Bertha in an asylum but hides her away at the top of his house where nobody will ever see her. Near the novel's end, Bertha escapes and burns down the house and cripples Mr. Rochester for life.

For a certain kind of enlightened reader, Bertha is the queen lunatic of our struggle against the unjust portrayal of the mad. *The Madwoman in the Attic* is the title of one of the twentieth century's most famous works of feminist literary criticism; one of our most celebrated novelistic critiques of colonial Europe, *Wide Sargasso Sea*, is a heroic reimagining of Bertha's life. Many readers imagine that Bertha is not mad at all, that she represents some martyr for discarded wives, for oppressed women in general. But when Bertha emerges from her attic in Brontë's prose, she appears like a lunatic from a medieval medical textbook. Bertha is neither *beast or human being*, Bronte writes, she has *bloated features* and a *purple face*. Perhaps her arson was a righteous act, but before she lit the fire, she *snatched and growled, like some strange wild animal*.

. . .

If it is still difficult to imagine how the reality of such a dreadful disease could be transformed so preposterously, writes Susan Sontag of the nineteenth- and twentieth-century romanticism of tuberculosis, *it may help to consider our own era's comparable act of distortion, under the pressure of the need to express romantic attitudes about the self . . . In the twentieth century, the repellent, harrowing disease that is made the index of a superior sensitivity, the vehicle of "spiritual" feelings and "critical" discontent, is insanity.* Insanity is *thought to bring consciousness to a state of paroxysmic enlightenment.* It reflects *in the most vehement way the contemporary prestige of irrational or rude (spontaneous) behavior.*

But that was 1978. In a 2018 article on French artist Jean Dubuffet's habit of collecting paintings from lunatic asylums, *The Paris Review* calls *the notion that insanity and art go together* a *harmful myth, perpetuated in part by a desire to justify bad behavior.* In the next paragraph, it reports on several studies of artistry and madness, including one from Johns Hopkins by the psychologist and mad memoirist Kay Redfield Jamison, which found that "distinguished artists" *tend to have depressive illnesses at a rate of about ten to thirty times higher than the population at large.*

Going mad does not make you a creative genius, of course, for the same reason being tall does not make you a basketball player. But *there's no getting around the fact that artists have especially high rates of mood disorders,* the *Review* tells us. They do not explain why they are perpetuating the *harmful myth* that they themselves identified just a moment earlier; they do not tell us why they possess, by their own reckoning, *a desire to justify bad behavior.* The article moves on.

. . .

In *An Unquiet Mind,* Kay Redfield Jamison writes that she believed her book *might provide a somewhat different perspective on a disease that had been well-described by many.* In *The Quiet Room,* Lori Schiller writes that she's *written this book hoping that my story can help others the way that I was helped.* Elyn Saks writes that she is *not someone whose illness consists primarily of having high and low moods.* This is why she chose to write about her schizophrenia. *Many people who suffer from manic depression and depression lead full and rich lives,* she goes on, but *people with thought disorders do not keep a list of famous and successful people who share their problem. They can't, because there is no such list.* But there is now, because Elyn Saks is on it.

In his *Memoirs,* Daniel Paul Schreber writes that *owing to [his] illness, [he] entered into peculiar relations with God.* While he cannot maintain that everything he writes *is irrefutably certain,* he is sure that he has *come infinitely closer to the truth than human beings who have not received divine revelation.* His memoir was written primarily for its religious and scientific significance, he says.

In 1834, the lunatic John Perceval published *A narrative of the treatment experienced by a Gentleman during a state of mental derangement designed to explain the causes and nature of insanity, and to expose the injudicious conduct pursued towards many unfortunate sufferers under that calamity.* He believed his work could reform the entire field of psychiatry and revolutionize the care of the insane. Gregory Bateson, in a twentieth-century introduction to the *Narrative,* called Perceval's *theoretical position . . . midway between that of Freud and William Blake.* Perhaps he was a genius, but he did not change psychiatry like that.

The critic Mary Elene Wood says that the work of the asylum memoir is the work of *narrative repair,* the means by which *identities troubled both by life events and by the traumas of institutionalization* can *claim control of their life stories.*

The question for the patient becomes how to acknowledge the narratable self, how to become a narrator, how to create through language a space for one's self and one's desires in a situation where . . . movement, the body, the self-imagined body are under constant surveillance and management. For Wood, the mad memoir is an act of defiance or subversion against the power of psychiatry, or the power of a stigmatizing public. The act of producing the narration is the point and the point is personal and political, and these two points are probably the same point, in Wood's view. What I always want to ask is: Why do sympathetic critics imagine that the highest ambition of the lunatic memoirist is to give themselves therapy in public?

Is that the point of writing this? *For myself*, as the cliché goes? To change perceptions, to *change the world*? Are these the same thing? We are meant to engage in *narrative repair*. I suppose what I am wondering is why the mad writer is always first and foremost a *political* and *social* object, whose success and merit are measured by the extent to which they advance the presumed political and social interests of the respectable mad? The well-intentioned academic ally encourages the mad memoir to remain in a state of permanent infantile respectability mongering. Maybe that's all that is possible. Maybe this is true of all memoirs now, all reporting now, all fiction now. The author performs self-psychoanalysis under the guise of public art. They think about the world in order to think about themselves, rather than the other way around. They are assessed by the degree to which their self-assessment corresponds to the way the world would like to think about itself, and what it therefore takes to be the only possible truth about what some particular person must be thinking. Every year now, books and films and television shows are met with universal acclaim for being *risky* and for being *brave*. I wonder: Why does the *risk* never fail to pay off? When does this *bravery* ever end in disaster?

Maybe the mad memoir is only a particularly acute case of this contemporary phenomenon, where the metaphorical work of identity-formation and self-actualization slips over the border from the metaphorical to the literal. Among the mad, the endless chain of expectation and counter-expectation, performance and counter-performance, suspicion and condemnation and hedging and adherence to approved scripts—in sum, everything that spoils nearly all writing these days—is only enhanced by the fact that the mad memoirists have spent a lifetime dealing with psychotherapists: We already know how these make-believe sessions go. We know what we're meant to say, what we're meant to believe, what our audience will believe that we believe, what they will believe that we are saying, no matter what we say.

Lately I've noticed myself defaulting to weary, eye-rolling cynicism when confronted with this type of memoir, writes the critic Houman Barekat of what he calls the genre of affliction. They are *literary anti-matter*, often *fragmentary* and too short. *Brevity is key*, he says, *for the diminished attention span of the internet-addled twenty-first century reader.* He is exhausted *from having had to indulge too many twee, insubstantial or only tenuously pertinent vignettes for too little intellectual payoff.* Well, here is a long book, but there is still no payoff to be found. The *affliction* in question is an affliction of the rational mind. What precisely do you expect?

There will be comma splices, and a quote, somewhere, from the personal correspondence of Virginia Woolf, Barekat writes. He knew what to expect.

I do not believe, at any rate, that I am writing this *for myself.* I do not believe that I am writing to *educate* or *enlighten* because this is tedious and impossible. I am not writing to *change* anything. I don't believe that you can write a book so good that it changes the world, even if you want it to, and I won't pretend that I am trying. I began writing and I kept on writing and that's all.

• • •

From his novels, it is easy to imagine that James Joyce was mad. But if madness is inherited, it is likely that his daughter Lucia caught schizophrenia from her mother Nora's line. Nora's sister spent time in a lunatic asylum; James Joyce just wrote effusive books.

Joyce did not believe that his daughter was crazy. *Whatever spark or gift I possess has been transmitted to Lucia and it has kindled a fire in her brain,* he wrote. It was only that she spoke a private language. Joyce even claimed to understand it, *or most of it* at least. He blamed himself for her condition and dedicated a great deal of his income to her treatment. Among the attempted cures endured by Lucia Joyce were hormone therapy, analysis from Carl Jung, and the direct injection of seawater into her blood. In 1941, James Joyce died of an ulcer believed to have been brought on by the stress.

In "A Sketch of the Past," Virginia Woolf recounts the speed with which she wrote her novel *To the Lighthouse*, and how, having written it, she cured herself of her decades-long obsession with her dead mother: *I suppose that I did for myself what psycho-analysts do for their patients.* But *To the Lighthouse* is a novel, not a memoir; they keep it in the fiction section of stores. You can read it and allegedly learn nothing about Virginia Woolf at all.

...

If you have not been subject to an undergraduate philosophy course, a contemporary explanation of the qualia problem goes like this: Imagine a very powerful computer, programmed to recognize the color blue. The computer has been given trillions of examples of blue objects. It has analyzed them and knows the precise light refractions that appear blue to human eyes. It possesses hardware capable of scanning the visible spectrum and recognizing when the light coming off an object is blue. Its scanning abilities work in all lighting and weather conditions; in years of field testing, the computer has never once failed to locate every blue object in a room. But despite this incredible engineering feat, most of us intuit that the computer does not actually see blue like we do. It doesn't have that subjective, sensory experience. There is a what-its-likeness to seeing blue beyond the physical data necessary to apprehend blueness, and this what-its-likeness is the "qualia" of seeing blue.

Instead of seeing *blue*, make the computer experience *psychotic*. This is the trouble with mad memoirs. This is the trouble with all psychological realism, with ordinary memoirs and even fiction. Description only gets you so far. Mimesis, particularly in the extreme of high modernist fiction, was meant to solve this problem, but it falters in the face of madness. It descends inevitably into parody. Literature is meant to help the reader *embody new experiences* but to do that, it must somehow lead the reader to the alien from the familiar. This is difficult to do when the alien is made so strange by the suspension of correspondence, metaphor, and sense. It may not be possible to reproduce madness at all.

It may not even be possible to portray it, except in a passing, external way—enough for the computer to say, *Yes, that's blue.*

An editor tells me that this book may *really help people understand the experience of mental illness.* Is that what I've set out to do here? Am I succeeding? Is it possible to tell you what it's like? Is that why you bought this? One day when I was sixteen or seventeen years old, my life as a sentient animal began to disintegrate and I have spent a long time trying to hold what's left together. That's as simple as I can make it. The most intense symptom of psychosis that you feel on the inside is the absence of anything at all. The falsity of the world, the hollow half-reality of other people, the sea fog enveloping your thoughts. The heavy nothing of a blank mind, occasionally pierced by a terrible, intense fear.

The fallacy of dividing people into sane and insane lies in the assumption that we really do touch other lives, observed the lobotomized historian and grifter Joe Gould.

• • •

Marya Hornbacher writes, *At first it's bliss. It's drunken heady, intoxicating. It swallows the people we were—not particularly wonderful people, but people who did our best, more or less—and spits out the monsters we are becoming. Our friends despise us. We are an epic. Everything is grand, crashing, brilliant, blinding. It's the Golden Age of Hollywood, and we are a legend in our own minds, and no one outside can fail to see that we are headed for hell, and we won't listen, we say they don't understand, we pour more wine, go to the parties, we sparkle, fly all over the country, we're on an adventure, unstoppable, we've found each other and we race through our days like Mr. Toad in his yellow motorcar, with no idea where the brakes are and to hell with it anyway, we are on fire, drunk with something we call love.*

Bassey Ikpi asks, *You know how you can get a song stuck in your head? Imagine hearing that song even in your sleep—waking you up in the middle of the night to ensure you're aware of the lap it's running in your head. Then imagine you have to find out everything you can about that song and its singer. Where it started? Who wrote it? What inspired it? Why? You have to do all of this before there can be quiet in your head, before you can rest, before you can sleep.*

I couldn't sleep or eat for several days, writes Kurt Vonnegut's son Mark. *Then I started hearing voices. Not gauzy, special-effects voices, but actual, real voices coming from outside my head. It's the kind of thing that can't be ignored. When somebody says hello, it's impolite to not say it back. Hi. Hello. Hello?*

There is something to the fact that at the height of psychotic experience, what I remember most is not some *vision* or *belief* or anything like that, but the absence of any single mind capable of entertaining *visions* or *beliefs* at all. What I remember most is an inability to concentrate, a complete inability—beyond anything inspired by stimulation or exhaustion or depression—to focus on any single object without it scattering and getting lost and going under again. The feeling that everything was different, too much and too little, and could not be explained, the certain knowledge that something wonderful or terrible was at hand. This is, of course, completely inexpressible: even this paragraph contains far more focus than the feeling that I am trying to represent.

As is the case with epileptic seizures, schizophrenic breaks are often preceded by an aura, writes Louis Sass. *Klaus Conrad . . . named this preliminary stage Trema, a term of theatrical slang referring to the stage fright an actor feels before the performance begins. At these moments, the patient will be suspicious and restless, often filled with anticipation or dread. Normal emotions like joy and sadness will be absent, the mood veering instead between anxiety and a kind of electric exaltation . . . the person has a sense of having lost contact with things, or of everything having undergone some subtle, all-encompassing change. Reality seems unveiled as never before, and the visual world looks peculiar and eerie—weirdly beautiful, tantalizingly significant, or perhaps horrifying in some insidious but ineffable way.* And the *trema*, already so alien, is only the prologue to the incomprehensible break.

Does this help at all? Do you see blue?

...

Over the course of writing this book, I moved from Iowa to New York City; the COVID-19 pandemic came and went; J. and I got engaged and then got married. The world changed and so did I—my medication, my routine, my motives. My ambitions in this book became obscure, even to me. *What I write today I should not write in a year's time,* Woolf tells us in her memoir. What I wrote a year ago was written for reasons that I can scarcely understand at this time. When I began, I think I told myself that I knew better, that I knew something that other mad writers, other writers on madness didn't know. But like any honest person, the process of writing what I know has shown me that I know very little after all. I am not trying to deal with the *representation problem* of the mad. I am not hoping that *my story can help others.* I have never believed that at all. I cannot tell you what it's like to go mad, not really. I resisted writing about madness for so long because I wanted to dispose of that part of myself, to not be thought of as a sickly, unreliable *patient.* When that became impossible, I decided that while I could not hide my illness, I could contain it, put the matter of my derangement in this box and move on. It was *for myself* after all, but now I don't believe that, either. Authors are not reliable narrators of their own motives, even to themselves. *It is a confessional work that—like many such exercises—confesses something different from what the confessor thinks he is confessing,* observed the critic Janet Malcolm about a different memoir. *[By] making himself into a subject, the autobiographer sets himself up for a betrayal no less profound than that invited by the subject of someone else's writing.*

I believe that I am telling you about a particular way of being in the world, about the way one person was, at one time. That's all. Perhaps that's all any memoir can be. A little squeaking whisper about the way one life seemed to be for a while, obsolete already by the time the ink dries on the page. Woolf calls the narrator of "A Sketch of the Past," that is, herself, *the subject of this memoir.* The subject of this memoir is not anywhere in the world anymore, but he was alive at the precise moment this was written. You want to know what madness feels like.

Why do you believe that I could tell you? I suffer from a condition that makes it difficult for me to be certain about the basic facts of reality. It's like that. Do you see? I can barely see myself at one, two, three, five, and ten year's distance. *I abandon the exhausting pursuit of an old piece of myself,* writes Roland Barthes in his memoir. *I do not say "I am going to describe myself" but "I am writing a text, and I call it [Roland Barthes]."* For Barthes, life did not move toward the integration of a subject into a coherent self. It moved toward disintegration. Madness is only when you disintegrate too fast, so totally that others take notice. Barthes wrote that the memoiristic impulse is pretentious and suicidal. Paul De Man called it *defacement.* There is no such thing as self-knowledge, he says. How do you expect to get someone else's secondhand?

Among the mad, these efforts may even constitute a kind of betrayal. Foucault called madness a kind of silence in the face of reason. Derrida knew what this meant. *The misfortune of the mad,* he wrote, *the interminable misfortune of their silence, is that their best spokesmen are those who betray them best; which is to say that when one attempts to convey their silence itself, one has already passed over to the side of the enemy, the side of order, even if one fights against order from within.*

• • •

It is ironic that the liberal faith in literature as an empathy trainer went mainstream at precisely the same moment that the epistemological limits of empathy became an intense motive for self-flagellation among those same liberals. The whole rhetoric of *lived experience* is about qualia. To be a member of a group is to have the subjective mental phenomenological experience of being-a-member-of-that-group, to possess direct access to the what-its-likeness there. While one can describe that experience to others, any resistance to that description, any failure of *empathy*, is not taken to be a failure on the part of the describer, but a failure on the part of the audience. They're taken to be like the computer—perhaps able to grasp what the color blue is in some objective sense, but incapable, ultimately, of actually seeing it. In such cases, the audience is expected to defer their own judgment and accept what they are told.

Something about this way of looking at the world is intuitively appealing. But all people are ultimately idiosyncratic in their lives. Nobody, having lived anybody else's life, can grasp anybody else's qualia at all. I am not the first to point this out. What then can I tell you about madness? Nothing. What can you understand? Even less.

You may believe that I want to tell you that the hermetic seal of *lived experience* is silly, that we must resist it, that otherwise literature and memoir will be impossible. But instead, I am going to tell you that I love it. I have so many points of conflict with my doctors, with doctors in general, with researchers, with cultural critics writing on *mental illness*, with the poor anxious strivers pretending they are insane. Now I can just say that these disagreements stem from those critics' failure to bow to my superior and specific epistemological access to the lived experience of being mad. I am so uncertain what I am doing here, why I am writing this, what I am trying to tell you. Now I can just say: shut up and listen to what you're being told. A therapist suggests to me that this is a dangerous attitude to take if you're prone to hallucinatory experience, delusion, grandiosity, and paranoia. But fuck him. What does he know? Not me.

The phenomenon of transference—how we all invent each other according to early blueprints—was Freud's most original and radical discovery, writes Janet Malcolm. *The concept of transference at once destroys faith in personal relations and explains why they are tragic: We cannot know each other. We must grope around for each other through a dense thicket of absent others. We cannot see each other plain. A horrible kind of predestination hovers over each new attachment we form. "Only connect," E. M. Forster proposed. "Only we can't," the psychoanalyst knows.*

The fact remains that getting people right is not what living is all about anyway, counters Philip Roth. *It's getting them wrong that is living, getting them wrong and wrong and wrong and then, on careful reconsideration, getting them wrong again. That's how we know we're alive,* Roth writes, *we're wrong.*

...

The truth is I admire anyone who believes that the point of writing is to let the reader *walk a mile in somebody else's shoes*, anyone who thinks that a story can put your head into another person's body. Doctors are afraid to even try it. In the early twenty-first century, an Italian physician conducted a series of controversial experiments on the possibility of a full head transplant. At first, his theories showed promise. With a team of doctors, he had severed the spinal cords of fifteen rats and reattached them to one another; all but one, he said, survived an astonishing thirty days. Now he wanted to try his procedure on a human subject. He found a volunteer from Siberia, a man who suffered from spinal muscular atrophy and who was willing to die for the possibility of having his head attached to a working body. The proposed surgery was extremely complex. It required an enormous team of doctors operating with total precision and employing a number of purely theoretical techniques.

A newspaper article about the plan quoted several doctors who said that the proposed procedure was reckless. The Italian would not be able to pull it off. One quoted physician agreed with the assessment of his peers, but added a wrinkle: he was more worried, he told the paper, about what might happen if the surgery *was* successful. Proteins, hormones, enzymes, and other chemicals produced by our organs interact with our brains in complex ways, he said, ways that we do not fully understand. If a brain woke up and found itself bathed in the bile and blood of a new body, it might induce a form of madness hitherto unknown in human life.

But It Is Embarrassing

Esmé Wang is embarrassed by a schizophrenic on the bus. *Because I am capable of achievement, I find myself uncomfortable around those who are visibly psychotic and audibly disorganized,* she writes in *The Collected Schizophrenias. I don't want to be lumped in with the screaming man on the bus, or the woman who claims she's the reincarnation of God.* Wang has tricks to keep herself lumped out. She is an award-winning novelist and essayist. She dresses fashionably and deliberately. She is available for speaking engagements, and she speaks with ordinary coherence. She is, as she calls it, *high-functioning,* and she does not want to be confused with those who aren't.

Wang is ambivalent. *I'm uncomfortably uncomfortable because I know that these are my people in ways that those who have never experienced psychosis can't understand, and to shun them is to shun a large part of myself.* Still, she has succeeded in shunning them, qualms or not, and seems to believe that her respectable presentation—her ability to *pass*—is key to her success. She does not seem to consider whether it is in fact the other way around, whether her status as a graduate of Stanford and of the University of Michigan, her status as a successful writer—that is, her status as a producer of marketable commodities—is what allows her to maintain her respectability. The man screaming on the bus may be the graduate of an elite college, too, but it is far more likely that he is the victim of a conservatorship and the graduate of nowhere. If he stopped screaming, it is not likely that somebody would offer him a book deal as a reward.

Like Wang, I am embarrassed by the screaming man on the bus and by the woman who believes she is the risen God. I am embarrassed by the middle-aged man who cannot remember to take his medication but can remember to scream whenever his mother doesn't buy him beer. I am embarrassed, still, by the patient in the wilderness who was arrested after knocking out his own grandmother, and by how I thought, even then, that this was the kind of story the staff must tell their friends when asked what the patients were like. I know that these are not fair things to be embarrassed by but *I'm uncomfortably uncomfortable because I know that these are my people*. What I mean is that it is easier to be embarrassed by other lunatics because I am sure that all of us, even the *high-functioning*, are embarrassed by what an embarrassment we have been, at times, to our schools, our jobs, our friends, and ourselves.

I have tricks for staying *respectable*, too. I have a limited wardrobe but I've spent time on my choices. I can wash myself if I really need to. I have verbal tricks to make pressured speech sound like only a mildly obnoxious *discourse* and self-aware jokes I've memorized to paper over the possibility that I am unaware of whatever I am doing that's aloof or rude or embarrassing at any moment. I know how to disguise the moments when I've lost the words I want; if I hear something, there or not, I'm careful not to comment on it right away. And like Wang, or Schiller or Jamison or Kayen or Saks or any of the others who have produced a book like this in the last generation, I have the privacy and distance afforded by typing in a room. I have the possibility of revision and the intervention of editors. I am speaking to you through several layers of control. This too is a trick, a gambit for respectability.

Almost all mad memoirs are full of vague allusions to ruined relationships and destructive behavior, but the incidents described in any detail tend only toward the strange and sad. They're almost all sympathetic at bottom. It is hard not to believe that one of the most common tricks for keeping yourself *respectable* is concealing the extent to which, even among the high-functioning, many of us are indistinguishable from the man screaming on the bus. *Sometimes, my mind does fracture, leaving me frightened of poison in my tea or corpses in the parking lot,* Wang writes. *But then it reassembles, and I am once again a recognizable self.* This is a statement about the subjectivity of a particular case of madness, but it is a statement about how these books work, too. The trouble for the man on the bus, for the woman lashing out, for the patient screaming obscenities is that they cannot just consign these moments to an elliptical. They cannot reassemble themselves like Wang can—like I can—by the end of the chapter, by the end of the book or the paragraph or the page.

• • •

There was a time when the ambition of the high-functioning lunatic was to pass as completely sane. To be insane was to be the man screaming on the bus; if you could get on, sit down, keep quiet, and get off without incident, then you were not crazy, no matter what medications were required to keep you that way. A diagnosis was best when it never came up at all. That was all I wanted for years, why I stuffed tissues into pill bottles and asked the few friends who knew not to mention it. It is a version of what Wang wants, when she writes that her *sickness is rarely obvious*, that she doesn't have to tell new people in her life unless she wants to. She writes about a guest at a writer's residency and a patron at a *literary party*, both of whom compliment her on her apparent sanity and coherence, and how this is a *backhanded compliment*, a reminder of the acute *shift* which occurs when she discloses. But she also tells us about this in a book with her name on it and *schizophrenia* in the title. And I am talking about it in a book with my name on it and the word *insane* on the cover. Perhaps we both want to appear respectable sometimes, but neither of us is really looking to just pass anymore. Today there are those who cannot pass, and those who can cash in.

Every lunatic who has ever written a memoir has written with the acute understanding that they are speaking to a sane and uncomprehending public, that the goal established by all their antecedents is to intervene and clarify that public's misconceptions. But in the nineteenth century, when some of the first American asylum memoirs captured public interest, the point of intervention was frequently an insistence by the author that they were *not insane at all*, that the asylum was a prison, and that even the real lunatics in there ought not to be kept in such conditions. Nearly a quarter of those early testimonials were published at the author's own expense and often sold for cost. In the twentieth century, particularly after the birth of the anti-stigma and survivors movements, these books tended to clarify points of fact—schizophrenia is not split personality disorder, recovery *is* possible in the aftermath of medication, not all lunatics are criminals—and to tell a sympathetic story of triumph over adversity to a public sincerely divided on these questions. I do not know what impact, if any, the books themselves had on the public mind, but their appearance signals a period of ideological shift, whether as cause or as effect. Whether the *mentally ill* were truly understood or not, whether understanding, even if possible, meant redemption or not, the market of the late twentieth century wanted to believe it all: for a while, every mad memoir was a memoir of *hope*.

By the twenty-first century, then, the success of *awareness raising* and *stigma fighting* by way of *hopeful* memoir was so thorough that today, the cruel and stigmatizing reading public lingers on today only as a vestigial conceit. Contemporary mad memoirs pay lip service to the idea of being feared and hated by their audience, insist that they hope to promote *understanding* instead, but know—as everybody knows—that the audience for these books is now made up almost entirely of well-intentioned liberals who already believe stigma is a crying shame. These books are purchased by readers eager to do some more *understanding* and to imagine that it is other readers who will benefit from the intervention. The corrective and plea are no longer enough to sustain a purpose between scenes of dysfunction and psychiatric sensationalism; we are left to intervene on ourselves. Interior neurosis as an animating narrative force is a common, cloying feature of all American memoir and personal essay writing now. We live in an age of openness! Why am I still ashamed? Or ashamed on somebody else's behalf? Aren't we over that by now? Why am I still so uncomfortable with the screaming man on the bus? Even if he is a reminder of *what could happen to me*, isn't that all right? Shouldn't he be open and unashamed, too? Of course, nobody will be asking him to speak at the next gala for the National Alliance on Mental Illness. All of those hopeful stories did not, at bottom, mean that the typical story had become more hopeful. The first decades of the twenty-first century have seen relentless campaigns against the *embarrassment* and *shame* of madness. To go insane in America now is to be told that going insane is *nothing to be ashamed about*, that shame, while understandable, is a surrender to stigma and fear. But this triumph is only ever possible in contrast. *Don't let the screaming man on the bus define you*, says the anti-shame campaign. *Write your own story!* The man on the bus is still—must still—be there.

The legacy of stigma is after all still essential to the public's fascination with madness. Insanity, particularly at the safe distance of a book or a film, is alluring precisely because of its strange suspension of reason, of morality, of sense. The appeal of the madman still contains the semi-erotic threat of violence, of loss of control, of uncontained lively imagination and suffering and *meaning*. The romance of insanity is that the insane are not *modern* in Max Weber's sense, not bureaucratic and rational and dry. But in a morally paranoid age, that romance must be mediated by respectability. *Understanding* is conditional, particularly in the liberal, *understanding* age, because the sympathy—the pity—is the point. It cannot risk being overwhelmed by the threat or the disgrace. To fight *shame* and *stigma*, or at least to give an already sympathetic audience the thrill of once again being persuaded to extend their sympathy, you cannot yourself be too unsympathetic, shameful, or embarrassing. The man screaming on the bus, the woman fighting with her nurses, the homeless man making vulgar comments to passing pedestrians, the prisoner in Los Angeles County Jail, awaiting a hearing on his competence to stand in his murder trial—these are the subjects of nonfiction by sane authors, but they are not the sorts of lunatics who are fit to testify to their condition. They are too far past the razor's edge, embarrassing precisely because they have something to be embarrassed by. Their very lives promote stigma. The purpose of the campaigns against *stigma* and *shame* is to highlight the *other* lunatics, the ones who are sitting perfectly quiet in their seats, concealing a mind on the verge of that alluring collapse, working to bring you an inspiring story.

All of this is to say that the ambition of the respectable lunatic is no longer concealing madness, but being the right kind of madman, the kind who provides an opportunity for *understanding* and *sympathy* by not being mad in the kind of way that would be too difficult to understand or sympathize with. That's the double trick. *Promoting understanding* is not a political goal, but a goal for the relationship between a particular author and her audience. The respectable lunatic, the member in good standing of the insanity high culture, serves as a container onto which the liberal public can pour its *understanding* because there is nothing but dusty, old, and unfair bigotries to stop them from being so enlightened. It is not a coincidence that over the past thirty years, the plot structure of most lunatic autobiographies has been borrowed from the drug memoir.

The model modern lunatic provides the charm without the curse, the threat without the act, gives you madness without madness, at least by the time it reaches you. *Don't be embarrassed* means *don't embarrass us.* It means, be insane but don't be crazy. It means feeling uncomfortable like I do, like Wang does, like all of the high-functioning insane do, with the screaming man on the bus, not because we might be tarred by associated stigma and sentenced to marginalization for his crimes but because we are all one missed week of medication, one bad impression, one *crazy* act away from sitting next to him, cast out of the bright proud halo of the high-functioning, banned from the ranks of the respectable and sent back to the obscure silent true condition of the mad.

The decision to write an autobiography is never as brave as it seems, particularly in an age where nothing self-conscious can be unforgivable, the scholar Roger Rosenblatt explains. *Indeed, the only autobiographies we ever tear apart are those that appear to be hiding something.* But all of us are hiding something. The difference between memoirs is only whether or not they are willing to tell you what they're hiding, and how artfully they hide it.

• • •

I was embarrassed in class when all the sound in the seminar began to converge and in the middle of someone else's comment I said *PLEASE BE QUIET,* then *sorry,* then didn't explain.

I was embarrassed on a date several years ago when after twenty minutes of sitting at a crowded bar, we finally got our drinks, and I said, *I don't know about this place, sorry,* and then I walked out to get away from the sticky residue of every eyeball in the place.

I was embarrassed when strangers found me, lost and crying on a street corner in the desert in California. When E. and I went to Montreal, and I refused to speak to anyone at a party. I was embarrassed when I yelled and stormed out and stayed mad until the next day. I was on lithium, but it barely worked, and I was still too embarrassed to tell E. that I took it, so I ruined the trip with no better excuse than I'm a jerk. I was embarrassed by how fat the lithium was making me.

I was embarrassed every time a friend of a friend or a girlfriend's friend or a stranger saw me acting out and thought *what a fucking jerk* and embarrassed that I'd embarrassed whoever I was with. I am embarrassed when I show up to plans and smell bad and can't look anyone in the eye. I am embarrassed when J. tells a joke and I don't get it. I think she's being literal and start to cry before she says, *I'm joking.* I stay in bed for hours, trying to figure out who convinced her to turn on me so suddenly. I am embarrassed when I remember a time when I was not so sensitive. I am embarrassed when I realized that I got lost when

I was a teenager and woke up as an adult and was sure that I missed things—rules and manners and graces—in between, but I am over thirty now and it is embarrassing to ask.

Two years after I began Seroquel, I noticed stiffness in my legs. I have written about this already. A few days later, I started feeling twitchy, like I had had too much caffeine. A few days after that, my left arm started acting up. At first, I was just having trouble keeping it still but then it began to move and shake, my fist began to clench and unclench at random, my fingers wiggled on their own, sometimes for hours at a time. Even when my hand calmed down, it shook.

I panicked. I went to Chicago for a weekend and went off meds cold turkey and spent two nights shaking and sweating, chilled and too hot and throwing up. I called my doctor and went to see him the next week. I'd developed a tremor, which is an unusual but not terribly rare side effect of my antipsychotic medication. My case wasn't as bad as it could be; it is not the similar but far more stubborn condition called tardive dyskinesia, which is far more difficult to suppress. I do not believe "your medication is interfering with the ordinary function of your dopamine system" is a fact for which I bear moral responsibility, but I didn't go back to class until my arm went back to normal. I didn't want people to see me like that.

Embarrassment occupies a strange position in the world of lunatic respectability. It is meant to be rejected, which means it must exist. The activist line is that no lunatic *ought to feel embarrassed* by their illness, but in practice this means that they ought to maintain a keen awareness of embarrassments so that they may be named and rejected with great public ceremony. You cannot declare that you *refuse to be embarrassed by the time I acted out and ruined the party* unless the memory of the party and your part in ruining it remains on file, dutifully tracked and recorded. I am embarrassed by many things, but it seems to me that it is not up to me to decide that I *refuse* to feel what I already do. I am telling you about it because I am expected to.

It is embarrassing to be ignorant, to accidentally offend, to misread other people, to be told after the fact that somebody has had to apologize for me, which happened to me a lot and still does. The activist rhetoric around embarrassment is premised on a conflation of embarrassment with guilt. Every time I am told that I shouldn't be embarrassed by the consequences of my illness, what I am actually being told is that being ill is not my fault. I didn't choose it. The symptoms, particularly before medication, are not my responsibility. So, the reasoning goes, I shouldn't be any more embarrassed by it than I would be about a physical disability resulting from a birth defect, or about an unattractive facial feature, or about farting loudly right after calling my tenth grade teacher "mom." But what does humiliation have to do with culpability? Transgression and moral failure can and often do embarrass those of us with a working conscience, but they're hardly the *only* category of thing that can cause embarrassment. I am embarrassed to fart in public, to call my teacher "mom."

The simultaneous embrace and refusal of embarrassment is a trick to walk the line between the allure and safety of the mad subject. It provides the veneer of disrepute while risking nothing. It is a variation on the most tiresome trick in modern writing: the Unlikeable Narrator, who posits a judgmental audience but knows the true audience likes them that way precisely because they like the flattery of being told they're not like those other narrow-minded readers. The Unlikeable Narrator who is never on the wrong side of sympathy, who is terrified of actually being disliked. The Unlikeable Narrator who understands keenly that embarrassment can be turned to advantage because embarrassment—its recitation, its acceptance, its rejection—is a placebo for shame, and shame is embarrassment that is not so easily refused, because it is embarrassment justified by guilt.

• • •

I am ashamed of many things.

I am ashamed of the time I became so convinced that an old friend from Los Angeles was stalking me (I had no evidence) that I had a friend in Chicago call them and tell them I was dead.

I am ashamed of the time I met a friend at their hotel in Los Angeles and, upon being told that I would have to leave my shoes in a locker in the lobby and change into some kind of robe, decided I had walked into a trap, stormed out, and sent dozens of text messages asking what kind of shitty, selfish friend would try to trick me like that. We didn't speak for a year.

I am ashamed of everything I stole—cash, pills, a razor blade, a credit card—from friends who very easily caught me and who could not understand why I insisted I was innocent. I am ashamed that this mattered less to me than asking myself why, if everything was fine, I kept doing this kind of thing.

I am ashamed of the thousands of angry and conspiratorial messages I have sent. I am ashamed of every time I melted down and insulted friends and colleagues and strangers, and I am ashamed that, unable to accept their pain, wrote off their protests as small-minded persecution. I am ashamed of the many times I didn't go to work, or didn't do my job, or embarrassed people that I worked with, only to say, in one way or another, no, actually, it embarrasses me to have to work with people like you. I am ashamed of the times—two times—that in the immediate aftermath of suicide attempts, I found the person I wanted to hurt the most and told them it was their fault.

I am ashamed of all the times I disappeared or stole or lied or cheated; I am ashamed by the six years that passed between the first time a girlfriend suggested I might need psychiatric help and the day I got it, and I am ashamed that even then, I only got it at the insistence of a doctor. I am ashamed of the girlfriends and friends who I emotionally terrorized, who sat bewildered while I paced and yelled and called them stupid or cowardly or weak or treacherous, while I drove away, telling them I might not be coming back. I am ashamed of the time I went out to my car and a woman stood in front of it and said, *Don't go*, and I said, *If you don't move I will just drive over you*, and I meant it.

I am ashamed of the time when I was seventeen years old and punched my best friend in the face. He wouldn't stop trying to extract secrets by plugging his hands into my brain. I am ashamed to realize that given that fact, I still think he should just get over it.

I am ashamed of what I've put my parents through. I am ashamed that even after all these years and pills, I can still tell when they're worried that I might freak out. There was a rumor, when I was a teenager, that I'd once menaced my mother with a knife. For years, I thought, *Christ, where do people come up with these things?* But now I realize I do not know if it happened or not, and I am too ashamed to ask, even now.

I am ashamed of the week my psychiatrist put me on a trial run of an SSRI. Those can be dangerous in cases like mine, even small doses can induce mania. I was told to monitor myself for anxiety and irritability, and while I began to feel anxious almost immediately, I also felt good and told myself I was only anxious about the possibility of noticing anxiety. I am ashamed that I let this go on until the Sunday morning when I lost my mind and smashed my head into our bedframe and the rocking cut up our wooden floor and I knocked over a chair and kicked a glass off a table and had to spend a week on tranquilizers until the bad drugs left my system. I am ashamed that I still think J. might poison me, and that sometimes when I hear her footsteps in a room when I'm laying down, or have my eyes closed, or am facing the other way, I brace myself for the knife about to pierce my ribs. I am ashamed that she knows this—and what? I am ashamed that I just expect her to live with it.

I am ashamed that between the ages of sixteen and twenty-two or so, I was not a friend or a boyfriend or a son so much as a blunt force instrument of abuse and pain. It would almost be better if I were just mean. The merely cruel retain a certain logic, a certain terrorizing network of moods and expectations. That kind of monster is predictable; their families and friends and lovers learn to anticipate them and coddle them and walk around the trip wires to survive. I am ashamed that lunacy throws everything into chaos—you cannot even predict when or why you will get lost in conspiracy and rage and fear and come out swinging. What I mean is: I am embarrassed of the fact that people don't like me, that I have always been difficult and made people uncomfortable, even before all of this, and even after. But I am ashamed that I have wanted and needed to be loved better than I was capable of loving anybody, and I am ashamed that I took this to be somebody else's problem for a long time.

A year or so after my initial diagnosis, I spent six months with a therapist in Chicago trying to *accept* the *fact of my illness*, as he said. I measured how fat the lithium was making me by how much my gut pressed into the sides of his narrow wooden chair. It was easy enough to reach acceptance, or at least to persuade me to say, when prompted, *I have a mental illness*, which is not precisely the same thing, but it was much harder to get me to disavow my guilt, which was evidently the second step. This is when I began to think about the difference between embarrassment and shame.

The therapist pushed back. He suggested to me, during one of our last sessions, that the distinction I'd made only refers to the consequences, not the culpability. I couldn't control the outside world, he said, only my own intentions and my own conscience. From that perspective, he asked, what is the moral difference between crying at a party *because you are having an episode* and punching a man in the face *because you are having an episode*? I said, sane people punch people in the face all the time. If I were sane, I might have done the same thing. If I were sane, I might have stolen, too. Might have cheated. Might have treated friends and girlfriends and family like shit. Not everything is attributable to insanity, even among the insane. Maybe, he said, but it would be even dumber to say, well, here is a person behaving erratically, and that person is also in the middle of a manic episode, but those two facts are unrelated. I said, who is to say that they aren't?

I said, even if you're crazy, they'll send you to prison for punching somebody in the face. They just send you to a special prison, a forensic psychiatric hospital, *not guilty by reason of insanity*, which is to say, *not guilty but still locked up for everyone else's good*, I said. Nobody protects society from someone crying at a party.

He said something about how it might be necessary to protect society from somebody, even if that person wasn't strictly *guilty*, in a moral sense, of malicious intent.

I said, well, okay, and I'm sure it's a great reassurance to those people in their bug house cells, refusing to feel ashamed.

The therapist was trying to reassure me, which was his job. Or he was trying to make the best of a bad situation and trying to give me *the cognitive tools to manage negative feelings* because stress and self-recrimination of this kind is associated with lower motivation for therapy, diminished medication compliance, and relapse. Maybe he really believed in this totalizing mens rea theory of moral life. I don't know. When I found out I was moving to Washington, DC, I cancelled my last month of appointments and disappeared without explaining why. I don't know if I'm embarrassed or ashamed by that.

I do know that his excuse is tempting, and consoling, and that perhaps I ought to be ashamed of that temptation, too. Perhaps I ought to be ashamed of all the days when I told myself it would be better to be evil than just sick because I was more embarrassed by how little control I had over my life than I was of all the lives that were a little worse for having run into mine. I am ashamed of how often I have thought of every time I have emerged into the wreckage of the days and weeks after a meltdown and tried to make a list of friends in need of an apology, and then thought: well, maybe it's best to just keep quiet. They'll just insist it's *not my fault* and nothing breeds resentment like feeling morally obliged to reject an apology. It's *not his fault*, I imagine them thinking, and if you hold his behavior against him, you're stigmatizing him, and the poor insane should never be made to feel *embarrassed*. Who wants to be told that in fact, they're the one who should feel ashamed of any lingering hurt?

I think now that what I ought to have told that therapist was that the real poor reasoning was this distinction between the person and the illness. I am the disorder in my senses and my thoughts, as much as I am anything else about myself, as much as I am my hair or my fingers or my eyes. One of the perennial tasks of moral life is learning to accept that deliberate malice is not the only way to bother other people; that there's something childish in saying, *Well, I didn't mean to, so it's not my fault*, when somebody says, *You hurt me.* Only the worst kind of narcissist can't ever stand to feel ashamed. Only the worst kind of childish striver must develop an elaborate justifying framework for explaining why nothing is their fault, and actually it's *brave* to feel good and prideful all the time, and actually, if you say otherwise, you're abusing them. If you set somebody's house on fire amid a psychotic episode, perhaps they'll be more willing to forgive you, but their house is still a smoldering heap. If you are flying a commercial airline and suffer an acute psychotic episode and crash into a mountain trying to escape imaginary UFOs, then several hundred passengers are still dead.

Perhaps unmanageable *feelings of guilt* send some patients off their meds, but if I weren't ashamed, I wouldn't take mine at all. They make me fat and tired. I'm not as quick as I used to be; I can't remember anything; I watch television all day more days than I work each week. I can still write, but it's becoming harder and harder to speak. But the last time I stopped taking my medication, I sent six hundred texts and Facebook messages to a woman I'd met one time in a progression from let's make plans, to why aren't you keeping these plans? To what you're doing is rude and cruel and terrible and you ought to feel ashamed and I hate you, to do you treat everyone like this? What's your fucking problem? Is this on purpose? Did someone put you up to this? What are you trying to get out of me? Who wants you to hurt me? Why are you doing this to me?

I am on my medication because I do not want any more houses to burn down. I do not want to crash the airplane. I stay on my medication because there is something wrong with my brain and interesting questions of moral philosophy do not change the fact that if untreated, I am not fit to be around other people, and I do not want to be alone.

...

When he still studied madness, Foucault wrote that there are *aspects of evil that have such a power of contagion, such a force of scandal that any publicity multiplies them infinitely.* That therefore *only oblivion can suppress them.* But when he turned away from the study of madness and toward the far more lucrative study of sex, Foucault noticed that a strange feature of his new field was that despite insistence that sexuality was repressed, that *nobody was allowed to talk about it,* the reality was that everybody appeared to be talking about it all the time: talking about how they weren't allowed to talk about it, talking about it anyway, everywhere, constantly.

Foucault argued that this apparent contradiction was a result of the transformation of sexuality into discourse, and that both the alleged repression of sex and the more modern incessant public discussions of sex—including the belief that such discussion constituted an effort to "free" sexuality from its alleged repression—were part of a larger system of power by which *a whole web of discourses, special knowledges, analyses, and injunctions* structured human sexuality, shaping not only its morality, but modifying the channels and content of desire itself. The make-believe of vanquished *repression* was a smokescreen for the present order, allowing order to disguise itself as liberation.

Some version of this insight can be applied to nearly every field of public discourse. In workplaces, in universities, in the media, we are surrounded by constant talk of topics that allegedly *cannot be talked about,* by arguments framed as subversive, even liberating, despite operating in the open and with the clear approval of institutional actors. Magazines run editorials arguing that the media refuses to discuss some topic, then it runs variations on the same editorial every week until public interest is exhausted and they've discussed not discussing it to death. Whole conference talks are premised on "the blind spots" of academic conferences: there are more talks concerning the alleged blind spots of the academy than talks defending the academic status quo. How many essays have been written in the past twenty years decrying "elitist" disdain for adults who want to like comic books and video games and Harry Potter, and how many have been written to enforce this phantom cultural hierarchy, attacking those poor philistines who only want to love the most profitable entertainment properties in the world? It is better for business, ultimately, if you believe that seeing every Marvel film as an adult constitutes some kind of radical act.

And so it goes for the insane. Activists insist openly and often that there is a great deal of stigma around open discussion of madness. Multiple corporations openly advertise psychiatric medication and therapy on television, often on the premise that there is a great deal of stigma around the very topic they're discussing. Authors of mad memoirs say the public is afraid of madness, that they don't want to hear about it, don't want to talk about it. There is an enormous and enduring market for books and films and television shows by and about the mad. Critics call attention to stigmatizing depictions of schizophrenics on shows like *Law & Order*. The actual show *Law & Order*, meanwhile, runs a three-episode arc about the schizophrenic sister of an ensemble member, with multiple characters offering reminders about how unfair all the shame and stigma surrounding mental illness continues to be. Even a decade ago, it ran episodes about how it is really pharmaceutical companies, and flop houses, and ignorant district attorneys and cops who make the lives of the mad such hell. Everywhere, we are talking about how nobody wants to talk about madness. Everywhere, the *shame* and *embarrassment* and *stigma* of lunacy is held up like a scarecrow, while every actual discussion of madness insists that it is trying to liberate us from that straw man's repressive gaze.

I have no doubt that many people really do fear madness in their own lives. I know directly that liberal ideals of *understanding* do not hold up very long when it is the actual difficult lunatic in your own life who you are supposed to *understand*. But in the public discourse, madness is no different from sex. We are talking about it all the time and talking about how nobody is allowed to talk about it. So the talking, all the talking, is taken to be an act of resistance no matter how common it becomes, and that frame—the specter of *shame*, the refusal of *embarrassment*—becomes the regime for governing the ways in which it is permissible to be insane. It is permissible to be embarrassed so that you can refuse to feel embarrassed. It is permissible to self-interrogate, to wonder why you *still* feel embarrassed, by yourself, and by other lunatics. Anything is permissible, so long as it takes the harmless difficulties of madness to be *suppressed* and discussion of these difficulties to be an act of enlightened liberation.

This is the line, between the insanity high culture and the bulk of the insane, the line that allows an ambivalent public to congratulate themselves for their compassion toward the marginalized mad without surrendering their desire to punish and ostracize the dangerously insane. The heroes are the ones *opening up*, *speaking out*, and *fighting stigma*. They are not the man screaming on the bus, the woman striking her nurse, the teenager breaking his best friend's tooth in half and blaming innocent people for his failed efforts to commit suicide. Those people are not even the embarrassments. Embarrassment, after all, presumes an audience, and those people do not have a social existence at all.

• • •

Where precisely the line falls between the acceptably embarrassing and the unacceptably shameful has moved throughout the history of the mad memoir. In the 1990s, Kay Jamison can tell us how she lashed out at a lover during a fight, how she said *a few truly awful things* and then went *for his throat in a more literal way*, but she cannot tell us more. The next year, Lori Schiller could confess to drug use and difficult behavior and suggest that she beat a dog to death, but that she has to tell us right away—before we can get too angry—that it was just a hallucination; she didn't really kill the dog. Esmé Wang can tell us in the 2010s that a boyfriend broke up with her because she was *undiagnosed and frightening*, but she cannot tell us what she did that was so scary. *Even back then my instability was clear to most*, she writes. But it isn't clear to us.

We are in the twenties now. Can I go further? When I was nineteen years old, during my first prolonged period of psychosis, I left a scarf in the apartment of a woman I met at a party. She didn't reply to the several messages I sent demanding that she give it back. I decided that she had stolen it for some nefarious end, that getting it back was the only way to avert imminent catastrophe, to correct the improper ordering and prevent the subsequent collapse of the world.

The next weekend, I went to her apartment building. I waited for somebody to go through the front door and followed them into the lobby. I went up the elevator to her unit and pounded on the door. She wasn't home, but a roommate opened the door, and I pushed in. I said, *Something of mine was stolen here. I'm here to get it back.* She didn't say anything. My hair was a mess; I smelled bad. She walked backward toward the far side of the living room. I crossed and went into the bedroom where I'd left my scarf. I emptied the closet looking for it. I left everything on the floor. I found it. When I went back toward the exit, I saw the roommate on the phone and terrified. I don't know if she was calling the police or the girl who'd stolen the scarf from me. I walked out and never heard from either one again.

In my mind, the matter was resolved. But how long did those two wonder if I would come back? Break into their apartment again? Rob them? Hurt them? Did they move? Does the roommate still get nervous at a pounding on the door? Does the girl who I left my scarf with still worry what will happen if a stranger from a party finds out where she lives? Is it embarrassing to admit this? Is it shameful? What I mean is, is this allowed? Do you still like me enough to offer your *understanding*? What about those poor roommates? If you do *understand*, are you denying their pain?

During a particularly manic summer, I cheated on a girlfriend with two of her best friends. Does that change anything? Am I still okay? One night in an apartment in Chicago, I took a knife and sat in the dark living room all night, wondering whether I should stab a roommate who spied on me with hidden cameras whenever I was home alone. Can we live with that? Is it enough that I didn't do it, or is it too much that I would have had I sat there long enough? Where is the line, now, where I become a dangerous, unstable lunatic? Where I cease to be an object of your pity, cease to be a respectable narrator? I have provoked a lot of fights and used to get beat up a lot on purpose, but I have never actually killed someone. Is that enough?

Maybe in a few decades all of this will appear tame. But I am trying to tell you that I am no different from the dozens of mad writers who have come before me. We are all, consciously or not, trying to confess a little more how horseshit this high culture is, how many of us are not afraid of having embarrassments held against us, or of the pain of *internalized stigma*, but of being hated because stigma, like all clichés, grew out of some plain facet of reality. Some lunatics are richer than others. Some lunatics are luckier than others. Some lunatics have sat for a long time with a knife and weighed their options. Some used it. Some didn't. That's all.

Part IV

Appalling Strangeness

I want to sit with the knife a little longer. I can't explain what happened to me without explaining this.

The year I found the alien presence in my throat, before I fled to E.'s and to the doctors and eventually into medication and consciousness and shame, I lived with two men I'd known in college in an apartment on the north side of Chicago. One I barely knew. The other was allegedly my friend; a slight, blond aspiring actor who was the child of well-to-do Minnesota professionals, very soft, but he carried himself as if he were the stern antihero of one of the "adult" comic books he loved. He never liked me. Living together didn't bring us any closer.

He was fastidious. He kept early hours and was prone to little tantrums. He liked to correct errors of cleanliness and order with the condescension of an exasperated stepparent left to babysit not-even-their-son. He was a drunk with a tremendous, hostile ego—notice how badly I want you to dislike him, do I even believe these things?—but he liked to issue corrections in matters of etiquette, too. He knew, at the very least, how everybody *else* ought to behave.

That winter, after we had been living together for about a year and a half, I began to suspect that he was watching me even when he wasn't home. It was something in his eye rolls, his disdain, the quiet malevolence of his corrections—what I'd left out, what I'd put away, a strain here, too much noise there, have I thought about showering today? He was connected to whatever was happening to my health.

Both he and our third roommate worked during the day, leaving me home alone between long walks and panics. One morning, as he went out to work, he told me not to use his bathroom. I had my own bathroom, but I hadn't gone inside of it in weeks. It was true that I'd used his bathroom the night before, sometime around two or three in the morning, but I was sure that he had been asleep and that I'd left no trace. I remembered an incident from two weeks prior, when he'd knocked on my door one evening and told me to wipe down the countertops if I used them to make lunch. He was never home at lunchtime. How did he know when I ate? I realized that there must be cameras in the kitchen and the bathroom. I thought they must have been very small if I hadn't noticed them before. As he went out the door, he told me to try not fucking up the place too badly while he was gone. I understood what he meant. He meant, *I'll be reviewing the footage. Show me that you can behave.*

I tried. For several weeks, I made sure to look respectable for him. Even when I was home by myself, I only went into the common rooms fully dressed. I cleaned up our empty apartment. I vacuumed and one day I even mopped, saying nothing to my roommate but knowing he would see. Nothing pleased him. He barely acknowledged me; when he came home, he went straight to his room. Sometimes at night he banged on the wall between us. I thought: he was probably reviewing the tapes and saw something that made him mad.

He was very protective of his space. The only time I had gone into his room had been the day we'd toured the apartment, when it was not yet his and empty. If I'd ever gone in, he'd see on the tapes, and I didn't want him any angrier than he already was. But one afternoon, I found myself pacing between my bedroom and the kitchen, unable to focus, more and more agitated by the possibility that there were even more cameras that I didn't know about. I decided that I needed to see the monitors. I needed to know precisely where I could be seen. I wanted to know if he was spying on our other roommate, too—maybe we could form some kind of defensive alliance. I thought the monitors must have been on the wall behind the door, in the corners of his room that couldn't be seen from the outside.

I went in. I looked behind the door. There was nothing there. I looked inside the closet. There were only clothes. I looked behind them, then looked in all the drawers and underneath his bed and anywhere else I thought a monitor might be. I found nothing. I dug around in the laundry hamper, and with my hand still rooting through his dirty clothes, I realized how stupid I had been. The cameras were probably digital. They probably transmitted directly to his phone. He was probably watching me right now.

That night, when he came home, he asked me how I was doing. I understood from his tone that he was gauging how well the poison was taking. I hated him, and for the next week, whenever I went into the living room, I put both middle fingers in the air and spun around. I mouthed "fuck you" into the fridge. I used his bathroom whenever he was gone and pissed on the seat on purpose. He never said anything, but he got angrier each week; more distant and hostile and annoyed. We barely spoke. He barely looked at me. I began to wonder if there were cameras in my bedroom, too. I moved my laptop so that the screen would face the wall just in case. I kept my light off and tried to save anything important I had to do until the sun had gone down.

One night I found myself in bed, unable to sleep. I was picking furiously at the lump in my neck, rolling it and squeezing it and I kept thinking how embarrassing it was, how the camera probably had night vision. He could see me, laying naked in my bed. I became intensely aware of my expression, of the speed and labor of my breathing. I tried to lie perfectly still. I tried not to betray what I now knew and after a few minutes, I turned over—playacting as if I were moving in my sleep—to face the nearer wall. I could feel the invisible lens of the camera out there somewhere in the dark. It was pressing somehow, very slightly, on a patch of hair just above my neck. It was intolerable. I thought he might somehow attack me through the lens. What if there was a laser? I could feel something in the dark behind me, ready to attack.

After a few minutes, I got up. I put on the dirty jeans I'd left next to my bed and walked quietly into the kitchen. I stopped and listened for any sound. After I was sure everybody was asleep, I found a short, sharp knife, drying beside the sink. I picked it up and sat down at our little kitchen table to think.

At first, I thought sitting there with the knife would be enough. He'd see the footage the next day and know I mean business, and he'd leave me alone. But then I thought: *This is it*. He'd see the footage and know I mean business—and if I didn't get him first, he'd get me.

. . .

For a long time, the lunatics of the Western world were punished like anybody else for their crimes. In his moral essays *On Anger* and *On Mercy*, Seneca the Younger argued that culpability was irrelevant: the common good demanded that mad murderers be put to death just like the sane ones. If the criminal's insanity was apparent before their crime, then their families should be punished, too. *If anyone be insane*, wrote Plato, *let him not be seen openly in the town, but let his kinsfolk watch over him as best they may, under penalty of a fine*. Some ancients believed that madness itself was divine punishment, but that divine punishment alone was not sufficient justice. Human punishment must be brought to bear as well.

The mad defense came later. We see it for the first time in the *Corpus Juris Civilis*, issued by the Byzantine Emperor Justinian in the sixth century AD. Citing the Roman jurist Modestinus, it allowed only that the madman *is excused by the misfortune of his fate*. For the Byzantines, insanity was punishment enough. In the eighth century, Ecgbert, the bishop of York, decreed that if *a man fall out of his senses and . . . kill someone, let his kinsmen pay for the victims and preserve the slayer against aught else of that kind.* The mad who could not be confined by their families were held in prisons or by the clergy. Some were chained to church pillars; some starved. In 868, a church council decreed that a madman who committed murder and later became sane should be punished for his sins, but if he stayed mad, then there was no point in effecting a punishment that could not be understood by the guilty party. In the West, it was not until the sixteenth century that the mad began to be regarded not as unfortunate souls whose insanity was *punishment enough*, but as people who did not bear moral responsibility at all. Early modern juries, tasked with judging mad defendants, began to carve out exceptions for lunatics who had committed heinous crimes.

This change inspired cynics. Cynics inspired cynicism in turn. Malingerers appeared. Almost at once, special tests were developed to judge the truth and extent of a defendant's alleged madness, tests that have carried forward into the modern legal theories of the West. Then, as now, jurists and juries intuited some special case for madness in moral life. But then, as now, they worried about malingerers, about the nature and degree of the forms of madness, about what was to be done when a crime demanded justice, but nobody could quite be blamed. Originally conceived as an act of rational mercy, the mad defense created an imbalance in the ledger of moral reckoning. What happens to guilt without an object? What happens when a crime cries out for justice, but there is no justice in punishing the criminal? Like us, the medievals wanted it both ways. Like us, they were unable to decide upon the moral status of the mad.

• • •

There was a small digital clock on the oven. It was one thirty in the morning, maybe two o'clock when I sat down. Then it was nearly three. It was dark, but I could see the room in the dim light of a streetlamp seeping through our flimsy curtains. I sat there a long time. My only sense of time came from the phases of my hand wrapped around the handle of the knife. My palm would sweat. The handle would get wet, then slick then sticky. After a while, my hand would go clammy and cold and dry until I brought it near my mouth and warmed it back up with my breath. After a while, I'd sweat again. I didn't know how long these cycles lasted, so they could only tell me that *time was passing* in a very general way.

There is a common belief that outside of mundane motives—greed, jealousy, revenge—one must be insane to commit a violent crime. But there is a difference between the insane and the Insane. The insane criminal has an unreasonable response to a real situation. He believes, for example, that his poor luck in love justifies a homicidal rampage. The Insane criminal has a reasonable response to a delusional situation. He believes, for example, that everybody on the street is an alien looking to harvest his organs. Under such circumstances, opening fire is a reasonable response.

I wish I could tell you that I waited so long because I was considering the possibility that what I was doing was wrong. But I believed that my roommate had planted cameras everywhere to watch me. I believed he knew that I'd begun to know. I believed that he was involved, in some yet unrevealed way, with what was happening to my body. From those beliefs came a reality where it was reasonable to defend myself, to strike before he could strike me.

My hand got wet then dry then wet again. I was having trouble thinking clearly. I had trouble keeping hold of thoughts. I felt weak and blurry, like I was missing something essential. I was trapped on the precipice of recalling what it was. I felt afraid. I felt, in a hazy and leaden way, like I might be dreaming, but that is a common way to feel when you're up in the middle of the night, agitated and exhausted but unable to sleep.

At some point, the knife slipped out of my sweaty hand and made a soft thud on the table. It hadn't fallen more than an inch or two, but even through the tablecloth, the sound of two hard objects meeting echoed off the walls. I froze. I waited for the sound of someone stirring, for cursing, for footsteps, for the creak of an opening door. But nothing came. My hand went cold and dry again, and I carefully picked up the knife.

•••

On March 30, 1981, the paranoid schizophrenic John Hinckley Jr. opened fire with a .22-caliber revolver outside an AFL-CIO conference in Washington, DC. He shot four people, including President Ronald Reagan and press secretary James Brady, who died thirty-three years later from his wounds.

Hinckley never went to prison. At trial, he was found not guilty by reason of insanity and remanded to a psychiatric hospital for care. Outraged congressmen, following the 83 percent of Americans who told pollsters that justice had not been served in the case, responded by passing the Insanity Defense Reform Act, which removed intentionality from the legal definition of madness, and shifted the burden of proof in such cases to the defendant. Now, to be found criminally irresponsible for reason of mental illness or defect, a defendant must affirmatively prove that at the time of their crime, they did not know that there was a difference between right and wrong, a vague and nearly unprovable standard that is not a symptom of any known mental illness. In the United States today, nearly all insanity pleas are reached by pretrial agreement; contested insanity pleas fail almost every time. Even if a defendant manages a Not Guilty by Reason of Insanity, they are often remanded to a specialized "forensic" psychiatric hospital, where they can be held for years in excess of the maximum prison sentence they might have received. There is no party, nor politician, nor serious activist movement in the United States attempting to change these facts.

The reactionary position on the mad defense is straightforward and differs little from that of the ancient Greeks: justice must take precedence over mercy. It is more important to protect society, to make any victims whole, than it is to consider the special moral status of any criminal. Faced with a dilemma between the uncertain culpability of the mad criminal and the broader demands of justice, they seize the second horn. In the decades following Hinckley's assassination attempt, several states have done away with the mad defense entirely. In others, the legal definition of madness has been narrowed so thoroughly that the circumstances under which madness is sufficient to impose an obligation of mercy rarely, if ever, arise.

This may seem like a crude solution, a moral dodge by technicality, but consider John Jonchuck, who in 2015 dodged his way through traffic shouting *You have no free will!* before he threw his daughter Phoebe from a bridge. Consider Orion Krause, who in 2017 beat his mother, his grandparents, and a nurse to death with a baseball bat in Maine. Consider Yoselyn Ortega, who in 2012 went to the apartment where she had been a babysitter for the past two years and took the two children that she watched—Leo and Lucia—into the bathtub, where she stabbed them both to death and left their bodies in the water. It is easy to begin to feel that mercy is a moral luxury. Perhaps the reactionary solution is not so crude after all.

. . .

I wish that I could tell you that I didn't stab my roommate because I knew that it was wrong. I knew that killing, in general, was wrong, but believed that the circumstances constituted an exception. This man was a spy, an assassin, a monster who would kill me if I didn't kill him first. Is that enough? I wish that I could say that I was scared, that I decided he might be waiting or might overpower me. But I got up from the table. I went to his door, and I cracked it open and I saw that he was asleep. There is no way he could have stopped me. I could have stabbed him a dozen times before he knew what was going on. I could have let him bleed out screaming on his sheets. The truth is, I didn't decide anything at all.

Standing in the doorway, I felt certain that I was missing something.

I felt dizzy and wet and tired. I went back to the chair to think it over and sat there for a long time. Eventually the sun began to rise. The distinct orb of the streetlight through the curtain got washed out in the light, and then the kitchen turned hollow blue and yellow-grey and white. I could hear cars out on the street. I heard my other roommate turning over in his bed, then stirring. I put the knife back on the counter because I'd run out of time. I went back to my room and lay down in my bed because it was too late to act—that's all.

Shortly after, I left the apartment and moved in with E. for a few weeks. I was terrified by then, terrified that I was sick, that I was dying, that the doctors I kept seeing wouldn't tell me what was growing in my throat because some malignant, invisible force was getting to them first. I was afraid that if I stayed—even if I finally found a doctor who would save my life, even if I survived what was happening to me—then one day my roommate would find the footage of me sitting all night in the kitchen with a knife and one night he'd open my door while I was sleeping and do what I'd failed to do to him. Or perhaps I was afraid because I knew that if I stayed, I would follow through next time.

A few months after I began lithium, he moved out of the apartment. A few weeks later, I moved out, too. Outside of accidental run-ins and obligations to mutual friends, we never saw each other on purpose again.

• • •

While conservatives work against the mad defense in the legislatures and the courts, liberals and their allies on the cultural left have begun to work against it where they work against everything these days: in the universities, the culture, and the press. A decade ago, they might have maintained a firm commitment to erring on the side of mercy. But the liberal world has grown more paranoid in recent years, more fixated on *harm* and more zero-sum in their moral meritocracies. Now their commitment to the mad defense is confined exclusively to matters of formal criminal justice, where they stand as always against anything favored by the Right. But in their personal affairs, and in the affairs of their institutions, where punishment is administered not by the state but by human resources departments, they have joined the reactionaries in grasping the second horn of the dilemma. They too are looking for a way to narrow, or eliminate, the special exception for the mad.

The liberals are more circumspect than the reactionaries. They do not even call what they are after "punishment." They call it "accountability," which is a synonym for "punishment" among people for whom an explicit punitive impulse is politically unfashionable. Unlike the reactionary who merely asserts that the protection of society outweighs the special moral status of the insane—or claims that most cases of alleged madness are brought forward by self-serving liars—the cultural liberal readily admits the madness of the transgressor but denies that their madness is the cause of their transgression. *Actually, the mentally ill are more likely to be the victim of a crime than the perpetrator,* they say. To suggest that madness may be the cause of transgression is *dehumanizing* they say, a *stigmatizing* bigotry. Therefore, the morally compromised part of the mad defendant must be located in some other part of their soul, and it is this defect, not the mental disorder, which must be condemned. Indeed, in this way the mad defendant who pleads their case is doubly guilty: first by their original transgression, and second by their stigma-promoting excuse. In a modern liberal culture that is paranoid above all things about the possibility of being conned, the second sin is practically the graver of the two.

Like medieval juries and reactionary senators unconvinced by Hinckley's story about loving Jodi Foster, modern liberals are worried about malingerers. The mad criminal, like many sane criminals, is suspected of being a manipulator; a *master manipulator,* if they are especially persuasive. The manipulator is a strange figure in the contemporary liberal imagination. Their core desire is not deception, but predation and *harm*; manipulation is only how they achieve this goal. They are devious. They are dedicated, above all things, to persuading you that they aren't dangerous. Any claims or even deeds that seem to paint them in a better light are deceptions designed to trick others into enabling them. If these claims or deeds are particularly compelling, then it is only evidence of how *masterful* they are. Finally, the *manipulator* is a monomaniac: They cannot be reasoned with, reformed, or constrained. So long as they live, they will always be trying to scheme their way back into a position where they can do more *harm*. They can only be *held accountable*, which is to say, completely extinguished from social life.

It is tempting to see the *manipulator* as a kind of hypocrisy on the matter of stigma, a plain description of a personality disorder inexplicably deployed as part of an argument against attributing danger to the mad. But even a personality disorder—even a psychopath—isn't as fundamentally beyond treatment as the manipulative predator of the liberal imaginary, nor so bereft of any other motive or personality. Despite the clinical language, the manipulator is not drawn from the mythology of psychiatry, but from a different tradition altogether: in their quest to resolve any lingering tension between their prior commitment to mercy, and their new desire to punish social criminals, these well-meaning and secular liberals have reinvented the Devil. Perhaps they are not so different from the Reaganites after all.

• • •

When I was nineteen years old and in my second year of college, I began dating a woman who had graduated from my university the year before. She was only a few years older—twenty-two, or twenty-three—but from the perspective of a teenager, those few years were a generation. She had an adult life. She went to adult parties. She had adult friends and an adult apartment. I did not understand why she would want me. We had very little in common and rarely got along. But when I was nineteen years old and in my second year of college, I was not in a position to be picky about which cooler, older women were inexplicably willing to date me.

This was the last serious relationship I would have before E., before diagnosis, which is to say before I had to ask myself if and when I should tell someone what was wrong with me because it was before I was aware that there was *something wrong with me* that might be explained or controlled. But this meant there was something wrong and I was not doing anything about it. I'd been having mood episodes for years. I would withdraw for months, become cold, sexually disinterested, preoccupied, and aloof. Then came months of neediness, enthusiasm, overbearing affection, fixation, and paranoid aggression. I was, I suppose, *bipolar* in the clinical sense and acted it out in a way that was *bipolar* in the colloquial sense. I believed that she knew everything, that she had encountered every kind of personality and every style of relationship before, that she was handling me the right way and that all of this was normal. Now, a decade older than she was then, I realize she must have found it terrible and confusing, too.

It is shameful to reflect on all of this. Sometimes, she said I was manipulative, but the truth is worse: I do not understand guile at all. I understand lying, like, *Did you eat the last cookie? No, of course not!* but the idea that a person can put on a false face, can make false friends, can harbor secret motives for days or months or years while seeking some unspoken advantage is a fact of human life I have only seen on television and must take on faith. I suppose this makes me easy to manipulate, but it also makes me overbearing and rude and difficult to like; any social graces I've acquired I've learned by rote. I am not self-disciplined or charming at all. She took advantage of this sometimes. She knew how uncool and young I felt around her, and she wielded her approval as a system of behavior modification, given I cooperated. She became withdrawn if I displeased her. She liked to belittle me, or she did, at least, whether she liked it or not. She liked to tell me I was a fuckup, or irresponsible, or too embarrassing to bring around; she was in control of herself in a way that I was not, and she could ignore me for days or weeks or even months to make a point. On one occasion, she punched me repeatedly in the face in public in full view of a mutual friend, but I suppose she wasn't strong enough to really hurt me.

I don't know if she knew what she was doing. Did she seek out a younger, immature, visibly unstable partner on purpose? There are people drawn to the sort of people they can control; the sort of people who are themselves so unlikeable and morally compromised that you will never be blamed for how you treat them. Perhaps I really was the monster. Maybe she really did like me at first. Maybe she didn't understand any better than I did how terrible and abnormal things were between us. How, after all, do you defend yourself, when you find yourself in love with a man who is suffering the worst early stages of a psychotic break? How do you learn to deal with the irrational and frightening, with unpredictable and constant pain? Perhaps you just learn to be irrational and frightening, too. I can't trust my own memory, and not just because I was in the process of losing my mind. The truth is that it is very easy to see others clearly. It is very hard to see yourself, even at the distance of many years.

Anyway, I am telling you this because one night six or seven months into our relationship, I decided very suddenly that I should end it. It didn't take, but it is what sent her to California for a while. I don't remember my reasons, only that it felt very urgent. Everything had felt urgent for weeks. Ideas and impulses floated up and I seized them at random; I had a feeling like boiling water in my chest and skin, a belief that by doing *something* I might release it. I had tried several *somethings* already. Driving to her house as the sun went down behind light snow and saying *It's over* was just the newest unexamined urgency. It occurred to me to do it. It felt possible that I might afterward feel calm again. So I did it.

I don't remember how long I stayed. I don't remember if I cried or she cried or neither. We would get back together a few months later. But when I left and was driving home on the long southbound freeway, I boiled just like before. I felt an unbearable internal buzz, as if each of my cells were threatening to break free or else implode. A new impulse bubbled up to the surface, this time accompanied by one of the few command hallucinations I have ever really heard, like the sincere and audible voice of God: *Crash your car right now and die.*

I was on the off ramp by then, headed up from the sunken freeway toward a surface street on the South Side of Chicago. I swerved left, hoping to go over or through the barrier and plunge back down into the traffic on the highway. Instead, my car struck the concrete and bounced back. I kept pushing left, and it hit the concrete again. This time, the tires got caught on the small, elevated curb, and I banged back and forth for several yards before being thrown back into the lane at the top of the ramp into the side of another car parked at the light.

. . .

Phil Ochs says the liberal is ten degrees to the left of center in good times and ten degrees to the right of center if it affects them personally. Something like this is going on between the liberal and the madman. They gladly concede that there are members of society—the mentally unstable, the drug-addled, the frankly *weird*—who are unfairly maligned for the consequences of conditions they cannot control. They believe that they ought to be sensitive and merciful and understanding toward them, both in matters of the law, and in matters of interpersonal compassion. But that sensitivity and mercy and understanding are more and more only ever exercised when their objects exist at a sufficient distance, when the lunatic is only an abstract *social concern*. When the offender is instead somebody with whom the liberal shares an office or a classroom or a peer group, they begin talking about justice and stigma and excuses. They are in favor of tolerance, so long as it is somebody else's job to do the tolerating. It is patience, so long as someone else, ideally someone with a degree in social work, is the one whose patience will be tested. The mad defense is intuitive in theory but strains against our instincts in practice. There are limits to *understanding*. Understanding, at any rate, is not the same as mercy. Beginning in the 1970s, Americans were told that schizophrenia was a brain disease; its onset and effects were entirely beyond the control of the patient. Subsequent studies have found that while this belief inspires people to assign less blame to lunatics, it also inspires them to treat them worse.

APPALLING STRANGENESS   255

The philosopher Agnes Callard writes that it's easy to blame questions of mental health on factors beyond our control because the only
ethical desire at play is the ethical desire to avoid blaming people for
unfortunate outcomes that they cannot control. *The relevant outcomes
are either normal or abnormal,* she writes. *We are faced only with the need
to avoid blaming people for the subnormal condition . . . We get everything
we want by ascribing outcomes to genetics,* or to any other accidental fact
of human life. Let the madman bear no responsibility for his madness,
this argument goes, because to do so costs us nothing.

Callard goes on to contrast this situation with other cases, where the
possibility of a supernormal outcome—exceptional academic achievement, or athletic ability, let's say—makes us hesitate to make the same
attribution to chance. To do so would deprive us of the opportunity to
praise the supernormal, to celebrate greatness as a product of human
agency. In these cases, therefore, we are faced with a difficult choice:
Do we avoid blaming people for subnormal conditions, and in doing so,
surrender our ability to praise the equally accidental supernormal?
Or do we retain our right to praise the supernormal, and in doing so,
commit ourselves to blaming the abnormal for their failures? Which
horn of the dilemma do we prefer? *The question of who we praise and who
we blame is not a scientific question, but an ethical one,* Callard writes.
*There is no way to answer it except by deliberating seriously about the kind
of society we want to live in.*

I don't know what kind of case the lunatic should be. Perhaps it is
so difficult because it is three-part kind: we want to *fight stigma* by
praising the madman who has lived a clean life, and so find it difficult
not to speak of excuses when it comes to the unpleasant, dangerous, or
even criminally insane. But even if this is a simpler case we're dealing
with, I don't believe that mercy comes free like Callard says. Mercy,
even in these cases, costs us something dear to the human heart: a solid
place to put our anger and our pain. *The disease* is too abstract. It can
only be blamed at a distance, too far away when you are the one who is
hurting, when you are the one who has lost a friend or a child, when you
are the one who has spent years feeling as if you are catching madness

yourself by repeated exposure. But a person can be blamed. They can be punished, "held accountable," can become the receptacle into which the wounded can pour out their suffering and transform the intolerable powerlessness of being hurt into the vengeful power of hurting someone else. A disease without a face is no substitute at all. This is doubly so when the disease comes from a field as dubious as psychiatry. Even Callard knows this, arguing in a different essay by way of Aristotle that, *Anger is a desire for revenge*, one which *inclines people to apply exalted labels ("justice," "accountability") to acts of vengeance; it is a fog in which bad things look good, just because someone else did bad things first . . . The more perfectly one attends to the gravity of the wrongs done, the less sensitive one becomes to the gravity of the wrongs one is poised to commit in response.* You cannot take vengeance on a diagnostic label. It doesn't squirm or scream or know it *had this coming.* You cannot hurt it at all.

In Graham Greene's *Brighton Rock*, an old priest tells an angry, grieving girl that neither she, nor he, nor anyone, can comprehend the appalling strangeness of the mercy of God. Readers and critics tend to focus on the *strangeness* but I think the essential word here is *appalling*. Divine mercy erases guilt; ignores it. It annihilates it for nothing, dissolves the whole immense fury of an angry God for nothing more than the plea of the guilty—you ask, and you receive. It is terribly unfair. Human beings cannot forgive like that, not really, and perhaps this is what makes God's mercy *strange*. But there is a more troubling thought that comes after: Even if we could forgive like that, would we want to? Twelfth-century Christians called mercy a kind *of ethical irrationality*, but lately we have begun to wonder if it is ethical at all. Mercy precludes the possibility of justice. Is that virtue? The justifying power of hurt is a precious thing in human life. Is it *just* to simply let it go? The result is an imbalance in the moral scales of the universe, wicked and soliciting further wickedness. Once you allow one moral exception, it is difficult not to let it creep. It is difficult not to wonder whether all blame must dissipate eventually, whether the most troubling quality of mercy is how, once admitted in a single case, it begins to feel inescapable in every case. How much easier to harden your heart and say, *It's just an excuse,* than to say the demands of retribution—of *justice,* of *accountability*—come first. That is to say: Mercy isn't only strange. It is appalling.

• • •

The crash destroyed much of my steering column. It shattered my headlight and crumpled part of the hood. I had still been going fast. I'd hit the driver's side of the other car, crushing it into the vehicle. I don't believe that I blacked out, but I remember sitting for a minute, listening to the hiss of the weather on plastic and metal, unsure of what was going on. I thought, *You're not dead.* Then I thought, *Is somebody else dead?*

I got out for a minute. Cars kept coming up the ramp, merging right to get around us. I'd struck the backseat of the other car. Nobody was there. If I'd hit two feet farther up, I would have killed the driver. She got out, screaming.

We moved our cars to a gas station right off the ramp. When the police came, I claimed my brakes had failed on the icy ramp. My insurance card was out of date. The police had me follow them to the station to issue a ticket. My car ran but I could not turn left without a terrible, low creak, requiring me to turn my wheel all the way. I stayed at the station for a few hours. A few months later, I went to a courthouse in downtown Chicago at six in the morning to show proof of insurance to a judge. The charges were dropped; I paid a fine.

The breakup did not even take. The relationship lasted on-and-off for years. We lived apart. Then she moved to California. She moved back and we lived together for a while, then apart again. I went through college. I turned twenty then twenty-one then twenty-two; by then, total paranoia had begun to set in. One night, many years in, she visited me while I was spending the summer in New York, and we got into a fight so bad that I threw up for an hour on the sheets of a friend's bed. In the morning, I went with her on the train to Long Island, where she stayed. I went back to New York, and we didn't speak for the better part of a year. During another fight, I stripped completely naked and threw things at the walls; eventually she called the police. When I came back, I confessed that I thought I might be crazy, that *something* must be going on—I had been institutionalized, I kept being sent to psychiatrists, surely this was all abnormal, I even had theories of what might be wrong based on some internet-enabled self-diagnosis—but we never talked about that possibility again.

I think sometimes that if I had killed that driver then perhaps I would have seen a psychiatrist. Perhaps I would have been diagnosed years sooner. Perhaps my lawyers would have tried a mad defense. Mania and incipient psychosis leading to a suicide attempt and resulting in a criminally negligent homicide. *Just ask the girl he dumped that night. She'll tell you he's crazy.* I do not believe it would have worked.

· · ·

The French philosopher and critic Louis Althusser had been mad for years. He had been diagnosed with manic depression and schizophrenia; in 1976, he estimated that he had spent fifteen of the past thirty years in clinics and psychiatric hospitals, undergoing, according to his biographer, William Lewis, *The most aggressive treatments post-war French psychiatry had to offer.* In 1980, when he was sixty-two years old, he began to deteriorate once again. His doctor recommended he be hospitalized, but Althusser refused. On November 16, his wife, Helene, asked him to give her a massage. *Kneeling beside her, leaning over her body, I am engaged in massaging her neck,* he later wrote. *I press my two thumbs into the hollow flesh that borders the top of sternum and, applying force, I slowly reach one thumb toward the right, one thumb toward the left at an angle, the firmer area below the ears.* He notices something wrong. *Helene's face is immobile and serene, her open eyes fixed on the ceiling . . . Suddenly, I am struck with her terror . . . What is happening? I stand up and scream: I've strangled Helene!*

In the ensuing scandal, Althusser's case re-created the whole history of the mad criminal dilemma in miniature, with calls for mercy and for justice, talk of *excuses* and *stigma* and concern for the *greater good*. Ultimately, Althusser was found mentally unfit to stand trial. He spent the rest of his life in and out of mental institutions, and he died in 1990 of heart failure.

Althusser wrote about the murder in a memoir he left unpublished in a desk drawer. It was released in English in 1992 as *The Future Lasts Forever*. In it, he wrote about the *strange situation* of a man after a mad defense, in a case that once again had failed to resolve the contradictions of the dilemma. A criminal trial, at least, would have enacted a ceremony of justice, allowed him to confess or deny his guilt to the public. But Althusser felt suspended, forever between innocence and guilt, life and death, the special exception for the mad and justice for the victim of his acts. *Even though I have been out of psychiatric hospital for two years, I am still a missing person for the public who have heard of me*, he writes. *I am neither alive nor dead and, though I have not been buried, I am "bodiless." I am simply missing, which was Foucault's splendid definition of madness.*

I have been thinking lately about the brief American preoccupation with the question of whether one would go back in time and murder Hitler in his crib. The answer—whether one is a Kantian or a consequentialist; whether one is willing to *talk tough* in the realm of hypotheticals or not—is not terribly revealing. But the question reveals a great deal: it reveals the fantasy of justice. The time-traveler can really settle moral accounts, to live in a world where punitive violence truly balances the books by erasing the very crime that is being punished, ensures *the good of society* by actually protecting society, not simply mitigating future danger after the fact.

The madman is the same: unable to really bear responsibility for his actions but an imminent danger nonetheless. To solve him would require the same impossibility: the ability to remove him from social existence in advance, the power to murder him in his crib. Otherwise, we will always come back to the same place. We will always be trapped in the same dilemma, forced to bear the guilt of punishing the not-quite-guilty, or anguished over the victims' unmet need for justice; searching for some other object to blame, appalled by the empty quality of mercy. What I mean is that this dilemma cannot be solved. It can only be avoided entirely. The dilemma is that the insane keep on being born. It becomes easier to understand the old asylums; the constraints and chemical castrations and sterilizing surgeries on early operating tables.

The philosopher Bernard Williams wrote that when he first introduced the expression *moral luck*, he *expected to suggest an oxymoron*. But it isn't. His contemporary Thomas Nagel observed that *a significant aspect of what someone does depends on factors beyond his control*, yet we continue to hold him responsible for the outcome; that's moral luck in action. We are committed to moral luck all the time. We commit to it every time we render moral judgment on a case dependent, at least in part, on factors beyond the actor's control, which is to say, in the case of every human act. The problem of moral luck is the problem of the mad defense writ large. It is the dilemma of the mad defense stretched beyond the mad, to everyone, which has always been the real problem. If we are committed, as we believe that we are, to the idea that we should only be punished for what we can control, are there are any circumstances under which a person can be punished? What then is the mad defense but a distinction without a difference?

• • •

Sometimes medication does not work. We do not know precisely why. One fall, in Iowa, I was persuaded for a little while that I did not really exist. I was not hallucinating; I was the hallucination. My thoughts came from the real brains of other people, mashed together and mutated into the unitary illusion of an independent mind. This explained why I heard radio sounds: they're the static hum of thoughts coming in. This explained why my thoughts seem to suddenly disappear sometimes: they were coming from outside, and sometimes something interferes with the transmission. I worried that if I got too far from other people, I would run out of fuel and disappear. When I felt ashamed, I asked, *Why are you all imagining me this way?* This belief crept up and integrated itself seamlessly into my sense of reality. I do not know why this happened. I was on medication the whole time.

During those weeks, I became fixated on a particular man in Iowa City who I had never liked. We barely knew each other, but we had friends in common. I saw him sometimes in public, and although we rarely spoke, I was always aware of his presence and he was always of mine. I thought he was the source of many of the more distressing transmissions I received, the ones that made me feel restless and agitated and ashamed.

I began to wonder if these transmissions could go the other way. Could I will a thought back across the permeable barrier between minds? Could I push a thought out into other heads? If the right combinations of transmissions could make me kill myself, or just disappear entirely, could I transmit the same signals back? The schizophrenic legal scholar Elyn Saks tells *Scientific American* that there are times she is convinced that she has *killed hundreds of thousands of people* with her thoughts. I never believed that I was that powerful. But it seemed possible that with a great deal of effort, I could jerry-rig the strange mechanism that created me; that with a great deal of concentration, I could end just one life with my mind.

On one of the first very cold nights of autumn, I lay in my bed in Iowa, too hot under the blanket and too cold without it. I couldn't sleep and I began thinking of this man I didn't like. I began thinking of him, that night, as that man I hated. I considered that he must be among the many minds linked to my own, feeding thoughts into my head. I was alone in my apartment. He was probably alone in his. I'd had flashes of this terrible power before—the belief that if I think the wrong words, I will accidentally bring catastrophe into the world—but in the past, I had run from these thoughts. They inspired fear and revulsion, made me desperate to unthink them, to never think that sort of thing again.

But this time I just lay there for a while. I weighed the possibilities. I wasn't revolted or afraid. I wasn't tired. It was so cold in the apartment. It was so hot in my bed. Somewhere out in the apartment my cat was scratching a wall. I sat up. I thought, *Yes, I want to do it. I want to kill him.*

I imagined that it would go like this: I would close my eyes. I would run soft, invisible fingers over every line of influence, unspool the psychic wires converging in the orbit of my skull. I would trace each one back to its point of transmission. I would sense the network of thin, silk lines growing out from every mind in Iowa, separate the strands tangling around me, feel the unique pulsing electricity of every one. I would find the one that led me back to my antagonist.

It would be easy. Most of these lines were harmless, neutral and soft, with a regular, calm pulse of passive data coming through. The strand I wanted would be rough and erratic, vibrating with pricking malice. I'd get it between the tips of my fingers, nearly imperceptibly small but surely there, and focus. Then I would gather all the hate up in my mind, all the malice and resentment and anger and fear, and push it back the other way. Would the charge overwhelm the cord and electrocute the man on the other end? Would he light up like a fuse box blowing out? Would I dissolve his brain with psychic heat? Would his whole body melt? I wasn't sure. I tried to push the phrase *turn off.* Maybe he would fall down inexplicably where he was standing, cause of death unable to be determined.

I am trying to tell you that I didn't feel ambivalent. I didn't wait or sweat. This wasn't like the long night at the table with the short knife, filled with doubt and fear. I let the thought come fully formed and worded. *I want him to leave me alone I want to send the charge back I want him to die.* I felt my mind pushing outward, felt the fat fatal package enter the invisible wire and race out across the empty sky. I felt it stop somewhere blocks away and crash into its destination. A few minutes later I fell asleep without any trouble at all.

• • •

In one of the most famous passages of the *Confessions*, St. Augustine and several friends sneak into an orchard and steal pears. Augustine tells us that he didn't steal them out of hunger. He didn't even want the pears. *We carried off a huge load . . . not to eat ourselves, but to dump out to the hogs.* It seems silly, an inconsequential crime. *Odd thing to see a man making a mountain out of robbing a pear tree in his teens,* as the Supreme Court Justice Oliver Wendell Holmes Jr. allegedly said.

But Augustine remembers the pear tree not because of any consequences, but precisely because of how senseless it was. *Behold, now let my heart confess to thee what it was seeking there, when I was being gratuitously wanton, having no inducement to evil but evil itself,* he writes to God. *It was foul, and I loved it. I loved my own undoing. I loved my error—not that for which I erred but the error itself. A depraved soul, falling away from security in thee to destruction in itself, seeking nothing from the shameful deed but shame itself.* Augustine remembers because he knew right from wrong, and wanted wrong, without hesitation or excuse. It is this sort of evil that requires divine mercy, no matter how inconsequential the crime.

Nobody died that night in Iowa, of course. I cannot kill with thoughts. I know that now. I knew within a week, although for a while I worried that I had sent the signal the wrong way and that somebody else, somebody I did not know and didn't hear about, had suddenly dropped dead because of me. That thought also faded in time. But does it matter that it didn't work? My heart believed it would work and I wanted to believe it. *Even the wicked,* Dostoevsky writes, have *simpler hearts than we imagine.* Perhaps they do. But I believed that I could kill another person with a thought. I tried to do it, willfully and with clear eyes. Should I be spared just because I lack telekinetic powers?

Why should the accidental fact that an intended harmful outcome has not occurred be a ground for punishing less a criminal who may be equally dangerous and equally wicked? asks the philosopher H. L. A. Hart. How simple can such a heart really be? There is no dilemma here at all. I believed that I could kill him with a thought—that, I suppose, is madness—but because I believed that, and because I tried to do it anyway, because I deliberately and for no reason but spite did what I believed would end in a young man's death, I am guilty. I am guiltier than I was during the long night with the knife, guiltier than I was when I terrified and confused my parents and friends and girlfriends, guiltier than I was when I came two feet and a stroke of luck away from crushing an innocent woman with my car, guiltier than I was any time I got into a fight, or flailed to defend myself from a conspiracy, or lost my capacity to understand what I was doing or what was going on around me. Sitting on my bed in Iowa, imagining myself seeking out the invisible, fatal wire through the night, I just wanted to hurt somebody. I sought *nothing from the shameful deed but shame itself* and there is no mad defense for that. There is no defense at all.

Odd thing to see a man making a mountain out of trying to commit psychic murder from his bed. But it is this, more than any other act, which terrifies me. All the years of medication and therapy and *insight* and stability, and what did I have to show? *Behold, now let my heart confess to thee what it was seeking there.* That I went from a man who nearly killed a woman while I was trying to kill myself to a man who knew he could kill with a knife but chose not to, to a man, at long last well-treated, stable, responsible, and sane, who believed he could kill with a thought and tried it out of spite. The medication really helps. The therapy is working. I'm so much better now. I've come so very far.

Mullin

On October 13, 1972, a twenty-five-year-old former Goodwill delivery driver was winding along Route 9 near Santa Cruz when he saw somebody standing on the side of the road. The driver recognized the man as Lawrence White, a well-known local transient and hitchhiker, so he pulled over, got out of his car, and popped the hood. He'd be happy to offer a ride, he said, but he'd been having engine problems. Would White mind having a look? White looked under the hood. While he did, the driver struck him from behind with a baseball bat. He knocked him to the ground and kept beating him, striking him over and over until White was dead on the side of the road. The driver rolled White's body down a nearby hill, then got back in his car and drove away. The driver's name was Herbert Mullin and, before his arrest in February 1973, he would beat, shoot, bludgeon, and stab twelve more people to death in California.

Eleven days after he murdered White, Mullin once again pulled over for a hitchhiker. This one was a local college student named Mary Guilfoyle. Guilfoyle got into the car and Mullin stabbed her to death in his passenger seat before dumping the body. Nine days later, he walked into a Catholic church in Los Gatos, opened the door to the confessional, and stabbed the elderly French priest inside. The priest bled out while Mullin ran away. A witness described him to the police only as a white man with dark hair, carrying a knife.

Three months later, Mullin turned up at a cabin he believed belonged to an old friend named James Gianera. But he discovered that a young woman named Kathy Francis lived there now. Francis gave Mullin Gianera's new address; Mullin drove there, shot Gianera and his wife, Joan, then stabbed their bodies over forty times. When he was done, he returned to the cabin, shot Kathy Francis and her two sons, aged four and nine, then stabbed their bodies, too. A few weeks later, while wandering aimlessly through a state park, Mullin happened upon four teenage campers armed with a hunting rifle. Mullin was disheveled; he seemed confused and strange, and the boys told him to get lost. But shortly after, he returned with a revolver and shot all four of them in their tent. Their bodies weren't discovered for a week. Before they were found, Mullin, armed with their .22-caliber rifle, made a sudden U-turn while driving down a residential street in Santa Cruz. He stopped his car, got out, and laid the hunting rifle across the hood to steady his aim. Outside a nearby house, a retired fisherman named Fred Perez was working on his lawn. Mullin shot him once through the heart, then he got back in his car and drove away.

A neighbor witnessed the shooting, and within minutes, a police officer spotted Mullin's car on the Pacific Coast Highway. Seeing the rifle on the passenger seat, the officer approached the car with his gun drawn, but Mullin did not fire. He did not try to flee or resist arrest at all. He did not deny that he was the man who had just shot a stranger in broad daylight and later, in police custody, he did not deny that he was the man who had murdered over a dozen people—four men, three women, four teenagers, and two young children—over the course of five months because, as he told police, God had commanded the murders. The victims themselves had agreed. He hadn't wanted to kill, but it was the only way to save the lives of millions more.

II

During the summer of 1965, seven years before the killing spree and just after his senior year of high school, Herbert Mullin's best friend, Dean Richardson, died in a car crash. The two had gone to school together in Salinas, a small town near Monterey Bay where Mullin was born in 1947. They'd both attended San Lorenzo Valley High School, where Mullin had played baseball, basketball, and football, had been a member of the Key Club, and, just that year, had been voted most likely to succeed. Dean's death was a shock, but Herbert had a lot going on. He was a devout Catholic. He had a steady girlfriend. After the summer, he planned to attend Cabrillo College for an engineering degree, a first step on a path following his war-hero father into the Army Corps of Engineers.

At first, things continued according to plan. In the fall, Herb moved to Aptos, California, to begin his studies. There he met Jim Gianera, who had also known Dean. Perhaps because of their shared loss, the two bonded quickly. Jim introduced Herb to marijuana. Herb became interested in Eastern religion. Like many students at the time, he began to reconsider the war in Vietnam. Rather than looking forward to the Army Corps of Engineers, Mullin registered as a conscientious objector and took an alternative service job driving a delivery truck for Goodwill. He began experimenting with amphetamines and LSD. None of this was the plan, but none of it was terribly unusual. Herbert Mullin was in college in California in the late 1960s. A lot of people were getting high and getting woke and deciding that they'd rather not die in Vietnam.

During his second year at Cabrillo College, Herb's behavior became markedly bizarre. His interest in Eastern religion became an obsession. He began talking regularly about reincarnation, then he built a shrine to Dean Richardson in his room. He dumped his girlfriend and began telling people that he'd been sleeping with men. He stopped attending classes, and then dropped out of school entirely. He continued driving the Goodwill truck for a while, but by 1969, Mullin told his family that he had quit that, too. He planned to go to India to study yoga. He made it as far as Sebastopol, a hundred miles north of Santa Cruz, where he moved into a trailer on his older sister's ranch.

If his parents and friends had dismissed Mullin's behavior as a result of his youth or pot habit or just the culture of the 1960s, Mullin's sister and brother-in-law did not. He told his sister and brother-in-law that they had been communicating with him telepathically. He propositioned them both. One evening, during a dinner, Mullin began imitating his brother-in-law's movements and speech. Whatever his brother-in-law said, Mullin repeated. If he stood up, Mullin stood up with him. If he gestured, Mullin imitated the gesture. At first, the family took this to be a not-very-funny joke; then, they imagined that he might be high. But the mirroring went on for hours and hours, lasting far longer than the endurance of a prankster or somebody on a trip. The next day, Mullin's sister persuaded him to voluntarily commit himself to the psychiatric ward of Mendocino State Hospital.

In the hospital, Mullin was diagnosed with schizophrenia for the first time. He spent six weeks at Mendocino State. Doctors noted that Mullin was "generally uncooperative" with the treatment program, but he took antipsychotic medication and his condition improved. In May, Mullin asked to be discharged. Despite a poor prognosis, his request was granted. He immediately stopped taking his medication.

The origin of Mullin's schizophrenia is both mysterious and over-determined. Nobody else in his family is known to have had it. Substance abuse can accelerate the course of a psychotic illness, but it is not the cause of the underlying condition. Trauma, particularly in early life, can sometimes play a role. The trauma can be physical or psychological, typically either a serious head injury or an emotional wound. Mullin never sustained a serious head injury. Often, a single sustained period of severe stress—a period of homelessness, a stint in solitary, the death of a friend—can be enough to trigger or accelerate a psychotic disposition. Dean Richardson's death is often taken as the immediate trigger of Mullin's insanity, but it may not have been the first accelerant splashed on his brain. Over forty-five years after his arrest, Mullin wrote in a prison letter that he had *an idea that might shed some light on my problems, past & present.*

He continued, *When I was at St. Stephen's Grammar School in San Francisco, California, in September 1960, I was thirteen years old. That September, I met a new priest assigned to the parish.* Then, elliptically: *I filed a formal complaint with the Catholic Church in Rome at Vatican City.* He wrote that he has heard the priest was *demoted and can no longer act as a Catholic priest.*

Aside from the alleged complaint, Mullin had never made this claim— or at least, the claim implied—in any public forum. It is easy to imagine that he's lying, inventing a sympathetic origin story in advance of his latest appearance before the parole board. It is difficult, at any rate, to imagine a thirteen-year-old Mullin filing a complaint directly with the Vatican. But there was a monseigneur with the name Mullin provided, assigned to St. Stephen's school in San Francisco. In 2002, many years after Mullin stopped being able to follow his story, the priest told his parish that he was going on a leave of absence for health and personal reasons. The same year, the *San Francisco Chronicle* reported that the priest had been named in a complaint to the church involving *alleged improper contact with a boy* decades earlier. The priest never returned to ministry. He died in 2013.

III

After leaving Mendocino State, Mullin moved to Lake Tahoe on the Nevada border. He worked briefly as a dishwasher, then quit, then moved back to Santa Cruz. There, he was arrested for pulling a knife on a park ranger. He began routinely burning himself with cigarettes, at first on his legs, and then on his penis. One of the few books written about Mullin—a seventy-page self-published paperback by a retired police officer—finds this detail revealing. *Mullin began to burn his genitals with lit cigarettes*, the ex-cop writes. *This is not normal or rational behavior.* Indeed.

In late 1969, Mullin told a friend that he was receiving psychic messages from an unknown source. It was these messages, he said, which had commanded him to burn himself. Alarmed, the friend went to his uncle, a doctor, and on Halloween they had Mullin committed to San Luis Obispo General Hospital. The doctors there diagnosed Mullin with paranoid schizophrenia and deemed him "gravely disabled" and dangerous. Once again, medication appeared to improve Mullin's condition, but once again, the hospital couldn't keep him. He was discharged after twenty-three days. Once again, Mullin stopped taking medication shortly after leaving the hospital. He applied for welfare and used the money to rent a room in a nearby motel.

The next year, Mullin joined a local commune, but he made other residents so uncomfortable that he was quickly expelled. He took a trip to Hawaii with a friend, but they fought and the friend left Mullin stranded by himself in Maui. Mullin checked himself into a local mental health clinic where he was once again diagnosed with schizophrenia and once again discharged. He returned to California and was promptly arrested for disorderly conduct. Once again, he was committed to a county psychiatry ward. But this time, Mullin refused to be committed and refused to take any medication. Five days later, the hospital was obliged to release him.

Over the course of the next year, Mullin moved to San Francisco, began a macrobiotic diet, shaved his head, then grew his hair out long again (adding a mustache as well), began wearing a sombrero, faking a Mexican accent, and trying to become a boxer. He began reading about da Vinci and Einstein and the San Francisco Earthquake of 1906; he renewed his interest in reincarnation. Mullin discovered that his birthday was the anniversary of Einstein's death. He confessed to a friend that the voices he heard were telepathic messages from God. By 1972, Mullin had burned out in the Bay Area and returned to Santa Cruz, where he moved back in with his parents. He began actively contemplating suicide.

By this point, Mullin heard voices every day. These voices—sometimes God, sometimes his father, sometimes no identifiable person at all—all told him that a terrible catastrophe was coming and only he could prevent it. That April, Mullin turned twenty-five years old. It had only been seven years since he'd graduated high school "most likely to succeed," with a girlfriend and a best friend and a plan for his life. A year later, he would be in prison.

IV

In police custody, Mullin spoke frankly about his motives. In between bouts of shouting *Silence!* in response to questions from detectives, he explained the purpose of his work. God, he explained, intended to destroy California with an enormous earthquake. The only way to prevent this calamity was through blood sacrifice. *We human beings, through the history of the world, have protected our continents from cataclysmic earthquakes by murder,* he said. *In other words, a minor natural disaster avoids a major natural disaster.* He pointed out that since he began his killing spree, not a single earthquake had struck California.

An interrogator, presumably attempting to determine Mullin's capacity to tell the difference between right and wrong, asked why he ought to be locked up for his crimes if *it's natural and has a good effect.*

Your laws, Mullin said. *You see, the thing is people get together, say, in the White House. People like to sing the die song, you know, people like to sing the die song. If I am president of my class when I graduate from high school, I can tell two, possible three young homo sapiens to die. I can sing that song to them and they'll have to kill themselves or be killed—an automobile accident, a knifing, a gunshot wound. You ask me why this is? And I say, well, they have to do that in order to protect the ground from an earthquake, because all of the other people in the community, because all the other people in the community had been dying all year long, and my class, we have to chip in, so to speak, to the darkness. We have to die also. And people would rather sing the die song than murder.*

A detective interrupted him: *What is the die song?*

Just that, said Mullin. *I'm telling you to kill yourself or be killed so that my continent will not fall into the ocean. See, it's all based on reincarnation, this dies to protect my strata.* Further questioning did not make matters any clearer.

The police were not the only ones who sometimes found Mullin confusing or even obnoxious. While awaiting trial, Mullin was held in a jail cell next to the notorious serial killer Edmund Kemper, who had been arrested the same year. Kemper didn't care for Mullin, either. *[He] had a habit of singing and bothering people when somebody tried to watch TV,* Kemper said years later. *So I threw water on him to shut him up.* Kemper also reported that he gave Mullin peanuts as a reward for good behavior. *Herbie liked peanuts,* Kemper said. *That was effective, because pretty soon he asked permission to sing. That's called behavior modification treatment.*

The Santa Cruz County District Attorney's office indicted Mullin on ten counts of murder. Eight days later, with Mullin in jail awaiting trial, a 5.8 magnitude earthquake struck Southern California, causing over a million dollars in damage.

V

At trial, Mullin plead not guilty by reason of insanity. His attorneys told the court how Mullin heard voices ordering him to kill and about how he believed that his victims telepathically consented to their own deaths, willingly sacrificing themselves for the greater good. When Mullin took the stand to testify, he did not concede that he was insane. He told jurors that they were being drafted into a conspiracy to keep him from becoming *too powerful in his next life. Every* Homo sapien *communicates telepathically, it's just not accepted socially*, he said, under oath.

Nobody disputed Mullin's insanity. He had been repeatedly hospitalized and independently diagnosed by several psychiatrists long before his arrest. Nobody argued that his incessant courtroom talk about Einstein and destiny and "cosmic emanations" were an act. But insanity pleas in the United States were not adjudicated, even then, based on a defendant's insanity. The prosecution conceded Mullin's illness was irrelevant. What mattered was whether his insanity prevented him from distinguishing between right and wrong, or rendered him unable to act on that knowledge. The prosecution reminded jurors that after the first three murders, he had stopped killing for nearly three months. During that time, Mullin had tried to join the military, failing the Coast Guard psych evaluation but passing when he tried the Marines. He was only barred entry because he refused to verify his record of previous arrests. Further, Mullin had killed somebody he knew. James Gianera was a friend, the friend who had introduced him to drugs. In some accounts, Mullin blamed Gianera for causing his mental illness, and his murder could be interpreted as a simple case of premeditated revenge.

The murders of Kathy Francis and her children were also noteworthy: The prosecution argued that Mullin had only murdered them to eliminate a potential connection to the Gianera murder. If nothing else, this proved that he knew he was committing a criminal act, although Mullin claimed that Francis had told him via telepathy that she and her children didn't mind being killed to prevent an earthquake. Finally, Mullin had told police that he refused a psychic command to murder his uncle, and instead murdered his last victim, Fred Perez, as a *replacement* sacrifice. He was not, therefore, totally powerless to resist these commands.

On August 19, 1972, Herbert Mullin was convicted of two counts of first-degree murder and eight counts of second-degree murder. That December, having already been sentenced to life in prison, he pled guilty to second-degree murder in the case of one of his other victims. The remaining two were never charged.

The jury in Mullin's trial did not necessarily reject his insanity defense because they believed that the fine distinction between *madness* and *legal insanity* could tell you anything about justice. Two days after the verdict, the foreman published an open letter to then governor Ronald Reagan in the *Santa Cruz Sentinel*. *I hold the state executive and state legislative offices as responsible for these ten lives as I do the defendant himself,* he wrote. *None of this need ever have happened.*

> *We had the awesome task of convicting one of our young valley residents of a crime that only an individual with a mental discrepancy could have committed. Five times prior to Mr. Mullin's arrest he was entered into mental facilities. At least twice it was determined that his illness could cause danger to the lives of human beings. Yet in February and January of this year he was free to take the lives of Santa Cruz County residents.*
>
> *According to testimony at his trial, Herb Mullin could and did respond favorably to treatment of his mental illness. Yet the laws of this state certainly prohibit officials from forcing continued treatment of his illness, and I have the impression that they, as a matter of fact, discourage continued treatment by state and county institutions.*
>
> *In recent years, mental hospitals all over this state have been closed down in an economic move by the Reagan administration. Where do you think these mental institution patients who were in these hospitals went after their release? Do you suppose they went to private, costly mental hospitals? Or do you suppose they went to the ghettos of our large cities and to the remote hills of Santa Cruz County?*

I freely admit that I write this at a time when my emotions are not as clearly controlled as perhaps I would like them to be, the letter concluded, *but I cannot wait longer to impart to anyone who may read this my convictions that the laws surrounding mental illness in the State of California are wrong, wrong, wrong.*

For the jury, it was not even relevant whether or not Mullin was morally responsible for his actions. They just believed that if Mullin were remanded to a psychiatric hospital, even for an extended and involuntary term, they could not be sure that he wouldn't one day be released. And then he might go off his medication. And then he might kill again.

This is, of course, an old terror about the insane. It doesn't only arise in extreme cases. Once, in Iowa, I sat in a bar apologizing to a former friend for how I'd treated her during a manic episode. She listened. She was liberal and sympathetic. She could not bring herself, at any rate, to admit a desire to punish somebody for the consequences of a mental disease. But, she asked me, *How can I know you'll never go off your meds again?* And after a minute I said, *Well, I guess you can't.*

VI

I wrote to Herbert Mullin for the first time in fall 2018. I'd discovered him in a book about crime and madness, where he took up only a few pages as a kind of cipher for the worst consequences of deinstitutionalization. I wrote him because he was the most terrifying example I could find of the worst consequences of schizophrenia: a lunatic in prison not because his benign illness was misunderstood by a bigoted police officer or neighborhood watch, but because his illnesses lead to real and terrible violence. Of course, of course: Schizophrenics are not, in general, the frothing madmen who will kill you for looking at them like a space alien, but Mullin is schizophrenic, and he was, at least for a time, a dangerous lunatic. He was a murderer of strangers and children and old friends, and those two facts are inseparable from one another. I thought that if I could come to understand him, if I could figure out what we owe him both as a patient and as a criminal, then perhaps I could understand something about that old terror. *No matter what he's done,* I told myself, *Herbert Mullin is still a patient.* I didn't want to write him off as a monster or an embarrassment just because he reflects poorly on the rest of us. That is to say: when I wrote Mullin for the first time, I told myself that I was doing something righteous, something difficult and contrarian and brave.

In my first letter, I told Mullin that I wasn't interested in his case but in what had come after. I wanted to talk to him about his life since his conviction. Enough had been written about the crimes themselves. I wanted to know what happens after a sensational case leaves the headlines, and a madman sits decade after decade in prison.

He wrote back, effusively. In the first two months of our correspondence. He sent nearly two dozen letters to my three. He uses exclamation points and question marks, but no periods. Ordinary sentences ended with em dashes. Unlike any source who I have ever had for any story, he sent me, unprompted, a complete list of all his vital records, and instructions for how to access them. In his first few letters, he told me three separate times that I ought to read Joan Didion. No amount of telling him that I had read Joan Didion and asking about books of hers he may have read, had prevented him from writing back to recommend her, always noting in parenthesis that she is *a very famous writer, in the California registry of significant persons.* Mullin has read one book by Joan Didion—2003's *Where I Was From*—and he has cited it more than once in handwritten writs of habeas corpus filed on his own behalf.

I sent a list of questions, almost entirely about his day-to-day life, but he answered erratically if at all, and usually in passing. Each letter, which was invariably about some other topic, ended with a promise to get to my questions next time. He told me that most of what I wanted to know could be found on his website, which he composes by hand and mails to a friend in New York who types it up. The site, which is mostly short essays and self-reflection, contains no mention of Mullin's actual life in prison.

By the time I began writing to Mullin, he had been in prison for nearly forty-five years. In August 1973, after his conviction, Mullin was remanded to the California Men's Colony in San Luis Obispo, roughly halfway between Los Angeles and San Francisco. Over his first few decades behind bars, Mullin completed an array of vocational programs there, including gardening, landscaping, and carpentry. He read about astronomy and other sciences in an effort to prepare himself for life after a possible release. But in 1993, Mullin was transferred to the medium security facility at Mule Creek State Prison, farther north. At Mule Creek, Mullin saw the physical and scientific vocation training he liked replaced with emotional programs: therapy and support groups and twelve-step meetings. He said that he didn't like those quite as much, but he attended them just the same: it's something to do.

Mainly, Mullin looked forward to letters and spent a great deal of time composing his replies. I was not the first person who tried to interview him, and inquiring journalists were only a small fraction of his correspondents. Some were oddballs, or true crime or serial killer enthusiasts. But many were like the girl who told me she just likes *researching and learning everything I can about random topics. I'm an administrative assistant in real life*, she told me, *so boring. I became interested in Herbert Mullin due to the mental illness factor in his case.* She did not explain why this might interest her. Another, a man named Christopher who describes himself as Herbert's best friend, told me that he grew up with an absent uncle. *He became incarcerated for the attempted murder of my grandmother*, he told me in an email. *He suffered from schizophrenia for sure, but it wasn't nearly as understood back in the seventies. I always felt like there was a weird hole in my family tree that nobody talked about. I started writing to Herbert because I don't think he is a bad person. He is a kind and gentle old man. But he was, and still is, very sick. But a man who spent forty-six years in prison has some stories to tell, and I love listening to them.*

[Herbert] has been a man who has been taken advantage of and mocked for the vast majority of his life, he told me. *[He] trusts me more than anyone else because I have done nothing but good by him.* This was the friend who maintains the website, but that's not all. *He sends me on real-world*

scavenger hunts to find things for him, he told me, although he did not say what he was tasked with finding.

All of this is to say that nobody came to write to a man like Herbert Mullin if he was not a cipher for some personal stake. He's like a picture of the sun, easier to stare at and study than the sun itself. For this man, it's an absent uncle. A few months into my correspondence with Mullin, I continued to tell myself that my interest in Mullin was mainly intellectual, with a tinge of Christian charity. But it was the same fall that I had tried to kill a man with my mind, and I do not believe it is possible that I wasn't thinking of Herbert Mullin at the time.

VII

Mullin had questions for me, too. He wanted to know my birthday, what I did with my time, if I had any pets, and if so, what their names were. He had a scavenger hunt for me, too. In an early letter, he included a postscript saying that he noticed my return address was in Iowa.

> *As a side note of interest . . . my GREAT grandparents, MR. and MRS. Mullin, ARE buried somewhere there in IOWA! I do not know much about them except that they had a son on July 24th, 1867—HE is/was my grandfather—*
>
> *Maybe you could SEARCH on-line and find where my Great Grandparents were buried—when & where were they born?*

I told myself it would be useful to earn Mullin's trust and goodwill. Perhaps if I did this for him, he'd open up a bit more. I found that Iowa maintains online records of all grave plots, and while there are several hundred Mullins buried in the state, there was only one match for a couple sharing that last name and likely to have had a son in 1867. John Mullin, b. 1836, d. 1912, and his wife, Mary J. Mullin, 1838–1913. I discovered that their headstone was in a graveyard less than a mile from my front door, and the next day, I went and found it. I was excited to tell Mullin about my discovery, in the way you are excited to tell a friend about a fun coincidence. They're buried right here near my house! How strange! I wrote Mullin and told him about my find. I offered to send a picture I'd taken, if he liked. Then I asked again if he'd take a look at the questions I'd sent along.

What I got instead were tangents. Over the following few months, I received envelopes full of extended free-verse poetry, enumerated explanations of different astronomical and biological phenomena, and requests for photographs of national parks, which I sent. One letter told me that *Enclosed is another poetry/metaphysical/mysticism/natural sciences thesis*—and asked if I'd be kind enough to give him feedback. *I do enjoy writing/creating them,* he wrote. *It gives me the feeling that I am doing the right thing with my time and energy.* Enclosed were a dozen pages, some photocopies of typed documents, some hand-written, with sentences like:

> *Commentary: 186282.3971 miles per second is a more accurate estimate of the speed of light.*
> *That which is bright rises twice!*
> *That which is beyond vibratory creation is mystical!*
> *120 squared is 14,400!!*
> *186282.3971 squared is 3.470113145 times 10 to the 10th!*
> *186282.3971 cubed is 6.46209947 times 10 to the 15th!*
> *Today is March 8th, 2019, Friday. Herbert William Mullin*

Other letters arrived with headlines like "POETRY METAPHYSI-CAL MYSTICISM," "Calculus (this one includes a number of accurate explanations and equations)," "Buddhism's Philosophy," "Kepler," "THE NOBLE EIGHT-FOLD PATH," "Interesting," "APPLIED NUCLEAR PHYSICS," "Disposition—Noun from 14th Century," "Coordination Complex = noun 1951 c.e.," "Nature Religion in America," and "BOOKS I HAVE RESEARCHED."

Mullin's letters mainly came on carefully numbered sheets of loose yellow legal paper, but sometimes he sent little index cards or white pages with full-color drawings of clouds and stars and flags. One read:

GOOD HEALTH

GOOD WEALTH for

THE UNITED STATES

OF AMERICA _____.

Underneath were three stamps, all American flags.

Have you looked up the word "Metaphysics" recently? he asked in one letter. *What about "Mysticism"? If you haven't, I strongly urge you to do so! 5 minutes of thinking about the definitions will allow you to see your feelings about REAL personal philosophical questions—and it will assist you in knowing what inspires me to write to begin with!!* The two exclamation points at the end are connected, beneath the dots, into a smiley face.

I received dozens of letters over the next few months. As time went on, I found that I was growing frustrated by them. They were interesting at first—*good color,* I told myself in a cynical note—but there were too many. They were hard to read. He still had not told me what his actual life in prison was like. I was often bored. *The secret of florid psychosis—it's boring* (another note). I wondered, sometimes, if Mullin was trying to come off as unhinged. I got angry with myself for suspecting that at all. I reminded myself that if nothing else I had been telling myself that I was engaged in an act of charity here: Why not just be a sounding board for what this poor, sad lunatic has to say? *A man is hired to give advice to the readers of a newspaper,* writes Nathaniel West in *Miss Lonelyhearts. The job is a circulation stunt and the whole staff considers it a joke . . . He too considers the job a joke, but after several months at it, the joke begins to escape him. He sees that the majority of the letters are profoundly humble pleas for moral and spiritual advice, that they are inarticulate expressions of genuine suffering.*

I never considered Mullin a joke, and I do not want to make him one, but I worried—I worry—that many of these letters, these expressions of his real interest in science and math and mysticism and metaphysics, these letters asking about my cat by name, these *inarticulate expressions of genuine suffering*, that all of this is so eccentric, conforms so well to the generally imagined cadence of a lunatic, that if I can spare him from being remembered as an uncomplicated monster, it will only be to transform him into a punchline. I worried that even this was a smokescreen: these letters, beyond the point of filling out a portrait, were not helping in my work. He was not telling me what I would like to know, and it was not clear that if he did tell me, I would gain any insight into the *problem of madness and crime* like I kept telling myself I was after here.

VIII

Shortly after we began corresponding, I wrote to the state of California requesting any documents available in Mullin's case. After a number of delays, I received hundreds of pages of documents, which I began to read six or seven months after I'd begun speaking to Mullin. Most of what I got were scans of handwritten, summarily denied appeals to various courts. Many of the pages were missing, and some, before 1980, no longer exist at all. The bulk of the documents are transcripts of Mullin's parole hearings over the years.

Herbert Mullin became eligible for parole decades ago. Since then, he has applied for release whenever he is legally able. All his applications have been denied, and it is not difficult to see why. A 2001 psychiatry evaluation found he was still actively schizophrenic. At a hearing in 2006, Mullin told the parole board that he had "purged his mind" of his disease by cutting off contact with his parents. He told them that while he prayed to "the God of America" for the families of his victims, his parents ought to receive more blame for his crimes. *[What happened is that] somebody started me on this while I was in a state of undifferentiated schizophrenia, paranoid schizophrenia,* Mullin said at the hearing. *They started me on this and I had no intentions of hurting anyone. . . .*

PRESIDING COMMISSIONER BIGGERS: You said they. Who is they?

MULLIN: Well, it was my parents, my mother and father.

BIGGERS: We'll talk about your social history a little bit later on, but I wanted—

MULLIN: Well, those are the people who started me—

BIGGERS: How did they go about doing that?

MULLIN: By denying me maturity—

BIGGERS: How did they go about denying you maturity?

MULLIN: By not teaching me the facts of life or the idea of the pecking order in society, how to deal with the life and death of the ego. How to think about heterosexuality, bisexuality, homosexuality, any type of sexuality. They left me in a state of immaturity, naiveté, and gullibility while they allowed my peer group in grammar school and high school and college to mature and become strong and healthy and worthwhile so-called members of society.

BIGGERS: So you're telling me that the reason you went on this killing spree was the fact that your parents did not allow you—didn't teach you anything about sexuality?

MULLIN: Not just sexuality, but also the pecking order. How the life and death of the ego—

BIGGERS: When you say the life and death of the ego, clue me in. I don't . . . I don't understand what you're saying.

MULLIN: Okay. When we're in a social situation and people are conversing, and one person indicates that that person is the alpha male so to speak, then the alpha male can get everybody else to keep quiet while the alpha male speaks and makes his power and influence and desires known. Okay. [Pause] I was not given any of this information from my parents or my schoolteachers or the Catholic priests that I went to confession to, and that lack of information kept me immature to the point that I became undifferentiated schizophrenic. And then, just before the crime occurred, my parents pushed me over the line into paranoid schizophrenia and the crime spree happened.

BIGGERS: All right.

MULLIN: I feel that that's wrong on their part and that the State should have punished my parents. At least chastised them publicly in the newspapers and on the televisions and in the radio.

BIGGERS: Yeah.

In his nearly five decades in prison, Mullin only had two disciplinary write-ups. One was for stealing feathers from an art room, which he claimed were for a nonspecific "religious ritual" in his cell. The other was for a nonspecific sexual encounter with another inmate, because in prison, even consensual sex is a crime. In one of his letters, he told me—unprompted—that as a young man, his parents caused him to become confused about his sexuality, but he was *100% heterosexual and monogamous* now. He told me that he had another parole hearing coming in 2021 and that he believed he would prevail this time.

After reading these documents and rereading a number of Mullin's letters, I considered giving up. My alibi for all of this was flimsy. Mullin had too extreme a case to be revealing, and he was too disorganized in practice to reveal anything to me. What could come of this? I didn't reply to a few letters, but Mullin kept writing, and after a while, freed of the belief that I must *gain something* by reading them and studying their author, I found that they were funny and friendly. I looked forward to them. I remembered that I too have heard the voice of God and believed the world to be conspiring toward my destiny, that I too have spent time in hospital after hospital and have known what it is like to feel that you are losing your mind and then losing it so thoroughly that you forget there is something wrong. There was a logic and an intuition in Mullin's writing that I recognized, and it is an incredible relief to talk to somebody else who is like you. Eventually I began writing back again, telling myself that the purpose of this story would reveal itself with time.

IX

Sometimes Mullin got angry with me. In many of my letters I repeated questions or reminded him about answers he'd promised to provide. I didn't always send the pictures he'd asked for or address the questions he'd asked me. I was still telling myself that I was the one conducting the interview here. In any case, I was not asking difficult questions. Several months in, I was still asking about his daily life. I had not, at that point, even asked him about the murders themselves. But he wrote sometimes, telling me, *I believe I already answered this question—! I wonder if you are paying attention!!* Then I would find myself in my apartment, trying to type up a reply that would not alienate him as a source and would not sour his effusive willingness to speak to me, even if it was not necessarily about what I was asking for. After eight or nine months, I decided the only way to reassure him was to mention, casually, that I too have been diagnosed with a psychotic disorder and am heavily medicated, so he needn't be worried or nervous about discussing his condition with me. I promised that I'd understand. He already knew my birthday and the name of my cat. I was not the first writer, or the first person, to correspond with a violent prisoner and realize I really could tell this person anything. What could he do? Judge me?

By spring, it had been nine months since I'd begun writing to Mullin. Soon, the university semester would be over, and I would have a few months to myself. I decided to go back to California and drive up to Ione and visit Mule Creek in person. Maybe it would prove a good interview, but even if it didn't, I told myself that it was the kind thing to do. Mullin hadn't had a visitor in years. What good did it do to lock this old, sick man up in prison all alone? He was nonviolent, eccentric—just look at his letters—but not evidently delusional. Even if he wasn't cured, he wasn't as sick as he'd once been. Maybe if he got out, he could be treated for his lingering symptoms. All of it, I thought, was just sad.

I also thought, as my initial frustration with Mullin receded, my motives were perhaps as obvious as anybody but me could see. Mullin was what every lunatic, myself included, is afraid they might become. It isn't precisely that I believe I am liable to murder anybody, much less a dozen people—I find, as the letters go on that I must keep reminding myself *this man murdered children, he stabbed children to death*—but as time has passed and I have realized that even rigorous adherence to medication does not guarantee prolonged recovery, I have come to appreciate how much of this is luck.

That is to say, the difference between a policeman and Herbert Mullin is that when the chief tells the officer to run headlong into a building, weapon drawn, because doing so will save more lives than it may cost, the chief and the emergency are real. That's all. I think sometimes that the difference between Herbert Mullin and me is that God mainly told me I was dying, not that other people were asking to die. That when I tried to kill a stranger, I used a method that was too insane to work. That's all. I don't like to think that, but it's true. Mean coincidence. Mean luck.

After my tenth or eleventh reminder, Mullin finally sent me his daily routine.

Awake at 5:00 a.m.

Breakfast at 6:00 a.m.

Mind-charting between 7:00 a.m.–8:00 a.m.

Book wrk + research btw. 8:00 a.m.–10:00 a.m. [*In this letter, I have enclosed some of my research projects*, Mullin writes. *They are indicative of how I spend my time day by day—I feel that is a good thing.*]

Outdoor exercise btw. 10:00 a.m.–noon

Lunch between noon & 1:30 p.m., with www.capradio.org/classical music

1:30–3:30 p.m. outdoor music + exercise

3:30–6:00 p.m. lock up for count; reading

6:00 p.m.–6:40 p.m. supper time

6:40–7:45 p.m. outdoor music & exercise

7:45 p.m.–9:00 p.m. shower time

9:00–10:00 p.m. Maybe a masterpiece theater movie on the PBS-T.V. station

10:00–10:30 p.m. www.coasttocoastam.com a radio program I get from the local KFBK-FM radio station

10:30 p.m.–midnight = "at the opera" with host Sean Bianco–it can be found at www.capradio.org/at the opera

midnight till 12:30 a.m.–mind charting and prayer until sleep

There is, he said, a little variety on the weekends.

This is not a terrible day. But it had been his day, every day, with only minor variations, for over forty years.

X

After the 2011 hearing, Mullin undertook what appears to be a deliberate effort to prepare a better case for 2021. In 2016, he posted a long essay, composed in pieces over several years, to his website. The essay, which he referred to as his "thesis," is called "Apologies and Insights."

Its sections have names like "Rehabilitation Attitude," "Rehabilitation Reflections," "Transformation and Rehabilitation," and "Rehabilitation: Forgiveness and Remorse." One section, "Sorrow and Remorse," reads in full:

> *In my daily prayer life I honestly express true sorrow and true remorse for having committed the 13 crimes.*
>
> *I am sorry and I am remorseful.*
>
> *I hope that the God of America will guide, protect, and improve the 13 victims and their families and friends.*
>
> *I hope that they will be reimbursed and repaid for their loss in the tragedy.*
>
> *I am truthfully very, very sorry.*
>
> *H.W. Mullin*
> *July 21, 2014*
> *Monday*

Almost every part is like this. *I am sorry*, he wrote over and over. *I pray for my victims and their families.* He said he does not blame his parents any longer, that he wanted to contribute to society, that he felt terrible and was not a danger to anyone. He accepted that he has, or at the very least had, a serious mental illness, although he did not receive medication of any kind. He reported that he had only ever been involved in a single instance of prison violence. But he was the victim, he said, not the perpetrator. Another inmate punched him so hard it dislocated his jaw.

Who am I? What is my purpose? he wrote in one section,

> *I am in the process of rehabilitating and reeducating myself. Over the years, since my arrest, I have sincerely healed and cleansed my mind and emotions of paranoid undifferentiated schizophrenia.*
>
> *Because I still believe I could and should become a free member of our U.S.A, California, society. I believe I could become involved in educating*

the younger generations as to how and why they should avoid living lives of crime. I take responsibility for my thoughts, my speech, and my actions. I am responsible for myself. I believe I am ready to become a law abiding, tax paying, worthwhile free citizen.

There is something incredibly rote, incredibly literal about these passages. They are like a checklist of parole qualifications. You must express remorse. You must take responsibility for yourself and your actions. You must demonstrate an understanding of any mental or emotional difficulties. You must have a plan to become a tax-paying citizen. So, Mullin said sorry, said he is responsible for his actions, that he knows he has schizophrenia, that he wants to contribute to the betterment of the United States. He said these things over and over and over.

In a sane prisoner, the "Apologies and Insights" would be laughably cynical—less a manipulative document than a document with ambition to manipulate written by an author too lazy to succeed. But when we were corresponding Mullin believed all of this, and he believed that if he only repeated over and over his sincere commitment to meeting the general terms of parole, then he would be released next time. But Herbert Mullin murdered thirteen people, including several children. Whether or not you believe he ought to be paroled, he never would have been. The Board would always find that he was insufficiently sincere, insufficiently responsible, prepared, or remorseful. What is laughably cynical is a prison system that allowed Mullin to go on believing that he could do it right next time.

The one thing that Mullin didn't do in prison, despite its possible value to his cause, was submit to psychiatric treatment. This wasn't always the case. I asked him about this in a letter. In the early 1970s, he said, shortly after his conviction, he worked with two prison doctors, Morton Felix and Gordon Haiberg, whom he liked and trusted. Under their care, he took antipsychotics for nearly two years. They helped him work with his family, although the particulars are frustratingly vague. *Dr. Gordon Haiberg arranged for me and my parents and Dr. Haiberg to meet all-together in the prison visiting room and talk about the whole mess of problems*—he wrote. *It was late summer or early autumn of 1976*—. *It lasted two hours with Dr. Haiberg asking questions and my parents answering and asking questions! I answered and asked questions myself, but*—and at this point, I nearly stopped writing him all over again—*I do not remember much of what was said that day.*

Mullin said that on the advice of these doctors, he ultimately cut off all contact with his family. Then he went off his medication. He claimed that he did this with the consent of his doctors, and that, in their opinion, his family—particularly his father—was the cause of his illness and that he was now cured. This is less suspicious than it sounds. Through the middle of the twentieth century, schizophrenia was frequently attributed to bad parenting, and particularly "bad mothers." It is not impossible that two doctors who attended medical school before the 1970s would tell Mullin that his family was to blame. It is more difficult to believe that they recommended he cease medication and told him that he was cured. No paperwork attests to this change in diagnosis. Mullin said he was declared cured verbally, in session. There is no way to confirm this. Dr. Haiberg died in the 1980s. Dr. Felix, who is mainly remembered for treating Charles Manson, died in 2012. Mullin's parents died in 1982 and 1998. Mullin told me that he did not trust the evaluations of the current prison psychiatrists, but he remained vague as to why.

As my visit approached and Mullin became more and more fixated on explaining his plans for his parole hearing (then still two years away), I considered telling him that I did not believe he would ever receive parole. I imagined phrasing it as a kind of leading question, *Given the circumstances, do you think it's realistic that . . .* but I decided against it. I told myself that I was concerned for his emotional well-being—which was not my official concern—but I didn't think about it for too long, because I knew if I reflected, I would realize that I was not being kind. I wanted to believe that I was, but I wasn't. I was being cowardly.

What if he stopped speaking to me? What if he blamed me, or assumed I was "in" with the parole board, or simply didn't want to keep up with such a downer, no matter how lonely he might be? What if he didn't like me anymore?

XI

In the summer of 2019, I flew to Los Angeles, spent a few days with my parents, and then rented a car to drive to Northern California. The drive to Ione is nearly seven hours, so I went up on a Friday. Ione itself is so small you could look down at your phone while driving through and look up to find you'd missed the town entirely. I spent a night in Sutter Creek, about fifteen miles away. Sutter Creek is the kind of town with a main street called Main Street, with a purposefully rustic hotel, a bar or two, and several wineries and boutique craft stores, but is otherwise largely meth country. I stayed there because I remember, mainly, that it was very hot, and unlike the Southern California desert, it was humid and stayed hot into the nighttime.

I spent most of the night in one of the two bars, asking if anybody knew anybody who worked at the prison. Eventually, I fell in with a middle-aged man who said his wife might be able to help me, and when the bar closed, I followed him back to his home a few blocks away. I sat on an enclosed patio with the man and his wife, who told me, at great length, about how they were fostering a child they suspected of having an anti-social personality disorder, how this had led to a prolonged conflict with the local school board, how the wife used to tour with rock 'n' roll bands but had settled down here in the country with her right-wing husband, and how incredible it was to learn and grow with somebody from the other side of the aisle. They mentioned knowing someone who maybe worked on the psychiatric staff at Mule Creek, but they remained vague on whether they could get in touch.

We kept drinking. They claimed to know who Mullin was—*wasn't he*

some psycho who'd been in prison since the sixties or seventies or something?—
and asked me if I thought he was really insane. I told them what, after
nearly a year of letters, I took to be true: yes, but not so much as he once
was. I told them that the symptoms of these illnesses tend to abate with
age, that the brute routine of prison life might have curative effects with
time, that he hadn't had a violent disciplinary infraction in years, and
so no, I didn't believe he was dangerous. I told them he was probably
just a sad old man, that you could see the course of his delusions in his
testimony, and his parole hearings, and his letters. Like many schizophrenics, he attributes godlike powers to other people; in Mullin's case,
to his father. Once, he believed that his dad was literally a conduit for
God, commanding him to kill. By his parole hearings, the delusion is still
there but lessened: his father caused his schizophrenia, he says, by keeping
him "naïve" while "allowing" his peers in school to reach maturity (the
delusion is in this power over Mullin's friends in school). By now, I said, I
think it's even less than that: he thinks his father caused his schizophrenia
by being a bad father, and that cutting off all contact cured him. I said
I didn't even know if that was quite a delusion anymore. Psychiatrists
believed similar things for much of the twentieth century. I told them I
thought it was wrong—but you can be wrong without being crazy.

The wife told me that was patronizing, which it was. It was also
strange. I was, after all, a stranger in their living room late at night,
mounting an impassioned defense of a mass murderer as if he were my
friend. Then she told me to smile more. Then she said, *You don't have
a sense of humor do you?* because I hadn't laughed at anything she'd said
all night, which is one way to interpret that phenomenon. It was nearly
five o'clock in the morning.

I walked back to my hotel, drunk and sweating through the humid
sticky California dawn. I was meant to meet Mullin in six or seven
hours. I began to imagine the meeting, and it occurred to me, for the
first time, that I had not seen any photographs of Mullin taken in the
past twenty or thirty years. There are photos of him as a teenager, clean-
cut and still round-faced, wearing a too-big varsity jacket, about to be

voted "most likely to succeed." There are photos of Mullin in his early twenties, sometimes short-haired with a light mustache, sometimes longhaired and long-mustached, like a stab at Frank Zappa without the curls. Sometimes he is dressed as a boxer; sometimes he is dressed up like a yogi. Mainly he is dressed up like a hippie, which his clean-cut war hero Republican father took as explanation enough for his son's increasingly bizarre behavior. I had seen his mugshot and pictures from his trial in which, Mullin, twenty-five years old, was captured at odd angles, staring at nothing. But that was nearly fifty years ago. I knew from descriptions that the man I was going to meet was largely bald and missing several teeth. I knew that he wore thick glasses, made from the awkward, blocky plastic allowed in penitentiaries. When I read the letters, I imagined the man in the photos I'd seen. But I wasn't going to see a man my own age, who grew up in the California I grew up in, and who I realized I had been imagining for nearly a year. I would be talking to an old man, with little hair, and too few remaining teeth.

I slept for a few hours and then checked out of the hotel and drove to Ione. On the way, I became suddenly nervous about the interview. Specifically, I worried how Mullin and I would manage to talk. Letters are one thing, but even with old age, the negative symptoms of schizophrenia do not abate. I thought that Mullin would say too many words that meant too little, that he'd have a blunted affect, be circuitous and digressive and exclusively responsive in conversation—none of which would be such a bad thing, except that I was that way, too. No medication I take can treat those symptoms. I get into topics sideways. I find it impossible to make sustained eye contact. I rarely smile or speak in a way that sets other people at ease—I sound rude, like I'm not really interested or listening—and I tend to hop through topics on an obscure and exhausting path. I rely on other people to prop up conversations. But Mullin, I began to worry, could be even worse than me. He'd be stilted. I'd be stilted. I wondered if maybe I'd come all that way for something terribly awkward. What if we didn't get along? What if we could barely speak at all?

Those negative symptoms, by the way, are why I didn't laugh or smile enough the night before. But I do have a sense of humor. I know how to set up a joke. For example, arranging an interview between two people who are medically incapable of ordinary social graces and clinically paranoid, to take place under observation, in a prison for the purposes of a story the real impetus for which remains obscure even to its author, concerning, among other topics, the younger lunatic's patronizing theory of the older man's sad, lonely prison life, and the time the older lunatic, among other victims, shot two children and then stabbed their dead bodies dozens and dozens of times.

XII

Before I could go in to see Mullin, I twice had to walk back across the baking parking lot to my car to stow another item I wasn't permitted to bring inside. I knew there would be restrictions. You cannot, unless you are an attorney, bring a tape recorder into a prison. You can't bring a phone with a recording device. You might be able to negotiate some paper, provided it is loose-leaf, but you cannot bring any kind of writing implement inside. You can't wear a belt with a buckle, or shoes with any steel in them. You can't bring in cigarettes or matches or a lighter. What I didn't realize is that you really can't bring anything at all. The first time I was sent back to my car, it was to put my jacket away (it had too many metal buttons); then, when I returned, I discovered that I would need to stow my wallet, too. To enter Mule Creek, you need an ID card, but you must carry it in separately. They won't make you put your car keys in your unlocked car, but they will take them from you and keep them at the front in a small bag until you're done. There are vending machines in the visiting room, but they require a special credit card issued by the prison itself; to get one, you bring cash that you exchange for the card. You can bring that in, but I didn't have any cash on me.

There are several steps between the front door and the visiting room. First, you receive paperwork from a guard at the front desk. He's the one who takes your car keys, too. You then present your paperwork and ID to a guard roughly fifteen feet away. They take you through a metal detector and swab your hands with a chemical solution designed to detect contraband. Then, you pass through a secure door into a fenced-in holding area. Once the door behind you closes, the first gate opens, letting you into a slightly larger fenced-in area at the bottom of the main yard. That gate closes behind you and the next one opens. From there, you can walk onto the main yard and follow signs for the path to the building where your inmate is housed. When the second gate closed behind me, I felt something like what I felt the first time I returned to a high school as an adult: *I've come in voluntarily; what if they don't let me back out?*

When you reach the appropriate building, you enter a new staging room. There, a new guard checks the same paperwork and ID that were checked on the other side of the yard; if you're the same person you were five minutes prior, he buzzes you into the visiting room. The visiting room itself is enormous; thirty or forty tables with chairs, ringed by special vending machines. These vending machines can only be operated by visitors, big block letters on the floor explain that inmates MAY NOT PASS to this outer ring. All the chairs face forward. Inmates and their visitors sit shoulder-to-shoulder; forty-five-degree angles at most, because at the front of the room, on an elevated platform, is another guard, watching everyone. You approach this guard, who checks your paperwork and ID once again and then assigns you to an empty table. You sit and wait while a second guard takes your papers and disappears through another set of doors at the far side of the room, into the prison itself.

I had written Mullin a letter a week before, telling him that I would come on Saturday or Sunday, and he'd written back telling me that he was looking forward to it. But visiting hours are long and stretch over two days—I wasn't sure if Mullin would be busy at eleven o'clock on Saturday; if he'd be asleep, or at work, or if the guard who took my papers away was meant to fetch him or if he was meant to come to the visitor room on his own, through a separate series of checkpoints on his side, and if so, whether they would at least tell him that I'd arrived. I waited in the visitor's room by myself for a long time.

I spent most of this time watching and listening to other prisoners and their guests: a large older man, monologuing to his family about the state of the Democratic Party; an elderly Sikh man sitting with a man who might have been his twin brother, silently playing one of the board games available for checkout from the guards; a very tall and broad blond man with prominent tattoos and the sort of coloring and jawline that might have once found itself featured on an SS recruiting poster, holding hands with a woman on the outside of the MAY NOT PASS line, he inside, although from time to time, when the guard was looking somewhere else, he'd slowly and performatively raise one foot and set the tip of his toe down on the wrong side, then make a face like an old mime, while the woman giggled. Most of the prisoners were young men, with mothers or girlfriends or young children or all three there to see them, chairs from other visiting tables hauled over to theirs to make more room, and everybody acting, in the way that I suppose one must in this situation, as if the decoration and time limit and seating choreography were ordinary, and what they might have chosen anyway if everyone at the table were free.

I had been sitting over half an hour when I suddenly became aware of a short man standing too-close over me saying, *Emmett? Emmett?* I looked up, and it was Herbert Mullin, who apologized for the wait. He hadn't been sure what time I was coming and was taking a nap. We didn't shake hands and he sat down at the table, forty-five degrees to my left, nearly shoulder-to-shoulder, both of us looking at nothing halfway between the guard station at the front and each other.

He said, *I'm glad you're here.* He hasn't had a visitor in nearly four years.

Mullin was old, but he looked older. He was turned inward, concave chest and thin arms bent toward his torso, gaunt face, as if he was slowly folding in on himself and disappearing. He didn't have a soft voice, but he was soft-spoken; he spoke at the volume of a whisper without whispering and nodded his head up and down very slightly while he spoke. There was none of the manic energy of his letters. Nothing he said could rightly be punctuated with an exclamation point. He was in good health, he told me, but he could stand to work out more. At seventy-two years old, Herbert Mullin was a very old man.

There was a moment after Mullin sat down when I wished that he had forgotten my visit, or that something had gone wrong; that I'd be able to write about visiting the prison without the awkwardness and difficulty of an in-person interview. We both sat there for a minute half-mumbling, *Yes, thanks for talking to me, glad this worked out*, without either of us locating a way in to the conversation. Eventually, after several minutes, I asked him if he had his own cell. *No*, Mullin said, the cells are designed for one, but there's overcrowding, so he has a cellmate. *How is he?* I asked. *He's all right. We get along all right.* I asked if he could tell me about him. *No, I'm not going to talk about that.* After another pause, Mullin asked if I knew anything about Amador County, where Mule Creek is located. I said that I didn't. Then he started talking about Amador County and didn't stop for four-and-a-half minutes by the clock on the wall.

This is how it goes with Mullin. Like many people, he is more willing to talk about himself in writing; in person, he becomes embarrassed and looks away when I ask him about himself. Instead, he is eager to talk about what he's reading or rattle off trivia he knows. He told me that Saturdays are unusual because he doesn't get to go out on the yard as much—they keep them all off while visitors are passing through. But he'd been hoping to get back out that night. He told me that Jupiter was visible; either ascending or descending. He had been tracking it and didn't want to miss it that night.

Mullin told me about his job. He's a porter. He said a few times that he *keeps the house clean*, always with the same nod, as if it was a prison idiom about porters, which I supposed it must be. I asked him if the prison library was any good, and he told me that it probably was, but that he got his books sent to him by friends on the outside. Then, he was reading about the Free Masons. Did I know about the Free Masons?

I expected him to launch into conspiracy—what else does one expect from a schizophrenic?—but instead he told me that Masonry began as a bourgeois political society in early modern Europe, managing to accrue some influential members and therefore exert some force in shaping the networks that shaped the mass Western transition into capitalism and constitutional democracy, but that now it exists mainly as an empty social club. All of this is accurate. The book sounded interesting, but I didn't catch what it was called.

I am not a particularly skilled interviewer; I have trouble directing even sane subjects toward the point. I didn't mind hearing about Mullin's reading and astronomy and work, but at some point, I would have liked to talk about his case. Twenty or thirty minutes in, I tried asking around the edges—something about the numerous writs of habeas corpus he'd filed over the years, but I'm not certain; my notes, written in the Mule Creek parking lot after the fact, only say *tried asking about extraneous court filings*—but got nowhere. *You're asking about stuff I've already told you*, Mullin said. I said something meek about double-checking and the difference between a letter and hearing somebody explain something in person, but he shook his head and then we were back to another book he'd been reading, this one about Plato. He told me that if you really want to grasp his philosophy, it helps to write out every one of Plato's key concepts on index cards, and then lay them out in different patterns. Then you start to see the connections.

In person, Mullin didn't have any of the clichéd schizophrenic energy of his letters. He spoke quietly and slowly. After Plato, he told me for a while about what being a "natural scientist" meant to him, the music he likes (Ralph Vaughan Williams's "The Lark Ascending" was a favorite), and his memories of Santa Cruz in the 1960s. He asked me about my educational background. He wanted to know what I actually knew about psychology and law, which is admittedly very little. He talked for a while about the Milky Way and the closeness of other galaxies and how he admired Joan Didion, particularly an essay she wrote about *liking the wind in Los Angeles*.

After forty-five minutes or so, Mullin began to talk more about

himself. There was a pattern to his conversational style; he was uncomfortable answering even trivial questions about his thoughts or mood
at first, preferring to go on about trivia. But trivia gave way to how he
came to know that trivia, which gave way to his other interests, which
gave way to biographical detail, which gave way to introspection.

It's a way of working sideways into the personal. I am the same
way. It's the discursive species of making poor eye contact. It's why talk
sounds so stilted in psychiatric wards.

I don't want to give you the impression that Mullin was strange. If
you spoke to him outside of a prison and avoided discussing his criminal
or medical history, he might seem like an ordinary eccentric old man,
the kind we imagine on a porch somewhere, talking to local kids: *a little
crazy, but harmless.* Less grandpa, more perennial bachelor older uncle,
the one you only see every other holiday. And I told myself, an hour or so
into our interview, that maybe I wouldn't ask Mullin any of the questions
I went to ask at all. Perhaps it was more of a visit than an interview; a
kindness for somebody who needed somebody new to talk to for a while,
and it would have been rude to force him to *answer questions.* Perhaps
that was what he wanted, after all. Could he really have been so irritated
that I asked about his court filings after he'd mentioned them in a letter?
Or was he only angry to be reminded, as I had been careful to remind
him from time to time, but less careful as time had gone on, that we
are not friends or even correspondents, but a writer and a subject with
a relationship based at bottom in a kind of exploitation?

I regretted not bringing any money with me to Mule Creek. Everybody else in the visiting room was eating; the vending machines had
full sandwiches and salads and snacks. Mullin talked for a while about
Bach and Beethoven, and I thought for a while about how long the drive
was back to Los Angeles. Perhaps I could stay with friends in Oakland.
There was another hour or so left in visiting hours, but I was thinking
of ways to wrap it up. I felt bored, which was a strange way to feel about
a visit with a mass-murderer in prison, but it was a very hot day and the
visiting room was poorly air-conditioned and I was tired.

I asked Mullin if I was right that his last parole hearing was in 2011. He said, yes, that they gave him a ten-year delay and he didn't know why (it's normally five years between shots). His next one was coming up in 2021. I asked if he thought what he'd written online—the "APOLOGIES & INSIGHTS"—would be enough to persuade the parole board. I expected he'd say what he'd said in his letters, insisting on his sincerity, entirely oblivious to the fact that his sincerity was irrelevant to his case. Instead, he said that, yes, he did hope it would help, but really what he needed was to get a psychiatrist in for an evaluation.

An outside one? I asked.

Yeah. Yeah, he says, *but it's hard. They'd have to visit here and do an interview in the visiting room, and I've written to some, but nobody, I mean, I don't get replies. And I don't— They all want money.*

I asked him why he couldn't just see one of the psychiatrists at the prison.

By that point, Mullin had spoken for nearly fifteen minutes without stopping, and with an energy he had not had all day. I cannot give you the monologue verbatim, but it went in fits and starts, and was full of interstitial sounds, where before there would have only been prolonged silence. But it was not frothing. It was not insane; he was not screaming or stuttering or incoherent. He was remarkably cogent as he explained what I expected he had wanted to make clear throughout our entire correspondence. The prison psychiatrists, he told me, refused to acknowledge the work of his earlier doctors. They insisted that he was still ill. He said he was scheduled for a new state psychiatric evaluation in October of 2020, six months before his scheduled 2021 parole hearing, but he wasn't confident that these prison doctors would make an honest assessment. They didn't like him, he said. They *don't like to be criticized*, and they *feel pressured* to criticize him. *What does that mean?* I asked. *We have a disagreement*, he said.

He told me he needed an honest psychiatric evaluation because his parole depended, in his opinion, not on the sincerity of his remorse (he admitted, for the first time, that he knew the parole board was unlikely to find *any* remorse or *any* sincerity persuasive), but on proving his parents' culpability in his crimes. That would constitute exculpatory evidence, he said. It wouldn't make him innocent, but it would be a mitigating circumstance—he would be *less guilty* if they understood he was acting under the influence of others when he committed his crimes. He explained that because he ended that influence by cutting off contact with his family, he was unlikely to reoffend. After so many decades in prison, any kind of mitigation would significantly increase his chances at parole.

I asked him what he meant when he said his parents *influenced* his crimes. Was it just what he'd said before, that they *kept him naïve* and pushed him into schizophrenia?

He said no and told me his parents—at least his father—knew that he was committing the murders.

When I asked him to clarify, he said that they at least knew about the first one, and he suspected they knew about the other twelve. I didn't say anything.

My parents failed to intervene. That's misprision, he said.

What do you mean? Did you tell your parents what you were doing?

After he said, no, that he didn't tell them, I asked him to elaborate. *They inferred,* he said. *You know, as they say, they surmised.*

The trouble, he explained, was that the prison psychiatrists insisted that that was a delusion. I realized that the trouble was that I had not understood Mullin's situation at all.

I asked him if he'd considered that possibility. He'd had delusions before. He knew that. *Could this be one?* I asked. He said no.

I asked if he had considered telling the prison psychiatrists that he accepted it was a delusion, just to tell them what they wanted to hear. Leaning forward and back in the hard blue chair, looking directly at me, he said, *They'd know I was lying. I have to . . . I have to be my honest and true self, to be moral.*

I asked again if he was sure it wasn't a delusion, to which he responded, *I've had delusions before. I know what those feel like. This isn't one. I just need them to see the truth. Like Dr. Felix and Dr. Haiberg said.* He paused. *They agreed with me. We agreed that was the situation.*

A few tables away, the two Sikh men finished their board game in silence and put it away. Several of the families had left but somebody's child was running around the visiting room. Suddenly I stood up. Mullin stood up, too. The air shifted in some scarcely perceptible way. I said thank you and told him I'd write soon. He didn't say anything for a minute, then he marched to the front of the room to the guard station. I followed him.

I guess we're done! he declared to the guard. He seemed angry. There was another hour of visiting time. Maybe he'd thought I'd stay. He was heated, I thought. I was just asking questions, expressing doubt. I couldn't take notes, but I realized there was only one thing I needed to remember: *still insane.* I wondered if he'd ever write to me again. I headed toward the door. *Good luck!* he yelled after me. I'd never heard anybody use that as a sign-off before—besides me. That's how I've always said goodbye to everybody.

I walked back across the visiting room, back through the waiting area and across the yard, through the first gate, then the second gate, then into the check-in area, where I got my car key back, then back across the baking parking lot to my car, where I sat for nearly an hour furiously writing down everything I could remember from our conversation. When I finally finished, I drove to the gate, where my car was searched. I drove through the gate out of Mule Creek, then out of Ione, then out of Northern California entirely.

XIII

After I returned to Los Angeles, I sent Mullin a quick note, thanking him for making time to see me, and asking a few follow-up questions. Ordinarily, letters to Mullin reached him in a couple of days, and I received his reply, or as was often the case, his barrage of replies, within a week. But the better part of a month went by and he didn't write back. I left the country for two weeks, and then returned to Los Angeles. There was still no letter. I reflected on how abruptly I had left and the hardness in Mullin's voice when he said *I guess we're done!* to the attending guard, and wondered if he was angry with me. I'd been hot and tired and uncomfortable, but at the distance of a few weeks, I wondered why I didn't stay for the rest of visiting hours. I could have learned more. It would have been kinder. I thought, cruelly, that he couldn't possibly be so mad that he wouldn't write me back. He hadn't had a visitor in three years. He'd been in prison for forty. He couldn't afford to refuse me.

I was angry at Mullin, too, for a while. It was a kind of defensive anger; the sort lathered up when you're afraid somebody else is displeased with you, and you're determined to have your own cause of action so that you can be equal litigants in your dispute. I resented him for refusing to be the character I wanted, for not being a cipher, then for not being coherent enough to be cooperative; I resented him for writing, for not writing what I wanted, for still being ill, for refusing to even be a feeble old object of pity. I resented that we could not even be friends, because what he really wanted from me was confirmation of his delusions. I resented him for being an untreated waste, not even a person who had *changed over time*, but just this discard of the state, kept in semi-sane stasis for years while the courts waited for him to die.

That is to say: I resented him in the way the mad are always resented, the way I have been resented; I resented him like the sane do for failing to even *not make sense* in an interesting way. I resented him for being what you would expect an untreated paranoid schizophrenic to be after all those years: fully conspiratorial, fully delusional, clearly unfit for anything freer than an institution. The parole board may be cynical, and it may be punitive, but Mullin didn't conceive of his case as a case of redemption or treatment or mercy or sociology or psychiatry or ethics. He conceived of his case as a *disagreement* between a psychiatric establishment *pressured* by vague forces to criticize and disbelieve him, and his own righteous efforts to prove that his parents knew that he had murdered a dozen people and encouraged him to do so, and that he was cured in the 1970s, primarily by freeing himself from their psychic influence. He did not want to be forgiven; he wanted to be exonerated. He conceived of it that way because he was insane. As I got angrier, I turned Mullin back into a cipher, a cipher for how easy it is to become repulsed by madness and by the mad. Then I finally received Mullin's reply.

He was not angry with me. He thanked me for coming. It was nice. He enjoyed talking about his work as a "natural scientist." It felt good for some reason, he said. He asked for photos of the Sequoias—*Very old trees!* he said, and he hoped I had a chance to see them while I was in the area. I sent the photos back. *I didn't get to see them this time*, I wrote, *but I did on a field trip as a child.*

A few months after my trip to Mule Creek, I sat in the living room of a friend of mine in Washington, DC, as she nursed her newborn daughter, and I tried to explain my interest in Mullin once again. It was journalistic, I lied, but I felt sincerely sorry for him, too. This friend has leftward politics and a developed sense of mercy, but she shook her head at me. *I don't know*, she said. *I draw the line at child murderers.* And who wouldn't? What mother wouldn't? What person?

Finally, I told her—I only half believe it myself—that I thought of writing to Herbert as a kind of mercy, or at least a kindness. I told her that I wrote to him and told him about my life, and listened when he told me about his, and visited him, and would visit him again, and sent him pictures of the national parks he wanted to see, not because I didn't believe he was wicked, but because I believed that he was—and because I believe that mercy goes first to the wicked for the same reason that bread goes first to the poor: because they need it. *For those who are well do not need a physician, but the sick do.* In Herbert's case, and in my case, and in so many millions of cases, this is both literally and figuratively true. My friend changed the subject after that. It was for the best. I don't think I could have defended much of what I had to say.

In his next letter, Mullin was tempered. He said that he hoped I'd keep my promise to come back in a year and a half, after his parole hearing, either to Mule Creek, or—hopefully!—to wherever he was living after release. But he also said that he wasn't optimistic. It felt like his last try, and he didn't expect that it would be successful. The doctors and the parole board and the prison system weren't interested in the truth, and Dr. Felix and Dr. Haiberg had died—if they'd still been alive, maybe they could've helped. He told me that they'd told him, back in the seventies, that it would take thirty years for society to understand him and his case. *I've been waiting over forty years!* he wrote.

I took a long time to reply. When I did, I apologized for the delay. He wrote back. I replied, resolving not to just abandon him, even if it ended up being a bust. Eventually, the COVID-19 restrictions led to a stamp shortage, and I didn't receive another letter for a while. I was worried that he'd died, but he eventually wrote to tell me again about his need for an independent psychiatric evaluation ahead of his next hearing. I procrastinated, again, and sent another letter apologizing for how long it took me to write. He wrote back, requesting pictures of a national park. I wrote a reply and printed the pictures, but I never sent it.

XIV

Herbert Mullin was sentenced to die in prison, a fate that many people believe he deserved. It's better, after all, than dying because a stranger beat you to death on the side of the road, or stabbed you in his car, or stabbed you in a church, or shot you on a camping trip or in your front yard or in your home before shooting your children, too. *He got decades his victims never got.* That's how the argument goes.

Of course, the same people who make this sort of argument invariably acknowledge that genuine insanity alters the meaning of criminal guilt. But this concession only ever seems to apply in general. They very rarely find a particular case in which they're willing to extend their pity. It's easier to speak in generalities about the *incarcerated mentally ill* than it is to reckon with particular cases. It is easier to imagine that the manic-depressives and schizophrenics locked up in our prisons are all pitiable cases, guilty of being too weird or too loud or too poor, rather than as specific people with their own specific names who sometimes stalked and robbed and assaulted and killed other real people who had their own specific names, too.

In one of his letters, Mullin told me that he was deprived of the opportunity to be properly reformed. If he had been treated sooner, then he never would have gone to prison. I asked him what he thinks would have happened had his insanity defense succeeded, if he had gone to a hospital in 1973 instead of jail. Would he have been cured? *I would have and should have been!* he wrote back. *I would have met a suitable woman, fallen in love, gotten married, sired many children, and become a successful businessman—me and my grandchildren could be fishing for forty-pound salmon and enjoying our riverside campfire!*

This is less a life that Herbert Mullin ever could have led than it is the fantasy *good life* of a man who left the real world when he was twenty-five years old and who had not, in the nearly fifty years since, spent real time with anybody who was not in some way connected to a prison. Perhaps Herb would have recovered with early, consistent treatment—he showed promise on his antipsychotic medication—but even a life in which Mullin did not commit his murders is not necessarily a life in which he is a *successful businessman*, the father of *many children*, happy with a *suitable* wife. Many of us living on the outside—with far better medication treating far less serious conditions than Herb's—will still never live so well. In any case, this was all impossible. It was all hypothetical. Everything is hypothetical with Herbert Mullin's life. If he had been treated. If he had gone to a psych ward instead. If he had been released from prison. If he hadn't still been delusional. If he'd just told the prison doctors what they want to hear. If he had never gotten sick at all; if Dean Richardson hadn't died; if one of the hospitals had convinced him to stay on his meds; if somebody stopped him, even after the first crime; if he'd made it to India or been able to join the Marines. The only consistent fact is that none of these hypotheticals ever came to pass. He stayed the same while getting older. Herbert Mullin was never cured. Had they opened the doors of the prison the day after my visit and said *good luck* as he walked free, he would have been dead inside a week. Our efforts, over decades and centuries, to make a moral reckoning of what we owe to those who wrong us out of illness and not malice, to decide what they owe us and what we ought to do to satisfy these debts, has always been, and perhaps always will be, a hypothetical, too.

In 2021, Mullin once again went before the parole board; once again, he was denied. A local news story reported that he once again blamed his parents for his crimes. I finally wrote him again after that to see how he was doing. He wrote back to say that he wasn't doing interviews anymore but asked again could I send some more pictures of national parks please? I didn't reply. I am not a terribly good provider of mercies, even mercies as small as a timely trip to the post office. A few months later, his website went down. *In all honesty, it only invited in weirdos to contact him*, his friend and webmaster Christopher told me. *That was really the only response he received from it at all.*

If Herb's life was filled by hypotheticals, his life was itself a hypothetical for every one of us on the outside who has ever heard the gurgles and murmurs of illusory voices, too. It's a silly fear, but I don't believe that there is a schizophrenic in the world who has not worried at least once about turning into *some kind of psycho killer* and winding up locked up like Herb. Writing to Mullin made me uneasy; in a cruel way, not writing to him reminded me that I am not like him. I have the luxury of time, the possibility of a life that grows and changes instead of just going on; I am not reliant on the mercy of letter-writing strangers with ulterior motives yet. I thought, *I can always write him again if I want to. Or I can forget about him entirely.* My hypotheticals are still open. I thought, *I am nothing like Herbert Mullin, who can only walk between the prison and the yard. Who could only travel as far as the visitor's room before returning home to his shared cell. Who could only write down Plato's thoughts on index cards and fume in letters and postcards about doctors and parole boards in the long intervals between doomed official hearings. Who could only keep track of Jupiter, watching it rise and fall from his fixed point in space and time, waiting for nothing, like a man trapped in a burning building, melting away so slowly that it felt like a whole life.* I thought, *That isn't me. Not yet.*

In August of 2022, Herbert Mullin died in a prison hospital in California. I hadn't spoken to him for the better part of a year. I wrote to Christopher, who told me Herb had neuroendocrine cancer. *I was the only person he told about his situation as he really didn't want a big deal made of it, just wanted to go in peace,* he wrote. *It was extremely aggressive and inoperable.*

I spoke to his doctor regularly while he was in the hospital, Christopher wrote. *He was totally with it and having a conversation with his doctor in which he had asked her to call me and to let me know he was okay, then died within the hour.* Small mercies.

In a press release, the California Department of Corrections attributed Herb's death to *natural causes*, the inexplicable and rapid onset of a rare, fatal disease. "Herbert Mullin Dies; Infamous Serial Killer of Santa Cruz's 'Murder Capital' Days," summarized the local *Mercury News*. The building finally burned down. The final hypotheticals foreclosed. Herbert Mullin got what he deserved or never got what he was owed, or we never quite decided what to do with him, with people like him, with people like us.

Ordinary Time

I drove away from the ocean and into the basin of the Topatopa Mountains, looking for a clearer transmission. The signal was getting scrambled on the coast. Something in the odd angles of the hills that cup the city where my parents live, how the small city lays exposed to the endless dissipating openness of the Pacific, made it impossible for me to hear. Different frequencies overlapped, hard bursts of static hurt my head; words arriving from every direction were swallowed up by one another. I had a headache and I had to go.

I came around the long curve of Route 126 away from the sea and tracked between the hills and farms alongside Route 150, heading north, then west again. I thought I could find somewhere where the signal was clear. It was so yellow and green and blue out there. I could find somewhere where the distance between mountaintops evened out, where I would be in the center of the gentle, reverberating bowl and the bouncing frequencies, amplified by the smooth uniform fields. The frequencies would coalesce around my car and let me receive transmission perfectly. Then I would be able to make sense of all the noise and remember why I left home and started driving, remember what exactly

I was doing out there by myself in the middle of a too hot winter day in California.

The sun made the windshields very warm. I put my left hand up against the window while I turned the wheel with my right along a long curve past a mountain range, watching Thomas Aquinas College appear and pass from my side mirror to my rearview. I kept driving. I felt calmer, but still, I could only hear distortion. I could only hear halves of words between bursts of static. The car felt warm but not too hot. I didn't need to use the air-conditioning at all. Small farms passed on the left side, then a town, a hill, more fields. The static became pleasant, like an old TV or radio coming on.

The highway petered out in Ojai, a small city at the foot of Los Padres National Forest. Ojai is mainly pueblo-style buildings and tourist spots, wine stores and new age shops and art galleries. I parked in a public parking lot across the street from a bad Mexican restaurant I'd once visited with my family. It was even hotter in Ojai. The air stunk like asphalt and the light shimmered above the ground. It was a sad, slow heat. I had a sense that somebody would come and find me. Somebody had said something about tracking me through my phone. They'd see I'd stopped, and they'd come and get me. I just needed to kill time. I crossed the street and sat down on a metal chair outside a sandwich shop with no one in it. I took one note in my phone: *I am in a parking lot in Ojai trying to fact-check myself.* I don't know what that means. Everything went slow.

After a while, I stood up and began walking around the block. There was a neighborhood behind the main commercial street, and I walked past houses, all in different eccentric styles—strange paint jobs and seashells on exterior walls, purple-and-white front doors, Buddha statues in the yards, the odd progressive NGO sign. Everything was one story and squat. I went around a dozen times at least. Sandwich shop, wine shop, turn the corner, the Mexican restaurant where I'd been before, houses, corner, houses, corner, houses, sandwich shop. White-purple seashells asphalt hot sun. My legs felt filled with heavy water—I could

only keep walking because the force of it sloshing back and forth pro-
pelled the limbs. The world felt very slow. I thought something might
be wrong. I kept thinking that something was wrong. But I couldn't
remember what was the matter.

My legs were very heavy and it was very hot. My stomach felt too
full even though there was nothing to eat. Very hot. I thought, what a
lazy day, walking in circles. The light was changing angles fast. Seashells. Purple door. *I've been here for a while*. NGO signs. Sandwich
shop again. *What am I forgetting?* I sat down and got up. Nobody came
to get me.

I stood for a while back in the parking lot, losing my train of
thought. The sun was very high. I watched a family get out of an SUV
and walk away fast without seeing me. I heard them squawking, *squawk
squawk squaaaa*. I got a headache again. The water in my legs came up
into my chest and I felt like laying down. Instead, I got back in my car,
where the seat was baking from its hours in the sun. I turned on the
air-conditioning for the first time and drove away.

J. was at home with my parents. It had been a year since we sat down
in Paris, when I told her that days like this would happen. I think she
understood in theory but is having a hard time in practice. My parents
are with her. At least they have seen me wander off like this before.
We've been visiting them for the holidays. It's been lovely; nothing has
been going wrong. We saw J.'s father and aunts and uncles for Thanks-
giving, but it's nicer to come to California in the middle of the winter.
It'd been very warm. We brought my black cat with us and have been
waiting, in the mornings, for the outdoor cat belonging to my parents'
neighbors to come into the backyard and play with mine through the
glass door. This is usually my calmest time of the whole year. Everything was going well. I'd been taking my medication every day. I was
stable. I was capable of *reflecting on* my illness, not merely *recovering
from* it. I'd begun writing this book already. My insight had never been
better.

Route 150 picked up again on the far side of Ojai and directed me over mountains before turning back out toward the coast. I headed to Santa Barbara. I don't think I can hear the transmissions anymore at all. But when I drove under heavy tree cover or get too high between inland hills, I would lose reception completely. I noticed that; it's like the sudden total silence of the white noise of an HVAC unit going out. You hear the absence of what you did not hear before. I knew that these were not real transmissions; I was not receiving signals from other minds. I tried to think of a reasonable explanation for it. The wind passing by the moving car? The far-off crash of the ocean? Electromagnetic frequencies stimulating the small bones in my ears? That would make sense of how the sound changes, how it buzzes and stops and oscillates depending on the surfaces around me.

In Santa Barbara, I parked in a covered lot to keep the car from getting hot again, but it was later now, and I was back out on the coast, so actually, it's cold. My legs still felt too heavy. I knew that I was getting messages on my phone, but I couldn't remember how to respond; more precisely, I forgot that responding is the natural response to receiving a message. I was aware I am meant to do something in reply to these incessant pings and buzzes, but I was not sure what it is—besides, it didn't feel too urgent. I walked past a small movie theater, the kind with an old, lettered marquee and flat seats that has been preserved for the antique pleasure of beach town tourists. I couldn't remember how to buy a ticket, and anyway, I didn't know what I'd want to see. Instead, I went into a coffee shop and used the bathroom and left. The really fatal moment in any attack is not losing the ability to resist, but losing the ability to track what you are meant to be resisting. I thought I was walking north back toward the car, but was not. I couldn't find the car. The breeze was cold now. I sat down on the sidewalk and told myself to cry but I couldn't.

I wasn't off my medication, but when I say, *My medication is working,* *it* doesn't mean that I do not hear anything at all. I don't, most of the time, but there are times when I can only ignore these sounds. It means that I don't respond to them most days, and that I recognized—or at least could say—that they were the symptoms of a disease inside my brain. Imagine yourself on the edge of sleep, alone in your dark apartment. The walls creak and the floors buckle. You have the passing thought—*Somebody is in my house*—and you believe it, but in the same moment, you also say to yourself, *Oh, this is that thing that happens when I'm falling asleep.* You don't jump out of bed. You don't go for a baseball bat. You aren't really worried. You go to sleep. I am hearing the person in my house just about all the time, but I don't get out of bed. It was like that, except when it wasn't. It just happens, even after the extraordinary period of the initial descent into insanity, after the hospitals and the doctors and the therapy and pills. *It just happens* sometimes.

I don't remember how long I walked in Santa Barbara, although I know I stayed outside, and when I finally found my car the sun had set. I had left home sometime in the morning. It was still early afternoon when I left Ojai. I drove the 101 down the coast and got off in Ventura; two turns off the freeway found me in the parking lot of a Barnes & Noble. I went in. I walked around the ground floor looking for anything to read. It was very quiet in the store. I went outside and heard the static in the parking lot; I panicked and went back through the doors. A clerk announced that they were closing in an hour. I decided that I couldn't leave before I knew what I was doing. The dark made everything feel very small. I was certain that I was running out of time.

I got in line for the store café then got out. I took the escalator to the second floor and went around the long banister, past cookbooks and travelogues and memoirs; I found an enormous wooden chair by a large cold window with old newspapers strewn around it. On a shelf nearby, I found *The Idiot* and sat down to read. I needed to read it all. I got as far as the moment very early on where Prince Myshkin tells the story of a man about to be executed, a story very similar to a real event in Dostoevsky's life. The man is being brought to the scaffold and suddenly begins to lament his wasted life.

What should I do if I were not to die now? he asks himself. *What if I were to return to life again? What an eternity of days, and all mine! How*

I should grudge and count up every minute of it, so as to waste not a single instant! But the execution is a fake; it's designed to scare the man, not actually kill him. He lives on. So, another character asks Myshkin what he did with the riches of time. *Did he keep careful account of his minutes?*

Oh no, he didn't! replies Prince Myshkin. *He said that he had not lived a bit as he had intended, and had wasted many minutes* since.

When I woke up, I was on the floor, back pressed against an enormous freezing window. An employee was standing over me, telling me that the store was closed. My hands were shaking and I couldn't speak. The heavy water in my legs had leaked. I felt light. I have very nearly no sense of smell—I haven't had it for years—so I didn't realize at first that I had pissed myself. I somehow got to my feet. I said, *I'm not drunk*, and the store employees called the cops.

When they arrived, the cops took me outside and sat me on the curb in front of the book store. The wind was very cold by then. I said, *I'm not drunk*. They took my phone. The officers looked through it for a while. One asked me why I was shaking. I said, *I didn't take the medication for my medication*. He said, *What?* Then the other one found the number for my mom. They called her. Maybe she explained. A few minutes later, she arrived with my father. He took my car keys and my car. I got in my mother's car to go home. I went in and out of consciousness and woke up in the garage. I think I said I was sorry.

At home, I took tranquilizers and went immediately to bed. J. had been crying. She'd been mad at me, I think, but felt she couldn't be while I was in that state. I couldn't hear anything at all. The bedroom in the basement was pitch-black; the bed seemed enormous and once in it, I found I couldn't move. I thought, *Time's up, I'm dying*, and I felt very calm.

I slept for a long time. I stayed on tranquilizers for several days, but I didn't get lost again. I spent a long time sitting on my parents' balcony, microwaved in the large sun above the sea. I felt fragile. It was hard to keep thoughts straight. I kept repeating a line from Virginia Woolf's *On Being Ill: The Amphibious Life of Headache*. But my head didn't hurt anymore. A few days later, when I spoke to my psychiatrist on the phone, she didn't seem too worried at all. *Just keep taking your medication and call me if anything changes,* she said. *Be careful.* In a few days I was fine.

MARCH 2020, IOWA

I was meant to meet J. in New York City during the second week of March. I didn't go, of course; or, I didn't go, of course, in retrospect. I could have gone without too much scandal. It was still a few days before everybody there began staying indoors, a few weeks before it became clear that even if you were set on traveling in the spring of 2020, you weren't likely traveling to New York. As it happens, I didn't go because two days before I was meant to drive from Iowa to the airport in Chicago, I looked at the spot on the wall in my living room where two white corners met just below the ceiling and realized that the angle was impossible. The space was distorted somehow; there was a bend in the laws of physics. It was strange and malicious and wrong. I couldn't say what the matter was, precisely, but I couldn't look away. I stared at the wall for at least an hour and remembered how badly I'd been feeling for the past few days and then I lost my mind.

No words quite work here. You know that by now. I had a *severe mood disturbance.* I suffered, over the course of the two ensuing days, at least two episodes of *aggravated, acute psychosis.* The language of the clinic feels too cold. I freaked out. I had a meltdown. I had the most trouble I had encountered in at least two and a half years, trouble that came in waves for the better part of two weeks, sometimes keeping me in bed, sometimes sending me running, sometimes getting me screaming, or bursting into tears, sometimes leaving me lying prone and tense and nervous on my bed or couch or floor all day, trouble that was only slowed, at least for a while, by what my doctor called an unsustainable increase in my medication regime, which has structured the decisions of all my doctors since. Iowa had only recently confirmed its first cases of coronavirus. I don't know if that had anything to do with it. I had been feeling worse—run-down, irritated, *off*—for weeks. In ordinary times, I would have been committed, but my psychiatrist was not certain that it made sense to expose me to a hospital.

J. flew out a few days later. Better to get her out of Manhattan anyway. Better for us to stay in empty Iowa. She flew into O'Hare four days after the night I'd screamed and cried for hours and told her I wasn't getting on my flight to New York, three days after I'd stayed in bed for twenty-three hours straight, then did the same the next day; one day after I said, *Okay, I am beginning to see that I am not behaving normally*, and left a message on my doctor's answering machine asking for help. I went to bed worried that I wouldn't make it to Chicago to pick her up. Normally, she could stay a night at her father's apartment if I couldn't reach O'Hare on the day of her arrival. But several weeks earlier, doctors had discovered a small mass in his pancreas, and while early detection meant his prospects were good, he had recently received his first dose of chemotherapy and J. didn't want to risk exposing him to anything she might have picked up on her flight.

Just a month before, on Valentine's Day, J.'s flight out of New York had been delayed by a blizzard but wasn't fully cancelled until I was already in Illinois. She flew late to Detroit, and I drove four hours farther through the snow to stay with her overnight in an airport motel before driving us back to Iowa. Now I didn't know if I could even make it to Chicago. Now an emergency appeared to be unfolding, and I was useless and ashamed and believed, very firmly, that if I got out of bed I would die. When I woke up the next morning, I panicked. I tried Ativan to calm me down. Ordinarily, I took a milligram or two whenever I needed to tranquilize myself out of an imminent catastrophe. But that morning, I discovered that if I took five, or six, or maybe seven milligrams, it somehow got me out of bed and let me go to the grocery store for the first time in weeks and stock up, let me get my apartment ready and let me get in my car and drive to Chicago and let me get

J. and let me take her back to Iowa in only a mild state of nervous agitation. I wondered how a tranquilizer in sufficient doses could feel like an amphetamine.

I kept it together for a few days. J. ordered masks and pretended my apartment was in order. She kept up with her father. He wasn't feeling well. We decided to visit once we had a better sense of how to keep everybody safe. It was still chilly in March in Iowa so it didn't even feel that strange to spend so much time indoors. I kept taking my extra Ativan, five or six or seven milligrams per day.

A few days later, sitting on the couch in my living room, J. admitted during a casual conversation that she was party to a conspiracy with everyone I knew to keep me stupid and steal my cat. She wanted me to stay drugged up, so I'd forget to listen to all the brains of every neighbor on my street trying to get through to me saying GET OUT WHERE YOU CAN HEAR US (sometimes loud) then getoutwhereyoucanhearusgetoutwhereyoucanhearus (sometimes quiet) then GET OUT WHERE YOU CAN HEAR US (loud again). I looked from the couch to the corner and noticed that the walls of my apartment were still wrong, so I GOT OUT on foot. I got lost. I found home, but then GOT OUT again, this time in my car, and got lost again and went back. I went inside to try to rescue my cat. I tried to kick a door in to get him. I yelled some more, as much to hear myself over GET OUT GET OUT GET OUT as anything, but then I froze. I forgot what I was doing. I felt paralyzed, lay down, and cried.

J. could only beg me to take more tranquilizers, to promise to keep taking all my medication the next day. I had been taking my medication. I was already taking too many Ativan on top of it. I still believed she was drugging me. She wanted to make me forget what she had confessed, to stop me from fighting back. But lying on my bed and unable to move, I decided that it would be easier to cooperate—to take the drug, to go into a haze, to forget what I had realized about this conspiracy, to just *give in*—than it would be to keep on fighting. I took one or two or three tranquilizers more than the five or six or seven I had taken earlier that day and fell asleep. The next day, I woke up a little better. I took five, six, seven milligrams more. A few days later, when my psychiatrist finally got back to me, she said, *You seem more like your-self than the last time that we spoke.* I didn't remember speaking to her recently. When was last time? *You don't seem dangerously psychotic right now*, she said. *Okay.*

All of this might have happened under ordinary circumstances. I suspect the blossoming pandemic hadn't helped, but I also have what the world had then taken to calling an *underlying condition. Underlying* is a relative term. It applies only when a more general condition lays over us. Even without a pandemic, there is still the difficulty and tension and slowness all the time. There is still the *compromised cognitive functioning* and *reduced impulse control* which do not, on their own, make me appear insane but which would not be happening if I weren't. In ordinary time, there is still the strange pallor that hangs over difficult weeks, the odd experience of living in conjunction with the world at a permanently inconvenient angle, and the thought, over and over, of how pitiable and useless I would be in any kind of crisis.

What I mean to say is that the worst parts of those weeks were not the brief hours of psychosis, but the days of in-between time. The worst parts were getting up in the morning or trying to go to sleep at night. The worst parts were getting angry too easily, scared too quickly, losing my train of thought over and over and over, missing the exit nearly every time I got on the freeway. The worst part was realizing that I had texted a friend who did nothing wrong and told him to fuck off over and over—I don't know why—and remembering how in the weeks before I had nearly gotten into a fight outside a bar, how two days before that I had flipped out on a waiter for almost no reason at all and stormed out without paying the check, thinking *You've been at this for years, you should recognize warning signs by now.* I was not being asked to do terribly much. Drive the car. Take out the trash. Keep up conversa-tion. Instead, I terrified J., and when I wasn't terrifying her, she tried to make a home in my apartment for an indeterminate stay, and whenever

I looked over, she looked worried. I told myself she was worried for her father, or for the state of the world, but I knew she was worried about me too and I resented it, and that was the worst part of all. I was not *freaking out* most of the time, but I was embarrassed to realize that even then—and by then, I had already written that first essay about the weather, had already committed to paper the idea that I could sit here in Iowa and tell other people what madness was really like—that even as I did that, I could not even recognize the signs.

J. worried about her father. He had become increasingly subdued. She worried about me while I yelled and cried and forgot things and freaked out. J. is surrounded by people with underlying conditions. She always has been. She had lost her mother, a manic-depressive, a decade before; her sister had died two years after that. I told myself, between bouts of embarrassment and self-pity, that my underlying condition is just as medical as her father's, just as immune to reason or willpower or the good sense to lay off when there's already a pandemic on. But I knew, sometimes secretly, and sometimes explicitly, that it is difficult to think of madness that way, even when you are the mad one. Sometimes I know, even when mad, that madness, like anything, is a resource. Total dysregulation is like a scream coming out of your whole body; it can let all the tension out and keep all the real terrors at bay.

The late Mark Fisher wrote that even when he was on the psychiatric ward, *I felt I was not really depressed—I was only simulating the condition in order to avoid work, or in the infernally paradoxical logic of depression, I was simulating it in order to conceal the fact that I was not capable of working, and that there was no place at all for me in society.* The delusions of psychotic patients are generally supposed to reflect, often in a carnival-mirror fashion, the secret fears of the patient himself. The night J.'s father stopped calling her back or responding to her texts and she had to implore her aunt to go to his house and make sure he was all right was only a few days after I'd become convinced that she and my doctors were trying to drug me up so they could manipulate and rob me. Or, in the infernally paradoxical logic of schizophrenia, I feared that I was being tricked into believing I was ill in order to conceal the fact that I was really somebody who, when confronted by a woman desperately worried about her father's cancer treatment in the middle of a generational pandemic, couldn't be bothered to do anything but accuse her of being the one who was actually hurting me.

When I had been stable for a few days, J. and I decided to take a walk through Iowa City. We went up a hill toward the highway, then through the back roads where the townies lived. I'd seen whole families of deer on this route before, sometimes in the middle of the street, but we didn't see anything this time, neither animals nor people nor clouds. It was a good walk. My legs hurt. I slept well. By Sunday morning, I'd begun to feel calm and considered scaling the Ativan back down. J. and I had breakfast on my couch while my cat sat beside us in a patch of dusty sunlight. It was an unusually bright morning for mid-March in eastern Iowa. Halfway through breakfast, J. got a call from her aunt who told her that her father was dead.

We didn't know, still do not know, precisely why. He had only had one dose of chemotherapy. His cancer was not taken to be advanced. He was not known to otherwise be sick. Since his appointment, he had barely left his apartment at all.

J. cried. Soon I was in an Ativan stupor. I locked myself in my bedroom and attended mass via online television and prayed to know what to pray for; I thought of the clichés about madness, the religious mysticism of the insane, thought of what a lie that is, how I was the worst person to insert into a crisis.

On Monday morning, I took six milligrams of Ativan, twelve pills in all, and we drove to Chicago. We got J.'s father's cat, appropriately named Tiny, and her box of toys, tree, and litter box. We found essential documents, and J. found out that her father's remaining relatives, an uncle and two aunts of J.'s who met us at her dad's apartment, would not be helping with the funeral, or the apartment, or anything else at all. Her uncle and I almost came to blows. I was not being helpful. My doctor called me, and I went outside and said, *Look, I am happy to*

debate, philosophically, the nature of my illness later on, and decide, delib-
erately, what is an acceptable dose of medication for the long term, but right
now I just need to bootstrap myself into stability for a few days. My doctor
said okay and told me to keep taking the Ativan and the Seroquel on top
of everything else; *I'm sorry for you all's loss.*

We took the cat back to Iowa and waited two days and then drove
back. The funeral was Thursday morning at a graveyard on the north
side. No more than seven people were permitted in the chapel. Ten
minutes total. J. and I and a cousin our age from her mother's side;
J.'s father's brother, brother-in-law, two sisters, and sister-in-law on the
other. One Our Father, one Hail Mary, then the casket went to the
plot, and we watched them lower it into the ground. J. didn't speak to
her family.

I went back to Iowa. J. stayed for three more days with her cousin,
calling cellphone carriers and life insurance companies and figuring
out how to get rid of furniture and close the apartment before the first
of the month because ordinarily you might call Goodwill to come take
your furniture for free but Goodwill wasn't taking donations at that
time. I spent three days by myself, introducing the two cats. I think that
I remained relatively stable. Most of the undergraduates had left Iowa
City. The houses near me were empty. That may be why they were so
quiet; why I didn't hear their pain and fear and loneliness and boredom
through the walls. I mainly slept. On Sunday, I went and got J. and we
went back to Iowa. J. kept telling me that she was grateful for all my
help those last few days, but all I did was sedate myself and sometimes
drive a car. I began to slowly taper down the Ativan and, after a while,
I was fine.

At some point during the months J. and I spent in Iowa, I searched
my closet for an old N95 mask I'd gotten in 2017 in California. There'd
been a fire that year, as there is every year now. The fire was enormous.
It had burned down whole neighborhoods in Ventura County, leveled
an apartment building only two blocks from my parents' house. I'd gone
home for Christmas only a few days after the evacuation order cleared,

when smoke was still covering every outdoor surface in soot. The city issued the masks to every resident to use until the air cleared up.

After the fire, dazed people around the small city kept saying—as people all over the world would begin to say a few years later—that despite all the horror and destruction, we would all Get Through This Like We've Gotten Through Everything Before. But J.'s father didn't. A million others didn't. Thousands will not get through any given day. History is written by the people who Got Through This. *That things "just keep going" is the catastrophe*, as Walter Benjamin says. In California, people were quick to remind one another that fires were a kind of good. *We don't let them burn enough. They rejuvenate the Earth.* The trouble, I thought, was that they don't rejuvenate what burns. The brush doesn't watch as the fire comes on and say to his neighbor, *This too shall pass, don't worry.* The fire comes, and the brush passes with it.

We kept going. In June, J. and I put her father's cat in the back seat of my car and drove east to find ourselves an apartment above a laundromat in New York.

SEPTEMBER 2020, NEW YORK

A few months after J. and I moved to New York, I went out in the evening to pick up our dinner from a restaurant deeper into Queens. It had been a difficult day. I was in the middle of the vague suspicion that I was prisoner in a hospital at sea and I had lost it a little bit earlier and curled up at an odd angle in the hall. I'd ruined the better part of J.'s working day; the takeout was a kind of apology. In the parking lot, I saw a text message from my father asking me to call him when I got a chance. I texted back, *Is it serious? I'm doing something right now. Yes*, he said, *but don't worry.* So, I didn't worry, but I called. When my parents picked up, they told me that my father had been to a neurologist, who had told my father that he had Parkinson's disease, and then we talked about it for a while.

I took the news casually because I did not really believe it. It took days for me to accept it as a real fact; I don't know why. *And it is notorious that the parents are the last to admit that their son is mad*, writes Simone de Beauvoir, *the children that their mother has cancer.* Close enough. I felt guilty. My father did not have cancer, he only had Parkinson's, a nonfatal disease. J.'s father had cancer and he had died. I got the food and drove home and told J. and we ate.

My father's disease is still in its early stages. It is moving slowly. For now, his hand just shakes. When it gets worse, he will take the same medication that I take for my tremor. When it gets really bad, he may begin to suffer delusions and hallucinate.

Some research has found that schizophrenia carries an elevated risk for Parkinson's. They are both disorders of a dopamine system. My psychiatrist reminds me that my father is old, past seventy already. He has had stents put in. Even if he lives many more years, he will likely die before he reaches the stage of Parkinson's where he goes mad. *Wherefore they are affected with madness in various shapes; some run along unrestrainedly, and, not knowing how, return again to the same spot.*

Every bout I've had of mania or psychosis I can remember had come with the terrified certainty that I was dying, that I was being poisoned or conspired against or was subject to psychic attack. But I am sure that one day, when I am really dying, I will tell myself that my worries—the lump I've noticed, the strange cough, the radiating pain, are just my paranoia acting up again. This is the best argument that I have ever heard for the idea that madness is just a coping mechanism, a way to avoid the unbearable reality. *The black-and-white universe of the paranoid may appear very certain*, writes Gregory Bateson, *but it is not founded on certainty . . . it is compensatory. It is a denial of those accumulated inner fears and weaknesses which long and bitter experience of being put in the wrong has built up.*

The first time I pushed death out of my mind was in my father's car. I was a child. My father turned right onto Topanga Canyon in the western San Fernando Valley and was heading south toward home. I looked at the browning grass of a high school track and field, baking under the haze outside. The sun made the window hot, and the cheap interior of the car smelled like chemicals and sweat. I put my finger to the glass of the passenger-side window, to trace and bounce along the blocks-long fence.

We were returning from my grandfather's house. He was dying. And I thought, *You will die too, gymnasium and fence. You will die and the whole world will go dark for you. Grass. You will die,* my hand against the warm, thick window. *No matter what, your life will end one day.* In my father's car on the southbound road through the hot west Valley, I felt for the first time the inevitability of my own dying; the inevitability of all deaths. I felt a tunnel of indeterminate length and a gray room and a hospital room like I'd seen in television shows, and I saw myself in bed, and I heard my own voice as an old man shaking inside my head saying, *Well, this is it.* This vision surely comes to everyone in some shape. You try to think around it, but you can't. You stew in it until it passes. It comes back and goes again. I suppose that I am trying to tell you that madness is like this in a way.

Each year before New Year's Eve, my father takes me for a walk. We used to go for miles, from our house up into the southern mountains of the Valley, into cul-de-sacs and out again, past the large houses on small lots that had replaced every one-story home that stood when we had moved there; my father liked to say that when we sold our house eventually, they'd tear it down too, and that would be that for modesty around there.

We would walk for hours. December in Los Angeles is never cold. The idea of these walks was to take stock of the year and my life and his life, but for most of each walk, we just talked about the news. It wasn't until near the end, when my father and I would turn south on Ventura Boulevard and cut toward the corner of our street, that he would say whatever was serious that year. For several years in Los Angeles, my father promised he would show me the combination for his safe. He would tell me that it's important that I'm able to find my parents' will, and instructions for what to do if he dies. But he forgot each time, and I still don't know the combination.

My father can no longer walk for hours. He couldn't even before the Parkinson's. Around New Year's, we drive down to the beach in Ventura and park there, then walk back and forth along the long flat stretch between the highway and the ocean to avoid going up any difficult hills. During the first few years of walks in Ventura, my father would say, half-joking, that he believed that he would die that year. On our first walk after his diagnosis, he didn't talk about his health at all.

My father is not in any immediate danger. Still, each time I get a phone call from my mother, I think she's going to tell me he's dead. And each time when we're walking and he forgets the light, and I have to put my hand out to keep him on the curb and out of traffic, I wonder what it will be like in coming years when my mother and I reminisce about the days when my father was still alive. The last time I told my parents I loved them was before they sent me to the wilderness. I do love them, but I can't say it anymore. I don't know why. *The parents are the last to admit that their son is mad.* I have put them through hell. I fantasize about telling my father on his deathbed that he was a good dad, the best I could have asked for—and it's true, but I don't know if that will make up for what I've put him through in life. *Sometimes, though very rarely, it happens that love, friendship, or comradely feeling overcomes the loneliness of death,* Simone de Beauvoir goes on, *even when I was holding Maman's hand I was not with her—I was lying.* In my fantasy, I am not lying but I still don't know if that's enough.

I believed for a long time that my thoughts were not my own. This is a fairly common delusion, although the imagined mechanism tends to vary between patients. I believed that I was in some way a projection of the collective unconscious of everybody around me. An intrasubjective hallucination that everybody was imagining together. I was made from a little bit of input from everybody who could see me; the closer you were, or the better you knew me, the more influence your subconscious had on the kinds of thoughts I had, and on what kind of person I was and became. Years later, a therapist suggested that this was probably my baseline delusion: everything else I have believed during far rarer and more acute periods of mania or psychosis—that I was Elijah, that I was dead, that the Holy Ghost lived in my body and was trying to kill me, that I was a prisoner on a sea hospital—was, if you accept the murky and incoherent logic of delusional thinking, a kind of elaboration on the idea that there is no barrier between my brain and all the other brains. Other people can read my thoughts, I can read their thoughts, all our thoughts are the same thoughts; the same premises that appear so often in psychotic patients.

This delusion isn't usually frightening, but there is one way it can get scary, even when I am not having a particularly bad attack: the fewer people I spoke to in a day, or the longer I was isolated, or entirely alone, the more likely it was that I would start to decohere. I imagined myself flickering, in and out of being. My brain would run on empty, and starved for fuel, my consciousness would start to leak out of my head. I think it was a way for me to explain some of my negative symptomology to myself. But whatever the reason, I spent years trying to physically put myself in as many places and situations as I could to receive a steady diet of mind-forming input from real people. I believe that's why I started going out all the time. And meeting up with friends if I could. Or strangers if I couldn't. Or, if all else failed, sitting in a restaurant or park or bar alone. Why I become desperate and clingy and overbearing in a way at odds with my ordinary personality sometimes. The delusion is largely gone, but the habit—and the irrational, vague anxiety that begins to form if I'm alone too long—remains.

A week after my father called me about his illness, I walked around New York for hours by myself, thinking of the new year in this new city. I slurped up thoughts from every mind I passed. I filled up on all the bickering, murmuring energy of all the people thinking there. I hate New York. It's loud and dull and vulgar, and although there is a sea, it is ugly and distant and cold. But I kept walking for a long time, until I felt filled with thoughts and could go back to my and J.'s apartment and act normal, stable, fine.

I didn't begin writing about madness until I believed I could write about it with insight, until I believed I had attained sufficient objective distance from my own condition. When you're really sick, you're lucky if you know it at all. Even now, I still don't feel quite right. Every time I have a major episode, every time the cracks turn into breaks, I recover but I never quite go back to how I was before. I began writing about madness because I believed, in a magical way, that by doing so, I could consign *going mad* to the past; turn it into an area of my expertise but not an area of my experience. But madness digs in its rut, deepens the groove, sets the bar even lower every time. When I told my new therapist about my father, and told her that I was having trouble with the news, she asked, *Do you feel crazy?* I didn't know. I felt like when you know your foot is cramping up. You freeze. There isn't pain, just the idea of pain, the twang, the taut string, anticipating the hurt. Is that what it feels like to feel crazy? How could I know? How could I tell her, or you?

The truth is that I am worried what I will become if I stay stable, what medication for a whole life means. I was funny once, and bold, and charismatic; I had energy, I was charming. The cost was only occasional horror and pain for me and everyone around me. Perhaps I will never have another episode again. But so long as I am *in therapy*, so long as my *medication is working*, I will remain this indecisive, slow, and doddering thing, this Prufrock who dares to do nothing at all. Is it so terrible to resent this?

Even when I am stable, even when I believe that I can write, it isn't quite right for me to say *my medication is working*, or *I have insight*, or that I am at an objective distance from the disease. I know that I have my own brain and thoughts and mind. I do not believe that I am about to die. I am behaving in an acceptable way, neither *a danger to myself nor others*. But what they don't tell you, even about successful treatment, is that it never stops. You don't forget that these are *delusions* the way you do when you're very sick but when I call them *delusions*, I am speaking in a second language, a language I learned as an adult and will never really speak like the natives do.

I'm good at saying it's a delusion. I'm good at saying, *I suffer from a psychotic disorder,* or *I'm schizoaffective,* or *I have a severe form of mental illness.* I'm good at knowing these things, too. But I don't believe them. Gut check, deep down, what-does-my-heart-tell-me, what-feels-true-in-my-bones: all of it was true, once upon a time. I didn't change. The world did. I used to live in a reality where I was just the amalgam of other people's thoughts and dreams and fears, where I was just a fantasy that all of them were having from time to time, imagining this fuckup into being. And then, several months after I turned twenty-four years old, I found myself in a reality where I was just an ordinary person. Where it would be delusional to believe all those old things. Where other people weren't a part of me, or I of them; where they could leave or I could leave them or they could get sick and die and I wouldn't be able to do anything at all. Where I would get sick, too, and wouldn't simply disappear but die.

I don't know, precisely, how I passed over. I don't know that I was transported from that old world into this one. I don't remember a portal or an act of God, just pills and time. I'm good at telling you what I know but not what I believe because I don't think anybody will believe me. I don't think anybody else came over with me from that old place, because nobody remembers that strange and frightening world at all.

I miss it. That's the secret. I miss when I was lost; I do. In ordinary time, in this ordinary world, I am too much aware of myself straddling between realities. I feel one foot in the world of floating thoughts and brain murmurs and sea ships and prophets and God, and another foot in this world, where even drugged and therapized, I am not a good or useful person, this world where people leave or get sick or die. I cannot come fully into this world. No medicine works so well. I can keep straddling for a while, but the truth is that I don't want to keep this pose forever. I want to fall backward, to let go of the medication and the insight and the slow push through thick sludge, to disappear back into the once familiar country where it's safe.

Ghost Stories

A schizophrenic woman is missing in San Diego. She was last seen on a Saturday afternoon, outside her Mira Mesa residence. The woman is five-foot-two, 136 pounds, with black hair and brown eyes. *She is familiar with bus routes and has the ability to travel throughout the San Diego region, and [she] has frequently been found at area casinos, unaware of her surroundings,* the police told reporters.

In Cleveland, a thirty-eight-year-old woman with bipolar disorder has been missing for over a year. The woman has disappeared before and is sometimes found hiding in the nearby woods. Cleveland police are also searching for a twenty-six-year-old man with schizophrenia. He was last seen in April.

A sixty-three-year-old bipolar woman went missing in Oklahoma. She was last seen on the morning she disappeared around 4:00 a.m., driving a black 2007 Saturn Vue. The woman only had a quarter-tank of gas when she left home, and she did not take her wallet with her. Investigators say she has been "very manic" lately.

In Los Angeles, the sheriff's department is looking for a sixty-nine-year-old schizophrenic man. He is five-foot-seven, 145 pounds, with brown eyes and black hair and chronic obstructive pulmonary disease.

In Georgia, police are seeking information on the whereabouts of a sixty-five-year-old man with bipolar disorder. He was last seen smoking a cigarette outside his home, wearing a short-sleeved shirt in royal blue. Police are also seeking the whereabouts of a fifteen-year-old schizophrenic girl with long, braided hair. She was last seen wearing a blue shirt. A nineteen-year-old schizophrenic boy went missing in North Miami, five-foot-seven and 230 pounds. He was last seen running away from his parents in the area of Northeast 125th Street, wearing a blue shirt. In Los Angeles, police are searching for a fifty-five-year-old man with schizoaffective disorder. He was last seen wearing a black shirt but can be recognized by an unusual tattoo on his forehead, depicting an open, bright-blue eye.

A sixty-one-year-old bipolar woman is missing in Missouri. She was last seen driving a red Nissan. The woman suffers from emphysema and only has one lung. She took her oxygen tank with her, but based on the timing of her disappearance, police believe that the oxygen has long run out.

A middle-aged woman with schizophrenia is missing in Tennessee. An elderly bipolar man is missing in New Jersey. In Dallas, the parents of a schizoaffective nineteen-year-old boy asked the public to help locate their missing son. He's run away before, they said, but never for so long.

In Savannah, Georgia, police are looking for a schizophrenic woman who left her senior living facility on foot. She was last seen wearing a purple jacket. Police are seeking a schizophrenic twenty-eight-year-old man in Florida. He has not been taking his medication. A man in Georgia went missing at a shopping mall; he is six feet tall, bipolar, with gray hair, wearing a T-shirt that says *Picture Perfect Renovations LLC.*

In Manchester, Connecticut, police are looking for a five-foot-six man with schizophrenia and autism. He left his house without his phone or wallet, barefoot, wearing a sweater that says *California.*

In Florida, authorities released footage of a missing thirty-one-year-old schizophrenic woman wading into a river full of alligators. According to her family, she had been missing for three weeks.

In Walnut Creek, California, officers responded to reports of a mentally ill man running down a busy street. They shot him.

In Houston, Texas, a police officer approached his forty-four-year-old schizophrenic neighbor in the area between their homes. The woman yelled, *I'm walking to my house!* He shot her.

In Tulsa, Arizona, police officers taunted a bipolar woman before forcibly arresting her. She is seventy years old.

In Orange County, Florida, police responded to a domestic dispute between a forty-year-old schizophrenic and his mother. When officers entered the home, the man shouted and waved a barstool at them. *[After] a taser didn't work*, a local paper reported, *a deputy shot the man dead.*

A schizophrenic woman was arrested in New Jersey for the murder of her mother. She had spent two years in a psychiatric hospital, awaiting trial, and was reported to be vigorously resisting attempts at medication. In Tennessee, the family of a schizophrenic man charged with the murder of his father said that they spent eight years pleading with doctors and police for help. In Boise, Idaho, a forty-year-old bipolar man was jailed on suspicion of driving under the influence of drugs. He died of dehydration and starvation six days later in his cell.

In Iowa, pretrial motions concerning the mental fitness of a schizophrenic man charged with stabbing a stranger to death have delayed the case for years. At issue in the dispute between prosecutors and defense attorneys, and the psychiatrists hired by each, is the defendant's mental competence to stand trial.

In Minnesota, a fifty-three-year-old bipolar man shot a police officer who was then taken to the hospital and survived. The police shot the man. He died. His ex-wife told investigators that he had twice been committed to psychiatric hospitals; once, he had threatened to *take her to the underworld* himself.

A Black manic-depressive in prison in Pennsylvania wrote a letter to a newspaper alleging abuse at the hands of prison guards. *They like when they get to pepper spray us*, he wrote.

In Connecticut, a police officer pursued a schizophrenic man driving a stolen car down I-95. Eventually, the driver got off and was blocked in by an officer on the road. The officer got out of his car.

The driver was still sitting behind his steering wheel, holding a knife. The officer shot the driver seven times through the window. He was nineteen years old.

In Texas, a sixty-one-year-old schizoaffective woman was jailed for criminal trespass. Her bond was set at three-hundred dollars, but she couldn't pay. The woman behaved erratically in jail. Officers said she was abusive. She was placed in the jail infirmary, where she refused medication and food. She refused over one hundred meals in all. She stayed in prison from December until June. Her family was not told where she was being held; they did not know she was in jail at all. The woman lost nearly one hundred and forty pounds while jailed. *The stomach is empty*, explained her autopsy report. Her official cause of death was an enlarged heart. Mental illness is listed as a *contributing factor.*

Charles Thomas called his mother from jail in Chicago. *He couldn't even form a sentence*, she told reporters. *I said, "Why don't you just go lay down?"*

I just want to hear you talk. Just talk to me, he said.

A bipolar man was arrested in Georgia after he tried to murder his friend. He told police that an organization had contacted him via Facebook. The organization told him that if he didn't carry out the hit, they'd kill his family instead.

In Florida, a schizophrenic man was arrested for the murder of his grandmother. The man said he was acting as a *sanctioned agent of the United States government.* He said the government had contacted him online.

A schizoaffective man in Nashville was indicted for the murder of a church parishioner. He faced a forty-three-count indictment. Prosecutors sought life without the possibility of parole.

In Berkeley, a schizophrenic man was arrested for choking a mental health care worker in a grocery store parking lot. The man's father was a schizophrenic, too. He hanged himself from a tree in a nearby public park.

In Arizona, a forty-three-year-old schizophrenic man was arrested for stabbing his father in the neck over and over with a switchblade. He had not been taking his medication, police said.

In Amarillo, Texas, a schizophrenic man was found not guilty by reason of insanity in the murder of his brother. He has been remanded to a psychiatric hospital, where his stay may be extended, one year at a time, forever.

In Portland, a schizophrenic man was arrested for murdering three strangers over three months. He was living in a group home but went out sometimes with a gun.

In Iowa, a schizophrenic woman was arrested for the murder of her sister. She stabbed her sister ten times while her children watched and screamed. The woman called the police herself. *Come get me*, she said. *You know where to look.* While the children cried, she went outside and stood in the middle of the street and smoked a cigarette and waited.

Police located a missing schizophrenic in Indiana. Police in Georgia found an elderly bipolar woman missing for over a month. In Ohio, a missing sixty-nine-year-old schizophrenic was found, stable and unharmed, after three weeks away from home. A seventeen-year-old bipolar boy missing in Farmington, New York, was located by police after just one day.

Police in the San Fernando Valley located a missing manic-depressive teenager, feared dead for several months.

In Arizona, police found a sixty-six-year-old schizophrenic man who had been missing for a couple of days. They found his body, which had been burned alive.

In 2013, a schizophrenic man was reported missing in Nevada. In 2019, a hiker found a skull in a public park. The next year, another hiker found a human long bone half a mile from where the skull was found. In 2021, a third hiker discovered several bones in a deep ravine two miles from where the other remains were found. K9 units found the rest of the remains, which had been scattered over several miles.

I keep a file on my computer called "Ghost Stories." It contains over a thousand clips. Nearly all of them are perfunctory local news stories about patients who have slipped through the cracks and gone missing or lashed out, the patients who often wind up, if there is any follow-up at all, on trial or in prison or dead. I suppose that I keep them as a reminder of what might happen, or as a reminder that all the studies and essays and books about madness we have, including this one, were written by the small sliver of the insane stable or lucky enough to stay stable in some place where they can write them. I keep them to remind myself to stop fantasizing about going back. I keep them because most ghosts don't get a press notice at all.

The first ghost story I ever saved, before I knew that I was saving a particular type of story, came out a little over ten years ago. The headline is, "Homeless Woman Freezes to Death." It's about a fifty-six-year-old woman who was found on the ground behind a deli in Pennsylvania.

The woman's name was Paulette Wilkie. After a brief, independent adulthood, she developed schizophrenia. She lived with family or in assisted living facilities for the better part of twenty years. But a year before her death, Wilkie went off her medication and self-medicated with drugs instead. She became disruptive and was thrown out of her group home for interfering with the *safety and recovery of other patients.* She became homeless. She was hospitalized at least once, but she was not held for long-term care. After getting out of the hospital, Wilkie went to her father but he turned her away. He'd wanted to take her in, but she refused to go back on her medication, and he was worried about what she might do. So, Wilkie stayed on the streets. She became a fixture of her neighborhood, and after a particularly cold night sleeping behind the deli, she froze.

Some contemporary coverage of Wilkie's death points out that, despite the freezing temperatures, the city had not yet activated the emergency housing protocols in place to save the homeless during cold spells. Emergency housing might have saved Paulette Wilkie's life, but she had refused emergency housing before. She often refused offers of help from strangers, and others often refused to help her.

In most ghost stories, there is an obvious point of intervention. If only the patient had health insurance, they could have gotten help. If doctors had been more sensitive or paying more attention, then the patient might have gotten the right care. If the family had been less terrified, or the police less trigger-happy, if the courts hadn't been quite so stupid and blind and vicious, then the story might have gone a different way.

But what could have saved Paulette Wilkie's life? She was a disruption and a danger to other patients. Should the group home have sacrificed the wellbeing of their other charges to keep her off the street? Wilkie refused to remain in the hospital. How long should doctors be allowed to hold someone against their will? Wilkie refused the help of other people who saw her on the streets. Can a person be compelled to accept charity? How much force is justified in forcing them? I think a lot about her father, about his terrible and enduring guilt. But so many of the ghost stories I've collected are the stories of family members hurt or killed by their unmedicated loved ones. Perhaps Wilkie's father should have taken her in, but if he had, perhaps she would have worked her way into these ghost stories just the same. In Pennsylvania, a fifty-six-year-old schizophrenic woman was arrested for the murder of her father. The jury probably would have rejected her insanity plea. The conclusion that a sufficiently uncooperative, aggressive patient, one who "chose," in some sense, to remain out of hospital and on the street, one whose own behavior has rightly terrified their family, has therefore consented by default to freezing to death in an alleyway behind a deli on a cold night is repugnant. But what should have been done? What specifically could have been done, would have been right to do, to save her life?

I come back to Wilkie's case again and again because what happened to her is what I imagine one day happening to me, what would have happened to me already in a different life. I've been lucky. I am afraid sometimes about not having health insurance for a while, but I'm not afraid that I will be entirely unable to afford care forever. I am afraid that I won't be able to keep a job or afford a home, but I am not entirely isolated in the world. Somebody will take me in. Somebody will care for me, I hope. I am afraid of reaching a point where I refuse my own luck. I am afraid that I will not cooperate, despite the work of doctors and family and friends. I am afraid that I will reach a point where I do not want help, do not believe that I need help, where I run away from anyone who tries to help me, or worse, where I become so terrified or angry or violent that I hurt those people until they are not willing to help me anymore. I am afraid that one day I will become so sick that I reach the end of other people's charity.

A few weeks ago, J. told me that I looked sad. But I don't feel sad. I feel nothing or I feel anxious or I feel myself on the precipice of some great torrential energy pouring forth; I feel all of this under the cracking paint job of my medication, waiting. I walked to the park near our apartment and looked at boats on the East River. I felt uneasy. The park is beautiful: green and red and brown, with two great bridges passing over it into the water. I watched a bird, then a squirrel. I saw a dog running through the grass, and thought that there was something wrong in its eyes, some automaton quality, the absence of *anima*. My face felt different; when I came home, it looked different in the mirror. This is *trema*; I know that. But I do not know what I can do about it. I don't know if anything will come of it at all. A few days later I felt fine.

During nearly every appointment I have ever had, every doctor in my life has asked me if I am suicidal. Usually, I say that I'm not, not now, but I worry about killing myself someday. Usually, I mean this in the ordinary sense: acute crisis, rapid loss of stability, despair, then poison or gunshots or hanging. Usually I mean it like, *killed in an officer-involved shooting*, or *sentenced to life without the possibility of parole*, or *police have stopped searching*, a headline for somebody else's set of ghost stories. But sometimes I mean it like so many of these ghosts. I mean it like a very long and very slow, confused and piecemeal, sure and steady suicide by refusal.

Acknowledgments

I'd like to thank Elizabeth Bruenig, William Callahan, Michael Maudlin, Charolette Goddu, Sam Kriss, Julia Lucas, Amelia Gramling, Tony Andrews, Kerry Howley, Bonnie Sunstein, Kiese Laymon, John D'Agata, David Rensin, Susan Peterson, Crissie Johnson Molina, and Pam McElroy. Every acknowledgments section says *this book would not be possible without* . . . but the trouble isn't what's possible. This book was always *possible*. The trouble is that without the encouragement, feedback, support, and work of these people, it would have *stayed* possible, or at the very most, would have existed as a far poorer work. I am so grateful to all of you.

In the same way, while my life would be *possible* without my wife, Jessica, it would be a poor life, one that I'm grateful I'll never have to live at all. I love you.